Ecospirituality
The Way of the Coyote

Charlton Hall, MMFT, LMFT/S, RPT-S, CHt

Copyright © 2019 Charlton Hall

All rights reserved. No part of this book may be reproduced in any form, except for the inclusion of brief quotations in a review, without permission in writing from the author. The author grants permission to reproduce the worksheets contained in this work only for the purposes of use in a therapeutic setting. Reproduction for any other purpose is forbidden without author permission. If worksheets are reproduced during the course of a program, copyright and contact information must be left intact.

You may contact the author at chuck@mindfulecotherapy.com

ISBN 9781091901353

CONTENTS

ACKNOWLEDGMENTS 1

HOW TO USE THIS BOOK 2

DEDICATION 3

A NOTE ON THE COYOTE STORY USED 5

Orientation - Introduction to Ecospirituality 7

PHASE ONE: DEPARTURE 25

Session 1 The Call to Adventure 27

Session 2 Refusal of the Call 45

Session 3 Supernatural Aid 57

Session 4 Crossing the First Threshold 69

Session 5 The Belly of the Whale 81

PHASE TWO: INITIATION 97

Session 6 The Road of Trials 99

Session 7 Meeting with the Goddess 109

Session 8 The Tempter 127

Session 9 Atonement with the Father 141

Session 10 Apotheosis 151

Session 11 The Ultimate Boon 163

PHASE THREE: RETURN 177

Session 12 Refusal of the Return 179

Session 13 The Magic Flight 195

Session 14 Rescue from Without 213

Session 15 The Crossing of the Return Threshold 225

Chapter 16 Master of Two Worlds 237

Epilogue - Freedom to Live 251

References 255

ABOUT THE ECOSPIRITUALITY PROGRAM 257

ABOUT THE AUTHOR 259

Books by Charlton Hall, MMFT, LMFT/S, RPT-S, CHt 259

ACKNOWLEDGMENTS

"The cleansing of the earth starts with the cleansing of our minds."

--Rolling Thunder

When I was considerably younger, I read a book called *Rolling Thunder*. It was a book about a Cherokee shaman and medicine man. I was fascinated with his world view and read the book several times. In 1979, when I was living in Pensacola, Florida, Rolling Thunder came to speak at the University of West Florida. Of course I attended the seminar.

During his workshop he spoke of a place near Carlin, Nevada called *Meta Tantay* (Chumush for "Walk in Peace") where he and people of like mind were living a communal existence. It sounded like my kind of place, so I packed up my bedroll and headed for Nevada. I spent about a month there at the ranch, watching teachers from various native tribes and from other spiritual paths learn and share with each other. I had my first Vision Quest there under the tutelage of a Hopi shaman. I learned how people of different paths, different races and different nationalities could come together in spite of their differences and work for a common good.

Meta Tantay was disbanded in 1984, about four years after my visit. I was sad to see it go. I took my first steps into the world of shamanism there. I will miss the wisdom of Rolling Thunder, who died in 1997. He was a great teacher and a good friend for the brief amount of time that I knew him.

Meta Tantay, Rolling Thunder.

HOW TO USE THIS BOOK

The human race is consuming natural resources at a rate that far outpaces nature's ability to replenish them. It is clear that we cannot go on with our present course of action if the human race is to have a future. The damage we're doing to the environment causes widespread anxiety. What is needed to heal this anxiety is a grassroots paradigm shift to a new way of being in the world. Ecospirituality is one of the paths to help to make this paradigm shift. Ecospirituality is a 16-week nature-based spiritual self-improvement program. Each session meets outdoors for about 90-120 minutes and is guided by a trained Ecospirituality Coach. This handbook was designed to accompany the 16-week program, but if the program isn't offered in your region you may also use this book to complete the exercises on your own. If you successfully complete the program, find it helpful, and are interested in training to be a coach for the program, visit www.mindfulecotherapy.org for more information on the Ecospirituality Certified Facilitator Training.

If you are completing this workbook as part of an ecospirituality program or workshop, your homework is to read the material for each session prior to participating in that session. The activities in each session will be done during the workshop, so don't try to complete them ahead of time. Just read over the materials so you'll have a good idea of what to expect in each session.

If you are completing the workbook on your own, feel free to do the activities at any time, at your own pace. Many of the activities require or suggest outdoor locales. You may use your own best judgment as to whether or not the weather is appropriate in your location for any suggested activities. If you've had to postpone an activity due to bad weather, make an effort to try it again when the weather is better. In doing so you'll get the full benefit of each exercise.

DEDICATION

There are those who are born to hear the Call of the Coyote. The Way of the Coyote is a lonely way, but it can be rewarding for those who know how to answer the call. I dedicate this book to the Coyotes and to their children, and to all my Ancestors who walked the path before I did. May these words in some small way honor them and their journey.

A NOTE ON THE COYOTE STORY USED

The Coyote story used in this book is not of Native American origin, nor did it originate from any other indigenous aboriginal tribe. It is purely a product of my own imagination. While the story was inspired by Coyote lore from all around the world, it is not entirely true to the stories in their original form. The stories I used for inspiration are Coyote lore from Native American, African, South American, and many other aboriginal cultures. It is fascinating to find that in all of these myths and legends from across the globe, Coyote remains the Trickster. It is almost as if the spirit of the Coyote inspired these legends.

Orientation - Introduction to Ecospirituality

In the time that was and will be again, all of the peoples of the world came up through a hole in Mother Earth to dwell in the sunlight. All the two-legged tribes and the four-legged tribes came up together to be born. In the beginning, all the two-leggeds and four-leggeds were brothers and sisters. All the tribes of animals and humans were one People. They came up from beneath the earth one by one.

Coyote was the last to emerge.

In the time of the beginning, the Earth was covered with trees, but none of the People knew how to make fire, so all of the people of the earth, the four-leggeds and the two-leggeds, lived without fire, and could not cook, nor stay warm in the winter, nor see at night.

In that time, each creature lived according to his nature. Brother Eagle was a stern hunter and visionary who saw far, so he lived a serious life. Brother Bear was strong and knew the herbs, so he lived a life of ease and healing. Sister Cougar was crafty and wise, and lived the solitary life of the hunter. Sister Salmon was quick and sleek, and lived a busy life jumping from stream to stream.

Brother Coyote was playful, so he spent his days running to and fro about the earth. He never took anything seriously, and loved playing tricks on all the other People. Sometimes his pranks unintentionally hurt the other members of the tribe. Because of this, many of the People were wary of Coyote, and did not trust his antics.

In the time of the beginning, the People had come up out of the ground during the first spring. They had never lived on the earth before, so everything was new to them. The Sun was warm, and the land was abundant. They went about their business through the first spring and summer, never planning for the future, because life was so easy.

Because they had never lived on the earth before, they did not know about the seasons. They lived as if spring and summer would be eternal.

But soon came the first autumn. The trees were ablaze with bright reds and golds of the season. The People did not know what this meant, as they had never seen it before. They had assumed that the weather would always be warm. But as the first autumn began to give way to the first winter, they soon came to know that things were changing.

Since this was their first winter, they had no way of knowing that spring and summer would eventually return to the land. As the nights grew cooler the People began to panic.

"Is this the end of everything?" they cried, "Someone must do something! What if the sun never returns?"

They all went to their Chief, saying, "The days and nights are getting colder! If you do not do something, we will all surely die!"

So Chief Buffalo held a Council to figure out what to do.

After many days of thinking about the problem, the People finally decided that they should elect a scout to go out and search the world for a warmer place to live. One by one all the animals were considered for this quest.

"What about Brother Eagle?" the People asked.

"Brother Eagle flies high and sees far," said Chief Buffalo, "But he is far too serious. He might choose a warmer place, but would he also be able to find a place where the children can play and be happy?"

"Then what about Sister Cougar?" the People asked.

"Sister Cougar is crafty and wise," said Chief Buffalo, "But she is also a loner. She might find an excellent place with plenty of sunshine, but since she prefers her own company, she might like it so well there alone that she would forget to return and share it with us."

"How about Brother Bear?" the People cried.

"Brother Bear is indeed strong, and wise in the ways of healing, but since the nights have grown colder, he has withdrawn to his cave to sleep and nobody has seen him since. He may never return!"

"What about Sister Salmon?" They asked in desperation.

"Sister Salmon has disappeared upstream," said Chief Buffalo, "And she too may never return."

One by one the People named all of the animals of the forest, and one by one Chief Buffalo found a reason why they could not go.

Finally the only creature left was Coyote. Because Coyote loved to play tricks, and because every one of the People had been the victim of one of Coyote's pranks at one time or another, nobody wanted to name him as the scout. They did not think him responsible enough to determine the fate of the entire tribe. But finally they had no choice.

"What about Coyote?" they asked Chief Buffalo.

"Ah, what about Coyote indeed?" asked the Chief.

"Coyote is certainly fleet of foot for such a journey, but who among you trusts him?"

The People admitted that Coyote was not very trustworthy, but they were out of options.

"Perhaps," they said, "His trickery may prove to be useful on the journey!"

The People were hesitant, but since they had ruled out all the other members of the tribe for one reason or another, they were finally willing to settle on Coyote.

So it was agreed that he would be chosen for the quest.

0.0 The Need for Ecospirituality

As the human race has become increasingly urbanized, we have come to spend less and less time in natural settings. Many of us now live in cities or suburbs rather than in rural areas. Even so, we still hear the calls of nature. The wilderness cries out to something in our blood. Although the Industrial Revolution has forced us into an urban way of living, we were creatures of the wilderness for millennia before that. Evolution has hardwired our brains for the woods.

Arne Naess was a Norwegian philosopher and founder of the Deep Ecology movement. He cited Rachel Carson's book *Silent Spring* (a book about how pesticides like DDT upset the delicate balance of nature) as instrumental in his development of the philosophy of deep ecology, which states that humans are not privileged above other living things and that all living things should be treated with equal respect and equal ethical consideration. Naess believed that all things have an equal right to thrive and to survive.

The Deep Ecology movement founded by Naess echoes the *Gaia Hypothesis*.

Although NASA scientist James Lovelock is credited with creating the Gaia Hypothesis, which says that the Earth herself is a living thing, and we are all a part of the much larger organism that is Gaia, the Earth, Native Americans had such a concept for thousands of years before Lovelock came along. The Oglala Medicine Man and Shaman, Black Elk, once said, *"The first peace, which is the most important, is that which comes within the souls of people when they realize their relationship, their oneness with the universe and all its powers, and when they realize at the center of the universe dwells the Great Spirit, and that its center is really everywhere, it is within each of us."*

Scientists have discovered what the Native Americans knew all along: That the Earth is a living organism and that we are all a part of the web of life. We are all connected. This idea of the interconnectedness of all things is what Naess meant by "deep ecology," and deep ecology is at its core a spiritual movement. If we are all connected, then what we do to the web of life, we do to ourselves as well. If we poison the water, then we drink the water, we take the poison into ourselves. If we pollute the food with pesticides, then eat the food, we take the pesticides into our own bodies. If we pollute the air, then breathe in the air, we take our own pollutants into our lungs. If we fatten our beef animals with hormones, then eat the beef, we take the hormones into ourselves. If we poison the minds and souls of our neighbors with hatred, anger, and bitterness, then interact with those neighbors in negative ways, we take the hatred, anger and bitterness into ourselves as well.

The deep ecology of ecospirituality teaches us to be one with nature. This oneness with nature is the ultimate in spirituality. This is true even if we are agnostic or atheist. We don't have to believe in supernatural beings in order to realize that nature is something larger and more transcendent than ourselves. The "divinity" in ecospirituality is nature itself. This is true whether or not we choose to personify nature as a separate, conscious entity. We are all interdependent, and ecospirituality teaches us that if we cannot live in a sustainable, ecological way, then the human race will have no future. This planet has limited resources, and we currently don't have anywhere else to go. Eventually everything will run out, and when this happens, how will we survive? The only way that the human race can survive is to embrace a way of life that honors all life on the planet. Such a way of life is what ecospirituality entails.

0.1 **Religion vs. Spirituality**

So what is ecospirituality?

The word "spiritual" comes from the Latin *spiritus*, which means, "breath." So originally, that which was spiritual was simply that which was breathtaking. From this perspective a spiritual experience is an awe-inspiring experience. People of all religions…or none…can experience such awe-inspiring events. You can be spiritual without being religious. Spirituality doesn't rely on a set system of teachings or dogmas. Spirituality is the joy of being present in the moment and experiencing the awe and wonder of living.

In my personal experience, those breathtaking moments most often occur when I have made some sort of connection. It could be a connection with nature, or with others, or with my own inner self. Such a connection opens up a channel of communication, or perhaps communion. Such a connection allows me to feel that I am a part of everything, and everything is a part of me.

In this ecospirituality workbook and the accompanying program, we will be exploring the possibility of making such connections through the eyes of Coyote.

0.2 **Coyote – The Trickster**

Many Native American tribes consider Coyote to be the Trickster, the one who teaches by becoming a mirror. Coyote's tricks and jokes reflect our own folly and stubbornness back to us until we realize what is happening and learn from it, if we are fortunate enough to realize what is going on. Coyote will continue to hold a mirror up to us until we learn to see our true selves, or until we become so angry and frustrated that we lose sight of our spiritual paths.

The Way of the Coyote teaches us that wisdom is the twin of foolishness. In an insane world, the sane man must appear insane. When following the Way of the Coyote we learn to see our own foolishness in the antics of others, and we learn from their mistakes, if we are wise enough. Likewise, when we follow coyote medicine, we show others their own foolishness by our own antics. If Coyote is your teacher, he will frustrate you, anger you, and make you furious. But if you can learn to see through the rage and frustration to the lessons beneath, Coyote can teach you much.

Coyote teaches through humor and the ability to laugh at life's absurdities and ironies, and to be able to laugh at ourselves. The Way of the Coyote is to strip away the masks we all wear so that we may get to the truth underneath. Coyote teaches us to cast aside all the fronts that we put on for others and for ourselves so that we may live fully and abundantly according to our own true nature.

Coyote energy is reflected in the phrase, "Simplicity is perfection." He teaches us to learn to distinguish what we need from what we want. Coyote won't give us everything we want, but he will lead us to everything we need. He will also teach us the difference between the two.

The Call of the Coyote stirs up something primitive and passionate in our souls, and reminds us to return to that place of the beginning; that childlike sense of wonder and fascination with the beauty of the world. That sense of awe and wonder is the essence of ecospirituality.

Coyote is a survivor, and is able to adapt to new situations by learning to bend and flow with skill and cunning. The Way of the Coyote is to understand that all things are sacred, yet nothing is sacred. If you have any sacred cows in our life, coyote will be sure to devour them. If you hold nothing sacred, Coyote will lead you to the knowledge that everything is holy.

Another way to put this, in the context of Coyote magic, is that if what you're doing isn't working, then Coyote teaches us that doing more of it isn't going to work either. In fact, it may make things worse. So when we begin to walk the Way of the Coyote, we may find ourselves lost in the unfamiliar. Some of the things Coyote may ask us to do will seem strange, even weird. But that's okay. If it didn't feel weird, we'd probably already be doing it. If we stay on the path of the comfortable and the familiar, we are in danger of doing the same things in the same ways and getting the same results we've always gotten. If, however, we have the courage to step forth and try something different, we may find that our world will change for the better.

But setting about doing things differently can be a scary experience. We often fear the unknown, and Coyote loves to take us into the mysterious. That is the art of the Trickster. It is also the reason Coyote can often be frustrating. He asks us to leave our comfort zone.

If you have heard the Call of the Coyote, learn to look for things you may have been avoiding or refusing to acknowledge in your own life. These sometimes manifest in strange ways. Look at what you criticize the most in others, and see if you yourself have those same characteristics. For example, if you find yourself constantly judging others for their anger, could it be that you have a problem with anger yourself? If you are constantly demanding other people to more forgiving, could there be someone in your own life that you need to beg for forgiveness? If you are constantly telling others to be more tolerant and loving, could it be that you may need to learn to be more tolerant and loving as well?

A pitfall of Coyote medicine is that those who don't understand Coyote's ways are often angered or alienated by the mirror Coyote holds up to us because they don't wish to acknowledge what it shows them about themselves. Sometimes the Way of the Coyote can be a lonely way because of this. If you have heard the Call of the Coyote, it could also mean that you need to look into your own mirror and see if there is something about yourself that you have been afraid to acknowledge. By refusing to acknowledge it, you give it power over you. But acknowledging our weaknesses and shortcomings is the first step to conquering them.

If Coyote has chosen you, look closely at ways you may have been giving energy to foolishness. This is especially true in relationships, since we often fool ourselves in relationships, and refuse to see what is plain to everyone else. As they say, *"Love is blind."* Remember that Coyote's ultimate goal is not to anger or frustrate, but to teach. In order for Coyote to teach, we have to be willing to learn. It helps to remember that sometimes the best lessons are also the most painful lessons. If Coyote is causing you pain, it is not out of malice, but out of love. It is so that you may grow on your own path. If Coyote angers you, it is because you gave him permission to do so. When this happens, always remember to ask yourself, "What is the lesson here?"

To answer the Call of the Coyote is to be a strong protector of family, relationships, and connections. Coyotes often mate for life, and will fiercely defend partners and cubs. If Coyote is your ally, family is probably very important to you. Coyotes will often adopt cubs who have become parentless. They realize that family is not always a matter of blood, but of spirit, so for those of us who follow the Way, Coyote medicine is concerned more with our spiritual families than our blood relatives. To follow the Way of the Coyote is to realize that members of the same spiritual family rarely grow up under the same roof. It is also to realize that our family need not be restricted to our two-legged brothers and sisters, but it can include our four-legged brothers and sisters as well, and all of nature.

Ultimately the Way of the Coyote is about achieving balance in our lives. Ecospirituality is also about achieving this balance. All life on Mother Earth is in danger largely because of the greed of human beings. If we continue our pursuit of trinkets and baubles, always wanting more and never satisfied with what we have, we will eventually destroy everything. A life of rampant materialism is a life out of balance. Things can never fill the void we feel inside when our lives are out of balance. Only true spiritual wisdom can fill that void.

The Call of the Coyote is about finding a balance between the material and the spiritual so that we cease to destroy our Earth Mother and each other. It is about learning to distinguish between our wants and our needs. The only true necessities in life are food, clothing, shelter and love. Once those needs are met, anything else is a luxury. Material possessions are a poor substitute for love and spirit. The Way of the Coyote teaches us to focus on the things that truly matter.

When we learn this lesson completely, we will be embracing the essence of ecospirituality and learning to walk the Way of the Coyote. When we seek to share this knowledge and wisdom with our fellow travelers along the way, we will have fulfilled our destinies as spiritual seekers. We will have achieved the ultimate in ecospirituality.

0.3 The True Self: Your Own True Nature

Ecospirituality is the path of embracing nature as a means of finding your own True Self. The True Self is the person you would be if there were no limitations on you. It is who you would be if you could live fearlessly. The path to True Self in ecospirituality is the path to living out your own true nature, free of the expectations or demands of others. Coyote, the ultimate Trickster, can lead you to this path, but he may infuriate you first. This is because he asks us to live up to our full potential. He requires us to do deep, soul-searching work and to be completely honest with ourselves. Such an act requires taking responsibility for our own lives. This is not an easy task. If we take responsibility for our own lives, we have nobody to blame but ourselves should we fail. The good news is that if we take responsibility for our own lives, nobody else can take credit for our own personal successes.

To walk the Way of the Coyote is to see the seeds of success in every failure. It is to acknowledge every crisis as an opportunity. It is to see every problem as a challenge and an occasion for learning and growth. Coyote teaches us that if we never make mistakes, we never learn anything, because if we didn't make a mistake when walking the path, we already knew the way. And if we already knew the way, we didn't learn anything new on the journey.

As we travel through this workbook together, it is my hope that you will take the time to learn about your own true nature from the exercises that follow. This book is a synopsis of what it means to answer the Call of the Coyote. It is a seeker's journey of self-discovery. It is an opportunity to discover your own true nature. Some of the material here may be useful to you as you answer your own call to adventure; some of it may not be. As you read over the material in this book, it is my wish that, as with everything else in life, you take what is useful and discard the rest.

Are you ready to begin?

If so, go on to complete the worksheet on the next page.

Worksheet 0.3 Ecospirituality and Connection   Page 1 of 1

Name _____ Date _____

This workbook and the ecospirituality program define spirituality as "connectedness." What are some things that help you feel connected to others?

_____
_____
_____
_____
_____

What are some things that help you to feel connected to nature?

_____
_____
_____
_____
_____

What are some things that help you feel connected to your own True Self?

(NOTE: Your True Self is the person you are in the process of becoming; who you would be if you had no limitations or constraints on being who you want to be; how you would live if you were free to live fully according to your own true nature)

_____
_____
_____
_____
_____

What are some barriers to connection that you may have experienced in your own life?

_____
_____
_____
_____

0.4 The Hero's Journey: The Monomyth

Joseph Campbell was an American mythologist best known for his works and lectures in comparative mythology and comparative religion. His personal philosophy is often summarized in the phrase, *"Follow your bliss."* This too is the path of ecospirituality and of the Way of the Coyote...to be able to live according to your own true nature by following your bliss.

One of Campbell's areas of study was the archetypal nature of world mythologies. He noted that myths from around the world followed a pattern. Campbell conceptualized this pattern into a framework or a template for the seeker's journey, calling it the *monomyth*. The monomyth is the archetypal mythological journey of discovery. Campbell's monomyth is often referred to as *the Hero's Journey*. Elements of this journey show up in sacred texts of most religions. It is the journey of Moses, of Jesus, of Krishna, of Mohammed, of the Buddha, of King Arthur, and even of Luke Skywalker. George Lucas relied heavily on the works of Joseph Campbell when crafting the original *Star Wars* saga.

The path of ecospirituality also follows the monomyth. This is because the Way of the Coyote is a hero's journey of self-discovery. The ultimate destination for this seeker's journey is to be able to live in True Self according to your own true nature.

The template for the monomyth, along with an explanation of the phases, is outlined below. There are three major phases, with steps for each phase. The three major phases are: *Departure, Initiation,* and *Return*. This book and the ecospirituality program are divided into three sections labeled after these phases.

As you read over the descriptions below, see if you can identify where you might be in your own spiritual path. This knowledge will help you as you progress through this book and through the ecospirituality program.

Phase One: Departure

In the *Departure* phase, the hero leaves the familiar on a journey of self-awareness that will ultimately make or break him. The Departure phase is about a way of doing things differently than they have been done in the past. It is an awakening to the world of wider possibilities. It has been said that, "Insanity is doing the same thing in the same ways and expecting things to turn out differently." In the Departure phase, we prepare for the journey by coming to the realization that if what we have been doing hasn't been working, then doing more of it isn't likely to work either. For a spiritual seeker, this means challenging your own accepted notions of what spirituality means. It means going against the dogma you were raised with and finding your own individual path. It means trusting yourself and your own supernatural aid enough to take that step.

The Call to Adventure

The Call to Adventure is the catalyst that sets the Hero's Journey in motion. It could be an inner need to change one's circumstances, or it could be an external event that triggers the journey. For Buddha, it was the inner desire to seek enlightenment. For Luke Skywalker, the Empire forced his hand. In either case, the hero recognizes that something fundamental has changed, and he/she can never go back to the way things were.

Refusal of the Call

Change is scary. The comforting thing about the familiar is its familiarity; we know what to expect. This can even be true if the familiar situation is grim. Such a sentiment is often expressed in the phrase, *"Better the devil you know than the devil you don't know."*

The familiar, however uncomfortable it may be, is at least familiar. When faced with change, there is an element of the unknown that must be reckoned with. Few things are as frightening as a trip into the unknown. No matter how bad things are, the thought that they could potentially get worse always hovers in the back of our minds. By making a change, chance has entered the equation. What may you expect to happen when walking into uncharted territory? Things might get better, but they might get worse as well. Because of this doubt and uncertainty about where the path may lead, many people refuse the call to adventure.

Supernatural Aid

Sometimes when we get stuck in our refusal of the call, we need a little push to get going again. When this happens, the stars tend to align in such a way that we have to act. If we choose not to walk through the open door out of fear or uncertainty, the universe begins to close all other doors one by one until we have no choice but to walk through the one that is open before us.

This supernatural aid doesn't have to come from some deity. Sometimes it is just as simple as a moment of inspiration or a flash of insight. Sometimes it may just be learning to see things in a new way. Sometimes it's just the knowledge that we can't live the rest of our lives this way. Whatever the ultimate form our supernatural aid takes, it sets our feet on the path in spite of our reluctance to embrace the journey.

The Crossing of the First Threshold

> *"It's a dangerous business, going out your door. You step into the road, and if you don't keep your feet, there is no knowing where you might be swept off to."*
>
> --Bilbo Baggins

A journey of a thousand miles begins with a single step. This means that for every journey there is a first step. The Crossing of the First Threshold is that first step. The significance of that first step is that it indicates a commitment to the journey. The reluctance and refusal are over, and the intention has been set. Once your intention has been determined, and you announce your intention to the Universe, there is no going back to the way things have been in the past.

Belly of the Whale

In order to learn new ways of being, we must first cast off our old assumptions about the way things work. Our assumptions create our perceptions, and our perceptions create our reality. If we're journeying to new realities, our old perceptions and assumptions have to be discarded. This can be an especially difficult task, since many of our assumptions and perceptions are involved in our own sense of identity. If we cast them off, we lose who we are. But in order to become someone new, we *must* lose who we were. Percival had to cast off his armor before he could receive the Holy Grail. Since he was a knight, this meant casting off all outward appearances of his former identity in order to discover something new.

Jonah spent three days in the Belly of the Whale after his Refusal of the Call. This was Jonah's casting off of his former identity so that he could step into his new role as a spiritual leader. This time in the whale's belly is a time of reflection and of challenging preconceived notions before initiation into a wider world. It is a preparation for the death of the old self so that the new self may be born.

Phase Two: Initiation

In the Initiation phase, the hero must "die to herself." Many religious and shamanic rituals involve a symbolic death and rebirth to a new way of being. Initiation is an emptying of your cup so that it may be refilled with new knowledge. For a spiritual seeker, Initiation means being open to new experiences and being willing to experiment with new ways of being.

The Road of Trials

> *"The word 'ashes' contains in it a dark feeling for death; ashes when put on the face whiten it as death does...some men around thirty-five or forty will begin to experience ashes privately, without ritual, even without old men. They begin to notice how many of their dreams have turned to ashes."*
>
> –Robert Bly, *Iron John: A Book about Men*

The *Road of Trials* begins with what Robert Bly calls "Time in the Ashes," or "Ashes Time." Sometimes things get worse before they get better. The Greek *katabasis* literally means "to go down" or "to descend." Katabasis is the idea that it is always darkest before the dawn. As the spiritual seeker's old identity is stripped away in the Belly of the Whale, there is nothing yet with which to replace it. To a spiritual seeker, this katabasis may feel like the end of the world. Sometimes it manifests as a sense that one's entire life has been meaningless up until this point. Author Richard Bach, in his bestseller *Jonathan Livingston Seagull*, describes this feeling best: "I gave my life to become the person I am right now. Was it worth it?"

The Meeting with the Goddess/God

"For she is the incarnation of the promise of perfection, the soul's assurance that, at the conclusion of the exile in a world of organized inadequacies, the bliss that once was known will be known again..." – Joseph Campbell, *The Hero's Journey*

The Goddess (or God) here isn't necessarily an actual divine entity, although she can be. Since the heroes in most of the myths Campbell studied were heterosexual males, the Meeting with the Goddess represents the ideal partner. Since we're talking about a spiritual and metaphorical level here, the Meeting with the Goddess symbolizes the idea of completeness and perfection. After having our former identities stripped away in the Belly of the Whale, and after our Initiation in the Road of Trials, the Goddess appears to us in ideal form with the promise of what could be, if we persevere. The Goddess represents perfect love. It is a love that is truly unconditional; a love that applies not only to others, bur to self as well.

The Temptress/Tempter

The original monomyth referred to "Woman as Temptress." The gender bias of referring to the Temptress/Tempter as a woman is a by-product of centuries of male heroes in mythology. The Temptress can just as easily be a Tempter, as when Lucifer tempted Jesus with all the wealth of the world if he would give up his seeker's journey.

Whichever gender you choose to picture the Tempter/Temptress, its purpose is to entice you with the easy way out. The Temptress manifests in shortcuts, laziness, and leaving things half-done. It is the counterpoint to the Meeting with the Goddess. The lesson of the Tempter is that if we cheat by taking shortcuts on the road to enlightenment, we are only cheating ourselves.

The Temptress will test your integrity and character, but there is a purpose in this trial. By testing you, the Tempter gives you an opportunity to display your honor. True honor is how we act when nobody else is watching, and the Temptress gives us the opportunity to practice that honor. She will attempt to sway us from the path and try to prevent us from owning the darker parts of ourselves. If this happens, we will fail to achieve Atonement with the Father.

Atonement with the Father

The poet Robert Bly, in *Iron John*, talks about the son receiving an injury from the father. Whether the father intentionally or unintentionally gives the son this injury, often it is this catalyst that sets the son off on a journey of self-discovery in the first place. In primal cultures this injury is sometimes ritualized and done deliberately. In some African cultures, the father knocks out one of the son's teeth in a rite of passage ritual. In some Native American cultures, the son receives some other form of injury, as in the ritual tearing of the pectoral muscles practiced during the Sun Dance of the Lakotas. This dark aspect of fatherhood is reflected in the idea of the *Shadow* from Jungian psychology (more on this later). The psychoanalyst Carl Jung believed that all human beings have the potential for all behaviors. The most moral among us have the potential to become serial killers, and the most immoral among us have the potential to redeem themselves and become saints. Since, according to Jung, all humans have the potential for all behaviors, the behaviors we choose not to express are suppressed in the unconscious. The part of the psyche in which these behaviors are repressed is what Jung called the *Shadow*. The behaviors we choose to express, the mask we wear in our daily lives, are what Jung called the *Persona*.

The Atonement with the Father is the integration of the Shadow with the Persona. Although the Shadow is where our dark, evil impulses lie, it is also where our creativity lies. Without it, we can have no imagination. So Atonement is literally "at-ONE-ment," meaning that the Shadow and the Persona become one. This does not mean that we consciously choose to act on those evil impulses. It means that by acknowledging their existence in the first place, we can move towards mastering them. When they are mastered, we can achieve apotheosis.

Apotheosis

This word, Greek in origin, means, "To deify," or to "become godlike." According to Joseph Campbell, apotheosis is, *"The pattern of the divine state to which the human hero attains who has gone beyond the last terrors of ignorance."*

Apotheosis is the ability to rise above the chess board and recognize that one has been a pawn in the game. By seeing the whole board, we gain a new perspective. It is a shift in perspective; the solving of the puzzle of existence. Once the hero has achieved apotheosis, he can never go back to the way things were before. Apotheosis is the gaining of a godlike wisdom. Adam has eaten the apple, and gained the godlike knowledge of good and evil.

The Ultimate Boon

The Ultimate Boon is the treasure at the end of the journey. It is the Holy Grail; the elixir of life; the reason for the journey in the first place. For a spiritual seeker, the Ultimate Boon may be the gifts of wisdom and enlightenment. In ecospirituality, the Ultimate Boon is the ability to live according to one's own true nature.

Phase Three: Return

In the Return Phase, the hero has gained wisdom about the nature of reality and consciousness, and is now faced with the challenge of returning to the world to teach those who are willing to listen. It is the process of coming home with the Holy Grail. It is the act of bringing the Ten Commandments down off the mountaintop. It is the skill of helping others to achieve what the hero has achieved, while avoiding the temptation to turn them into carbon copies of himself. For a spiritual seeker, this means applying lessons learned in the spiritual realm to daily life. It means learning to see the bigger picture and to trust the vision.

Refusal of the Return

When you have tasted the milk and honey of Paradise, why would you want to leave? When you've experienced perfection, it can be difficult to summon the energy to return to an imperfect world. There is also the consideration of trying to communicate your experience to others who have not had the same experience. You will lack a common frame of reference. Once your perceptions have been transformed and you learn to see things in a new way and speak a new language, it can feel like it's impossible to communicate with those who haven't learned the same language.

In Plato's Cave Allegory, the Seeker learns to see beyond the illusion and into the real nature of things. In Plato's Cave, these illusions take the form of shadows projected on a wall. The shadows are of people. The shadows are not the people; they are merely an illusion and a projection of the real people behind the shadows. In Plato's Cave, the Seeker sees the real people behind the shadows for the first time. But when he tries to explain the concept of real people to the others in the cave, they cannot understand what he means, because they lack a common frame of reference.

A return to the "real" world of shadows after living for a time in the world of true substance can be a frustrating experience if you hope to share your newfound wisdom with others. Because of this, it is easy to refuse the return, especially if you have attained paradise along your journey.

The Magic Flight

> *"If the hero in his triumph wins the blessing of the goddess or the god and is then explicitly commissioned to return to the world with some elixir for the restoration of society, the final stage of his adventure is supported by all the powers of his supernatural patron. On the other hand, if the trophy has been attained against the opposition of its guardian, or if the hero's wish to return to the world has been resented by the gods or demons, then the last stage of the mythological round becomes a lively, often comical, pursuit. This flight may be complicated by marvels of magical obstruction and evasion."*
>
> --Joseph Campbell

Sometimes the hero can escape with the Ultimate Boon. But sometimes forces conspire to prevent the hero from returning. Even paradise can be a prison if you can't leave when you wish to leave. For the spiritual seeker, the Magic Flight may consist of letting go of forms of spirituality that are no longer meaningful. Spirituality is only good when it isn't taken too seriously. This is the ultimate lesson of Coyote magic. If you find yourself in a space where the tools and the dogma have become more important than the message, then you may be in need of a Magic Flight.

Rescue from Without

As the end of the path draws nigh, the hero may be exhausted and spent from the journey. If you have cast off the weary world, you are probably in no hurry to return to it. If this is the case, then the world may have to come and get you. For a spiritual seeker, this rescue from without may come from a friend or a family member who needs the wisdom you have gained from your journey, or it may come from the knowledge that we are all connected, and what helps one must ultimately help all.

The Crossing of the Return Threshold

The Return Threshold is the doorway that lies between the spiritual world and the "real" world. In order to cross the return threshold, the spiritual seeker must complete three tasks. First, she must retain all the wisdom she gained on the quest so that she may share it with others. Next, she must find a way to integrate that wisdom into a human life without pain or regret. Finally, she must find a way to share that wisdom with the rest of the world in such a way that they receive it with welcome. This last task is especially important, as we humans tend to make martyrs out of messiahs. This is another powerful way that Coyote magic may be used. Sometimes people have to be "tricked" into enlightenment in order to bypass their preconceived notions of what is and what should be. In any case, these three tasks must be accomplished in order to cross the return threshold.

Master of Two Worlds

Once your basic needs of food, clothing, shelter and love have been satisfied, how much do you truly need? We often confuse our wants with our needs. The Master of Two Worlds has learned to reconcile these dualities. Such a Master has found a balance between the spiritual world and the material world. This seeker has also found a balance between his Shadow and his Persona; his light half and his dark half. Such a person has moved beyond seeing the world in black-and-white terms, and can see the gray areas, where most of life happens.

Georg Wilhelm Friedrich Hegel's famous philosophical device, commonly known as the Hegelian Dialectic, is a triad consisting of *thesis*, *antithesis*, and *synthesis*, where the thesis is an idea, the antithesis is the idea's opposite, and the synthesis is the blending of the two. If the material world is the thesis, and the spiritual world is the antithesis, then a synthesis of the two would be finding a way to live spiritually in the material world. The Master of Two Worlds has achieved this synthesis.

Freedom to Live

Once you've conquered your fear of death, what else can stand in your way? If the soul is the only thing in the Universe that is truly indestructible, then death is just another way of being. Even if you are atheist or agnostic, and have no belief in an afterlife, this is still true from the point of view of your own consciousness. If this life is all you will ever know, and there is no afterlife, then it is impossible to ever be conscious of your own death; therefore there is no way you could ever know that you have died. How can you be conscious of your own death, if death is the end to consciousness? So from the perspective of your own consciousness, you are immortal for all practical purposes. When you die, your Universe ceases to exist, and you are no longer the Center. With this knowledge of death comes the Freedom to Live. Soul musician Ray Charles said, *"Live every day like it's going to be your last, because one of these days you'll be right."*

Freedom to Live means that you have mastered death…and life.

A spiritual seeker can use this monomyth template as a road map for following the Way of the Coyote, or any other spiritual path. As you look over the phases and steps above, you can probably readily identify where you are on the journey. You can also identify what lies ahead, and get some idea of what skills and tools you will need to meet those upcoming challenges. The chapters that follow will go into more depth about what some of those challenges might be, and how to overcome them. The rest is up to you!

When you have read over the information in this chapter, think about where you might be on your own ecospiritual journey, then go on to the next page to complete the worksheet.

WORKSHEET 0.4 MY HERO'S JOURNEY

Name _____ Date _____

Based on the phases of the Hero's Journey described in this chapter, where do you feel you are?

Phase One: Departure
- ☐ The Call to Adventure
- ☐ Refusal of the Call
- ☐ Supernatural Aid
- ☐ The Crossing of the First Threshold
- ☐ Belly of The Whale

Phase Two: Initiation
- ☐ The Road of Trials
- ☐ The Meeting with the Goddess
- ☐ Woman as Temptress
- ☐ Atonement with the Father
- ☐ Apotheosis
- ☐ The Ultimate Boon

Phase Three: Return
- ☐ Refusal of the Return
- ☐ The Magic Flight
- ☐ Rescue from Without
- ☐ The Crossing of the Return Threshold
- ☐ Master of Two Worlds
- ☐ Freedom to Live

What are your reasons for choosing this stage of the journey?

_____
_____
_____
_____

Based on where you are right now on your journey, what skills, tools, and knowledge would you need to get to the next stage of your own Hero's Journey?

_____
_____
_____
_____

What are some things that might stand in your way?

_____
_____
_____
_____

What do you plan to do if those things get in your way?

_____
_____
_____
_____

PHASE ONE: DEPARTURE

In the Departure phase, the hero leaves the familiar on a journey of self-awareness that will ultimately make or break him. The Departure phase is about a way of doing things differently than they have been done in the past. It is an awakening to the world of wider possibilities. For a spiritual seeker, it means challenging accepted notions of what spirituality means. It means going against the dogma and finding your own individual path. It means trusting yourself and your own supernatural aid enough to take that step.

Session 1 The Call to Adventure

So the People went in search of Coyote to ask him to go on the quest to find a new place for the People. Chief Buffalo sent Brother Eagle and Sister Cougar to find him.

They came upon Coyote playing in a field of fallen leaves, and told him that Chief Buffalo had summoned him, so Coyote followed them back to Chief Buffalo's lodge. When Coyote approached, Chief Buffalo greeted him politely.

Brother Coyote said in return, "Why have you summoned me here on this fine but chilly day, Grandfather Buffalo?"

Chief Buffalo spoke, "I have asked you here to request that you go on a quest for the People."

"A quest?" Brother Coyote asked skeptically.

"Yes, a quest," said Chief Buffalo, "The days and nights are getting colder, and nobody can say whether they will ever grow warmer again. The People are afraid that the warmth of the Sun might never return, so we are asking you to go on a journey to find a new place for the Tribe to live."

Coyote was puzzled. His brothers and sisters of the tribe always seemed wary of him because of his love of tricks and practical jokes. Why were they coming to him now? This strange request didn't seem to make any sense to him. How could his brothers and sisters of the tribe, who didn't seem to trust him, suddenly ask him to take on such an important burden?

1.0 On the Nature of Reality

I moved to Pensacola, Florida shortly after graduating high school in 1978. I had begun investigating alternatives to the religious dogma of my Southern Baptist upbringing a few years before that time, and I was still trying to figure it all out. One day I was at the beach, wading in the water while meditating and taking in all the scenery, when I had a revelation.

If you've ever been to the Gulf Coast, you know that for the most part the water is crystal-clear. Or at least it was back in those days. I had waded out on this particular day to about waist-deep and was staring at my feet through the water. As I looked at my feet, I watched the image refract, expanding and contracting with the motions of the waves. I remembered from my high school physics class that matter is essentially vibrations of energy patterns. As I watched the patterns the water made across the images of my body, refracting them and bending the images at random, I began to see myself as vibrating waves and not as solid matter.

The ripples of the ocean waves made my body appear as if it were dissolving and re-appearing in clouds of probability around the center of my being. As I watched these ever-shifting images I had a revelation. The ripples represented the atoms and molecules that make up my body. They vibrated in and out of existence, just like subatomic particles do. Yet my body was still there. I looked out across the sea, watching the ripples recede into the distance. All of those ripples were separate and distinct, yet all were interconnected by the waters of the sea.

As I watched, I realized that this was a perfect metaphor for existence.

Each group of ripples could be seen as an individual entity. The subatomic vibrations that make up a human body or an animal, or other living thing, are all groups of vibrations resonating at a shared range of frequencies. The ripples could represent any inanimate object as well. By focusing on a particular group of ripples I could see that group as separate from the whole, but eventually they melted into other ripples, which melted into other ripples, and so on into the infinite horizon.

All of these ripples were separate in a way, but they were all interconnected to one another in another way. As I stared out across the surface of the sea, I saw it as a metaphor for the Universe and all the energy it contains in all of its myriad shapes and permutations.

At the time I had been reading materials on the ideas of clairvoyance and premonition. It seemed to me at the time that if people could really see the future, then this gift should work all the time, and not just intermittently, as was so often reported. My scientifically-minded viewpoint was that if there was such a thing as clairvoyance, it should work 100% or not at all. But as I stood there in the waters, watching the waves come and go, I began to see things differently.

As I stood in the sea, I saw one wave rise, only to be obscured by another wave. I could see the peak of one wave for a moment, but as another wave rose up, that wave was hidden from sight. Suddenly I saw the ocean as a metaphor for the fabric of time. What if time isn't linear, but vibrates like waves on the surface of the ocean?

I pictured the waves as the sea of time in which we live our lives. What if those with the gift of clairvoyance can see the future, but only when the waves of time are in proper alignment? That would explain why clairvoyants aren't able to be 100% accurate 100% of the time. From this perspective time is not a solid thing, but a pattern of waves, like an ocean. If an event occurs, it is like throwing a stone into the sea. That event produces ripples that change the pattern of time. If a large enough event occurs, like a war or a cultural revolution or change in consciousness, it is like a storm at sea. That storm makes a huge change in the patterns of the waves. As the waves spread out from the events that cause them, it changes the pattern a person with psychic abilities might see. So a vision of the future might vary from moment to moment as circumstances change.

What is the dividing line between one entity (or one reality) and another? How do we decide when one collection of vibrations is separate and distinct from another? For me, the answer is that there is no true separation. The idea of separation is an illusion that we have consciously chosen to accept for our own purposes. So if I perceive any separation between you and me, or between me and other living things, or between you and the inanimate objects in your environment, then that separation doesn't exist in reality. It's just a temporarily useful framework our minds have created in order to more easily make sense of things until a better hypothesis comes along.

Einstein demonstrated that there is also no separation between space and time. Space and time are part of the same thing. Time is just another aspect of space. Because of this "wavy" nature of reality and time, what we mean by "reality" isn't necessarily written in stone. So there can be multiple realities based on where you choose to place your perceptions and how your consciousness chooses to organize those perceptions.

The Way of the Coyote is the Way of the Shaman. One of the characteristics of a shaman is the ability to walk between the worlds. In most shamanic traditions, this means that the shaman has the ability to go into the Otherworld where the spirits of the dead lie. Some people like to think of this Otherworld as having an actual independent existence outside of our own minds. For these people, the Otherworld is an actual place where the spirits of our departed Ancestors dwell. Others prefer not to declare that the Otherworld is a real place, but instead is the realm of what Carl Jung called the *collective unconscious*. In this place of collective unconscious, the Otherworld lies in our own unconscious minds, and does not have any independent existence outside of our own thoughts and perceptions. In this case, the Otherworld, or the collective unconscious, is the repository of all our unconscious archetypes. It is the genetic memory shared by all human beings.

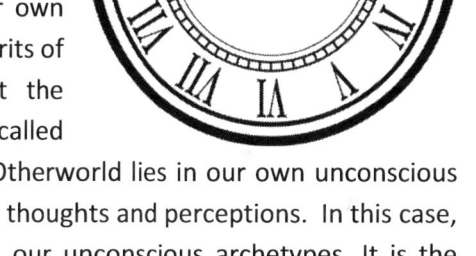

In either case, whether you believe in the Otherworld as an actual place or as a construct of the unconscious mind, what matters are our perceptions of the Otherworld. If the Otherworld alters our perceptions, gives us useful information, and teaches us about ourselves and others, does it really matter whether it is a "real" place? What do we mean by "real" anyway? From this point of view, the Otherworld of the shaman is simply a non-ordinary reality created by altering our perceptions and consciously re-ordering those perceptions.

I imagine that a great deal of time and effort has been wasted on arguing about the "reality" of the Otherworld. I for one don't care if the Otherworld is "real" or not. I'm far more interested in whether or not the Otherworld is a useful concept when it comes to re-ordering perceptions and changing consciousness. If the concept of the Otherworld is helpful to me in any way as I answer the Call of the Coyote, then it has fulfilled its purpose.

1.1 Creating Your Reality

Our assumptions about life influence our perceptions. Taken as a whole, all our perceptions add up to our own version of reality. If your assumption is that the world is flat, how would that influence your daily perceptions and your daily reality? What if your assumption is that the world is round? Each of these choices comes with perceptions about the way the world works. If you assume the world is flat, how would you feel about sailing in a ship to the ends of the earth? If you assume that the world is round, would you feel the same way? What reality would you create for yourself in each of the scenarios above?

You create your reality through your assumptions and perceptions. This creates a triad that looks like the illustration in the figure below.

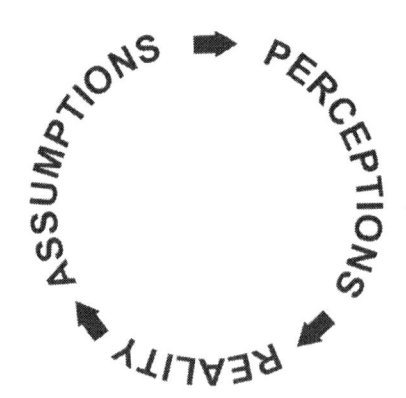

To explain how this process works, consider for a moment that you have an assumption that "Everybody is out to get me."

If your assumption is, "Everybody is out to get me," then that assumption is going to set your perception filter in a certain way. With this assumption, your perception filter is set so that you only notice instances of behavior that confirm your assumption. If your perception filter has been set by the assumption that "Everybody is out to get me," then you're only going to notice when people act in a way that confirms your assumption, and you will ignore any behavior to the contrary. If this is how your perception filter is set, then you are going to ignore it when people act in such a way that they demonstrate that they are *not* out to get you. Not only that, but when people act in such a way, you're going to take it as evidence that they *are* out to get you, because you'll think that the only reason they're being nice is that they're trying to get something from you.

Now this assumption and this perception will work together to create your reality for you. Here's how it works: If you assume that "Everybody is out to get me," and your perception filter is set to only see examples that confirm your assumption, how are you likely to treat people who *aren't* out to get you? If I'm a person who's not out to get you, and I'm doing nice things for you because I like you and want to be your friend, yet every time I do something nice for you, you treat me as if I'm up to something, how long do you think I'll stay around?

If you treat everyone as if they're out to get you, even when they're not, you will eventually drive away anyone who's *not* out to get you. At that point, the only people who are still in your life are people who *are* out to get you. So through choosing your assumptions and your perceptions about the way the world works, and by acting upon those assumptions and perceptions, you create a reality based on those assumptions and perceptions.

Let's look at another example. If you are seeking to follow the Way of the Coyote, you are seeking to walk the path of the shaman. To walk in the path of a shaman is to interact on a regular basis with the Otherworld. Therefore in order to be a shaman, you have to have some concept of the Otherworld. It can be a real place, or it can be a psychological place, but it is a necessary place for shamanism to exist and work its magic. So if you seek to walk the path of the shaman, but your first assumption is, "The Otherworld does not exist," then you are going to set your perception filter to only notice things that confirm your assumption that the Otherworld does not exist. As you continue to ignore any and all evidence for the existence of the Otherworld, it will retreat further and further away from you, until, for you, it does not exist.

On the other hand, if you assume the Otherworld does exist, then your perception filter is set to look for evidence that confirms this assumption. The more evidence you find to support this assumption, the more you make the Otherworld real in your own mind.

When considering the Otherworld, don't forget that just because something is happening in your own mind, that doesn't mean it's not real. The Otherworld might be a real place, or it might just be a place of psychological processes lying between the conscious and subconscious worlds. In either case, if you experience the Otherworld, then it has become real for you. I prefer to focus on the utility of these experiences instead of whether or not they're happening in a "real" place. The more I use my assumptions and perceptions to create my own reality, the more real the Otherworld becomes for me.

1.2 Characteristics of Shamanism

Shamanism is known throughout most indigenous cultures of the world. The word *shaman* itself comes from the Evenk language (Tungusic) of North Asia, and originally meant, "one who knows," so a shaman is a wise person. The word itself is North Asian in origin, but most primal cultures had some sort of concept of the shaman, even though they might not have been known by that name. In ancient Scotland they were called "taibhsear, or "vision seekers." In Lakota, they were called "Wicasa Wakan," or "holy men." In Hawaii, the word is "Kupuna," meaning "Elder" or "Ancestor." There are nuances of meaning from culture to culture, and some cultures get offended when people use an Evenk word to describe their own shamanic traditions, but the word "shaman" has become ingrained in common usage to refer to anyone from any culture who practices a spiritual path with the characteristics listed below:

- *Out-of-Body experiences* – These experiences are sometimes called "soul journeys" or "magic flights." In such an experience, the practitioner's soul leaves the body and travels to distant places and/or times to gather information for healing and other purposes. Most cultures that practice shamanism also have a belief that the shaman can visit the Otherworld; the realm of the dead that is the dwelling place of the departed Ancestors, and sometime of the gods as well.

- *Chanting, drumming and dancing* – These rhythmic and repetitive sounds are specifically designed not for entertainment, but to induce a trancelike state that can then be used to journey to the Otherworld.

- *A codified system of training* – This training system usually takes the form of an apprenticeship in which an experienced shaman trains a student in specific tools and techniques usually geared towards producing visions and otherworldly journeys.

- *An initiatory crisis involving a death and rebirth experience* – This is usually a ritualized event in which the student or apprentice "dies" to the old way of life and is reborn to a new way of being in the world. It usually also includes a new way of seeing the world.

- *Gifts of divination, diagnosis, and/or prophecy* – Shamans are able to see the future, diagnose sicknesses, and make prophecies. Divination and prophecy usually takes the shape of journeying to the Otherworld and bringing back information, or consulting with the gods about the fate of a person or situation. The diagnostic aspect can incorporate basic medical skills, but also moves beyond the physical to seeking diagnostic information within the spiritual realm.

- *Healing rites and rituals involving spiritual matters* – Shamans from most cultures journey to the Otherworld to recover lost souls who may have left their bodies behind during a sickness. They may also recover spirits trapped in various versions of Limbo.

- *A belief that diseases are caused wholly or in part by spirits, witches and sorcerers, or curses* – A modern take on this belief is the idea of doing *energy work* in order to prevent the influence of negative energies and to promote the influence of positive energies. Studies like the Adverse Childhood Experiences (ACE) study have demonstrated that mental wellbeing can have a powerful impact on one's physical wellbeing, and restoring mental and spiritual balance improves immune system functioning and overall physical health.

- *A belief in and interaction with totem animals and spirits* – Most shamans have at least one totem animal, and many have more than one. Totem animals assist the shaman in spirit journeys, and in completing magical tasks. They may also watch over the shaman and people under her protection.

- *The ability to shape-shift into different animals* – This shape-shifting doesn't necessarily imply a literal transformation. It could be creative costuming and mimicry. Shamans from many cultures wear feathered cloaks because birds have the ability to shift between the worlds of earth and sky. By impersonating birds, shamans gain their powers and abilities. So by dancing like a bird, the shaman gains the power to travel between the worlds.

- *Ability to cast and to cure curses* – Shamans have the ability to see things others cannot. This means that they can recognize the influence of negative energies in the form of curses. They also have the ability to hurl curses at others using their own spirit allies. A modern interpretation of this could be seen as having the ability to remove the influence of toxic relationships in our lives.

- *Ability to perform hunting magic* – Shamans have the ability to predict the movements of food animals, to bring them closer to the tribe, and to perform rites and blessings of thanksgiving for a successful hunt. A modern interpretation of this skill could be the ability to attract positive influences in one's life.

1.3 Modern Shamanism

Looking over the list of the characteristics of the shaman outlined above, a modern spiritual seeker can readily identify with some of those characteristics, while others might be more difficult to put into a modern context. It's easy to engage in ritual chanting, drumming and dancing around a campfire, and to have a ritual death and rebirth experience (in a metaphorical sense, that is). It may be more difficult to cast literal curses or to engage in actual hunting magic in a contemporary urban or suburban environment.

So what does it mean to be a shaman in modern times? How do we walk the Way of the Coyote in an industrialized society? A redefining of the role of the shaman is necessary. The way to begin this redefinition is to first answer the Call to Adventure.

In the Departure phase of our journey to ecospirituality, we are leaving the familiar world to partake in a journey of self-awareness. We are learning a new way of being in the world, and challenging our old assumptions and perceptions about the way the world works in order to create a new reality. We are allowing ourselves to awaken to a world of wider possibilities by being willing to do things in a different way. We are recognizing the interconnectedness of all things, and that we are all one. It may mean challenging the old dogmas by which we have lived our lives in the past. It may mean allowing Coyote to devour our sacred cows so that we can come to trust our own inner voices. It may mean learning to trust ourselves and our own supernatural aid enough to be willing to take that first step into a new reality.

The choices you make create that reality for you. What reality are you choosing to create?

The Call to Adventure is the catalyst that sets the Hero's Journey in motion. It could be an inner need to change one's circumstances, or it could be an external event that triggers the journey. In either case, the hero recognizes that something fundamental has changed, and he/she can never go back to the way things were.

If you are holding this book in your hands right now, you have received such a Call to Adventure. It is up to you how you choose to answer that call.

1.4 The Call

Looking over the list of the characteristics of the shaman outlined above, a modern spiritual seeker can readily identify with some of those characteristics, while others might be more difficult to put into a modern context. It's easy to engage in ritual chanting, drumming and dancing around a campfire, and to have a ritual death and rebirth experience. It may be more difficult to repel curses or to engage in hunting magic in a contemporary urban environment.

So what does it mean to be a shaman in modern times? How do we walk the Way of the Coyote in an industrialized society? A redefining of the role of the shaman is necessary. The way to begin this redefinition is to have a change of context. The first step in creating such a change in context is to answer the call.

Have you heard the Call to Adventure that is the Way of the Coyote? Here are a few characteristics to help you to recognize if Coyote is calling you:

- You have a deep concern for the environment and all life
- Family is extremely important to you
- You use humor as a teaching tool
- You like to challenge everyone's beliefs, including your own
- You are a fierce protector and loyal friend
- You have an ability to "walk between the worlds"
- You had dreams and visions of other realities as a child
- You have an inner sense that you were born for a higher purpose

- You are willing to acknowledge your mistakes and learn from them
- You have a no-nonsense approach to things that matter
- You have a way of cutting through the extraneous to get to the heart of the matter beneath the façade
- You feel more at home in the woods than in a city
- You have often been attracted to nature, more so than your peers
- Traditional forms of spirituality and religion don't seem to fit you
- You want to make a difference and leave a legacy
- You have a natural gift for teaching and explaining things to others

If these characteristics sound familiar, then you may be ready to answer the call. When you have read over the material in this chapter, go on to the next page and complete the worksheet.

Worksheet 1.4 The Path of the Shaman

Name _____ Date _____

Review the description of the Assumptions-Perceptions-Reality triad from section 3.1. When you feel you have a good understanding of the concept, go on to answer the questions below.

What are some of the assumptions that are creating the current reality you are experiencing?

_____
_____
_____
_____
_____
_____
_____

How are these assumptions filtering your perceptions of the world that you are experiencing?

_____
_____
_____
_____
_____
_____

How are these perceptions creating the reality that you find yourself in?

_____
_____
_____
_____
_____
_____
_____

WORKSHEET 1.4 THE PATH OF THE SHAMAN

Name _____ Date _____

What might you change about your assumptions that would lead you to experience different perceptions about the world?

_____
_____
_____
_____
_____

How might this change in the way you perceive the world lead you to experience a different reality?

_____
_____
_____
_____
_____

Review the characteristics of a shaman from section 3.2 of this chapter. Which of those characteristics might help you to change your assumptions, perceptions, and reality? Why?

_____
_____
_____
_____
_____
_____
_____
_____
_____

1.5 Naming Ceremony

Most indigenous peoples from around the world named their children after things found in nature. We are familiar with this practice through the names of Native Americans like Sitting Bull or Crazy Horse. These names have obvious sources in nature, but did you know that many other names have their origins in the natural world? My middle name, "Bruce," means "brushwood thicket." The name "Glen" originally meant "from the fertile valley," the name "Mary" means "wished for child," the name "Ann" means "merciful one," and so on. All of our names originally meant something and were usually taken from nature, characteristics of nature, or personal idiosyncrasies.

As you begin your journey to living in True Self by acknowledging your own true nature, you may wish to select a new name for yourself that reflects this new identity.

To do this, first go outside to a natural place. The wilder this natural space is, the better it will be for the purposes of this exercise. If you have the time and the opportunity you may wish to do this activity in a national or state park or other wilderness area that has been largely untouched by humans.

Prepare yourself for your naming ceremony by taking several deep breaths, and by grounding and centering yourself. Once you feel prepared, go into the forest. Keep your attention open and accepting. Set your intention and your awareness on the activity, and only on the activity.

Continue to walk in the forest until you find something that appeals to you. This could be any natural object, animal or plant that your find yourself attracted to. This thing that caught your attention shall be your new name.

For example, if you are walking on the trail and a hawk flies overhead, you might choose the name, "Flying Hawk."

Alternately, you may observe and describe your own thoughts and feelings to yourself as you walk. What personal characteristics would you like to cling to? Which do you wish to cast aside? These ideas may also be sources for your new spiritual name.

Once you have found your new name, you may wish to have a ceremony where you announce it to your family and friends. If you are completing this workbook as part of an ecospirituality group you may be asked to reveal your new spiritual name to other members of your group. This ceremony may be performed as formally or as informally as you like. This is your own rite of passage, so you may craft the ceremony to meet your needs and expectations.

Now that you have your new name, use it when exploring the skills of ecospirituality. At our workshops, selecting this name is one of the first things we do. Workshop attendees are addressed by their "nature name" for the duration of the course as we explore the Way of the Coyote together. This helps to reinforce the idea that attendees are becoming new people and are learning to acknowledge their own true natures, as are you as you progress through this workbook.

Prior to partaking in your own naming ceremony, you may find it helpful to complete the worksheet on the next page.

WORKSHEET 1.5 NAMING CEREMONY

Name _____ Date _____

Prior to partaking in your own Naming Ceremony, you may find it helpful to answer these questions. As you go on your naming quest, meditate on the answers you provided to these questions.

What is the nature of your own True Self? (Think about archetypes like "Warrior," or "Sage," or "Teacher," or "Hunter" or any other archetype that comes to mind)

_____
_____
_____
_____
_____

What are some characteristics or personality traits that if enhanced would help you to live more fully according to your own true nature?

_____
_____
_____
_____

What are some animals or other things in nature that might possess these characteristics or personality traits?

_____
_____
_____
_____

How might the lists you created above help you to select your "nature name?"

_____
_____
_____
_____
_____

1.6 Mindful Awareness

The first key to walking in the Way of the Coyote is to learn a new form of consciousness called *mindfulness*. Mindfulness means simply paying attention to the present moment. Think about something that stresses you out. Now ask yourself, "Is it something about the past, about the future, or about this present moment, as I'm reading this sentence?"

The vast majority of things that stress us out either have to do with the past or with the future. Very few things that stress us have to do with the present moment. While it is true that we can be stressed about things involving the past or the future in this present moment, when we are doing so we are in something called the *mind trap*. In other words, when we are stressing out, in this present moment, about the past or the future, we are living in our heads instead of in the present. We are stressing ourselves out in the present because of the past or the future.

There is, however, another way to be present in the moment.

The past only exists in our memory. The future only exists as we make educated guesses about what may or may not happen in the future, based on past experience. If we project our past experiences into the future, then those projects also only exist in our minds. In the present moment we can choose what to focus on about the past or the future.

Note that this is different than telling yourself "Don't think about the past" or "Don't think about the future." Telling yourself not to think about the past is thinking about the past. Telling yourself not to think about the future is thinking about the future. So the more you tell yourself not to think about the past (or the future) the more you're thinking about the past (or the future).

Instead of trying not to think about it, simply note those thoughts and let them go. Recognize that thoughts are just things that your brain does. You can choose whether or not to give those thoughts power by acknowledging them. The more you dwell on them, the more power you give them. The more you focus on the present moment, paying attention only to what your senses are telling you, the less you are caught in the mind trap.

It has been said that there are three ways to deal with a problem. The first is to solve it. If it is a problem that cannot be solved, then the second way to deal with it is to change the way we think about it so that it is no longer a problem. If we can't change the way we think about it, then we may just have to accept that this is the way things are. When we conceptualize problems and solutions in this way, we are mindfully aware.

The more experience we gain in achieving *mindful awareness*, the more we are able to move towards a state of radical acceptance. Such acceptance allows us to deal with life as it really is, in the present moment.

The most basic feature of mindfulness involves simply paying attention to the present moment. One way to do this is to focus only on your breathing, without thinking about anything. If a thought comes to mind, simply note it and let it go, without judging yourself or the thought. It's perfectly natural that thoughts will try to surface, because we are taught to be thinking creatures. However, as you practice with mindful awareness, it will get easier to let those thoughts go, so don't get frustrated if it is difficult at first.

Remember that it's not a question of trying not to have any thoughts.

A better way to picture it is as ripples on a pond. The water in the pond is your thoughts. The ripples are the troublesome or negative thoughts. If you try to smooth out the pond you'll only succeed in making more waves. But if you sit quietly and wait for the pond to settle down on its own, soon your pond will be as smooth as glass.

The features of mindfulness are tools that we may use to help to smooth out the surface of our own inner ponds. When we are able to achieve such a state at will, we have achieved mindful awareness.

Mindfulness is a skill like any other. It can be difficult to learn at first, because it is so diametrically opposed to the way we're accustomed to thinking, acting, and doing. Some of the techniques of mindfulness may feel strange, simply because they are different.

"Different" doesn't mean "better" or "worse," it simply means "different."

Remember that, "Insanity is doing the same thing in the same ways and expecting different results." To put it another way, if what you're doing isn't working, then doing more of the same isn't going to work either. If we've been doing things that lead to negative consequences, we're probably doing those things because they feel familiar to us. But the way to get different results is to do things in different ways. This leads to different consequences for our actions. It's only natural that doing things differently will feel strange or weird at first. If it didn't, chances are you already doing things that way. So learning to get different results means being willing to do things differently.

Mindfulness is a way to do things differently.

Although meditation is a part of mindfulness, mindful awareness is much more than a meditative technique. Mindfulness is a way of life. The techniques of mindfulness can be applied to any of our day-to-day experiences. They are not restricted to the realm of meditation.

Like anything else that has to be learned, mindfulness is a skill that requires practice. Leonardo da Vinci didn't paint the Mona Lisa the first time he picked up a paintbrush. Likewise, you probably won't be able to jump right into mindful awareness mode of being without a lot of practice. That's okay. Give yourself permission to practice once in a while.

The more you do so, the more mindful you'll become!

1.7 The Power of Intention

We can talk about problems all day, but until we start talking about solutions, nothing will ever get solved. The way to solve a problem is to take positive, intentional steps towards finding a solution.

All of the skills of mindfulness come together in the power of intention. A mindful life is a life lived deliberately and effectively. Such a consciously lived life is not driven about on the winds of whim and fortune. It is a purposeful life. The Way of the Coyote that leads to ecospirituality is also a purposeful life, lived intentionally.

The power of intention helps us to solve problems in a purposeful manner. It is possible to live a life of purpose through tapping into this power. The way to us the power of intention is to begin by asking two questions:

1. What am I trying to accomplish here?
2. Are my thoughts, feelings, and behaviors going to help me to achieve this goal?

When you are able to focus on your intention in a given situation, you are able to let go of problem-based thinking like blaming, shaming, and guilt-tripping and to move on to a solution-focused way of thinking. When you are able to do this, you are well on your way to the ultimate goal of ecospirituality, which is the ability to live according to your own true nature.

To practice the power of intention, go on to the next page and try the *Power of Intention* activity.

WORKSHEET 1.7 THE POWER OF INTENTION   PAGE 1 OF 2

Name _____ Date _____

The *Hua Hu Ching*, by Lao Tzu, says, "Those who want to know the truth of the universe should practice the four cardinal virtues.
1. The first is reverence for all of life. This manifests as unconditional love and respect for oneself and all other beings.
2. The second is natural sincerity. This manifests as honesty, simplicity and faithfulness.
3. The third is gentleness, which manifests as kindness, consideration for others and sensitivity to spiritual truth.
4. The fourth is supportiveness. This manifests as service to others without expectation of reward."

What do you want to accomplish in your life? It has been said that if you don't know where you're going, any road will get you there. Living a life of intention means knowing where you want to go with your life and what you would like to do with your life. Imagine you are lying on your deathbed, looking back on your life. What are the things you'd like to be remembered for? What are the things that you'd regret not accomplishing? If your life were to be summed up in a few paragraphs in a "Who's Who" at some future date, what would your entry say? What would your loved ones say about you and remember about you after you're gone? Think about these questions. Take all the time you need before answering.

My intention (purpose) for this life is:

_____

_____

_____

_____

_____

_____

_____

_____

_____

WORKSHEET 1.7 THE POWER OF INTENTION

Name _____ Date _____

In order to live a purposeful life, or a life of intention, we must live out our values. The final skill of ecospirituality is the ability to live in True Self. The way to live in True Self is to know who and what we are, and to use that knowledge to set our intentions and purpose. When we can do so we may live life fully according to our own true nature. The first step to True Self, and therefore to an ecospiritual life, lies in creating a roadmap. Looking back on your answers to the question on the previous page, think about which values and traits you have that might help you to accomplish your life's mission. Write these traits in the spaces provided below.

I demonstrate my reverence for all of life by manifesting unconditional love and respect for myself and all other beings in the following ways:

_____

_____

_____

I demonstrate my natural sincerity by manifesting honesty, simplicity and faithfulness in the following ways:

_____

_____

_____

I demonstrate my gentleness by manifesting kindness, consideration for others and sensitivity to spiritual truth in the following ways:

_____

_____

_____

I demonstrate supportiveness by manifesting service to others without expectation of reward in the following ways:

_____

_____

_____

Session 2 Refusal of the Call

Brother Coyote loved to play tricks, but now he felt that Chief Buffalo and the rest of the People were playing a trick on him. He felt the disbelief rising in his heart, and said, "You wish me to go on a quest? Are you mocking me? Surely this must be some sort of jest! Brother Eagle, I do not have your keen eyes and ability to fly high in the sky, so I could not escape danger, nor could I see it coming ahead of time. Sister Cougar, I am no great hunter like you. If I were to go on such a journey, I would surely starve!"

Why not send Sister Doe, who has the ability to sniff out predators and run away quickly? Or send Brother Bear, who has great strength, so he could fight an enemy should one overtake him?

"Sister Doe is much too timid for such a journey," said Chief Buffalo.

"And Brother Bear is sleeping, and has been for many weeks. Nobody knows if he shall ever wake again."

But Brother Coyote was not convinced. One by one he named all of the creatures of the People; but one by one Chief Buffalo gave him reasons why they could not go. He explained that if Brother Coyote could not go, it could be nobody else.

"I am not a warrior!" cried Coyote, "I am not a hero! I spend my days running through the forest, playing and joking with the People! I am not clever enough, or strong enough, or fast enough, or smart enough for such a journey! I cannot go!"

Chief Buffalo, Brother Eagle and Sister Cougar looked upon Brother Coyote with sadness. They thought about pointing out all the ways that he was wrong about what he had said. They thought about listing all the strengths that Brother Coyote could bring to their quest, such as his ability to track, and to hide, and to deceive a predator on the trail. But they had been down this road with Coyote too many times before. They knew that it would only lead to more arguments and more hurt feelings if they tried to talk him out of his decision. So instead they walked away with pity in their hearts.

As Chief Buffalo turned to leave, he said to Coyote, "I am disappointed in you. I thought you would be happy to help out the People, who have been victims of many of your cruel jests. I would think that you would like to make amends for your pranks. I can see now that I was wrong."

And with that, Chief Buffalo walked away.

Of all the things Coyote had heard from the People this afternoon, the words of Chief Buffalo stung him the most. He had always admired and respected his Grandfather Buffalo, and it hurt Coyote deeply to see him so disappointed. But Coyote did not see what others could see in him. In his own eyes, he was just a trickster and a fool, incapable of great deeds.

With a sad and heavy heart, he walked away from the Chief's lodge to return to his own den.

2.0 A Change of Context

Change can be scary. The comforting thing about the familiar is its familiarity; we know what to expect. This can even be true if the familiar situation is grim. Quite often we'll stay stuck in a bad situation because the fear of the unknown can be worse than the current (known) situation. Such a sentiment is often expressed in the phrase, "Better the devil you know than the devil you don't know."

The familiar, however uncomfortable it may be, is at least familiar. We often choose to stay in a familiar, yet miserable, situation rather than to fly off to ills we know not of. When faced with the possibility of change in such a situation, there is an element of the unknown that must be dealt with. We don't know what to expect. What if, by acting, we make things worse? What can we expect to happen if we leave the familiar for unknown, unexplored territory? Sure, things might get better, but they might get worse too. When we let our fears of the unknown overwhelm us, it is easy to, like Coyote, refuse the Call to Adventure. It's simply easier to stay in misery than to set sail on uncharted waters.

I was once traveling to a workshop on shamanism. This particular seminar was being held in a hidden-away corner of the Southern Appalachians. This was before the days of GPS, and I was having difficulty finding my way, so I stopped at a little country store to ask for directions. When I told the clerk where I was going, he jokingly replied, *"You can't get there from here. You have to go someplace else and start over."*

Of course he was being facetious, but his answer was a great metaphor for the journey into the world of shamanism. If you plan to journey to the Otherworld that is the realm of the shaman, you can't get there from here. This is one of the reasons for the metaphorical death and rebirth experiences so common to shamanistic paths throughout the world. The shaman must die to his old way of living and being in the world and be reborn into the life of the shaman. Sometimes the rites required to complete this task may seem odd or downright silly to modern eyes. Celtic shamans were required to stand on one foot like a crane, with one eye covered, while seeking visions or pronouncing prophecies. Some Native Americans stood for days with pebbles between their toes to keep them awake while seeking visions. Some shamans painted their naked bodies, lay down in boats at sea, ate special foods, slept wrapped in a buffalo hide, or engaged in drumming, singing, chanting and a variety of other behaviors all designed to put the shaman's consciousness in touch with the Otherworld.

So it's pretty obvious that some of the rites, rituals and tools of shamanism will feel weird at first. That's okay. If they didn't feel strange, you'd already be doing them. Given time you will become accustomed to these new ways of being and new ways of doing as part of your spiritual practice. If you cannot get past the unfamiliarity with drumming and chanting, or creating your own reality and taking responsibility for it, or performing rites, then you "can't get there from here." In such a case, you are not ready to enter the Belly of the Whale, and you are still in the Refusal of the Call. Answering the Call of the Coyote means setting forth with purpose, with determination, and with will. There's no, "I guess so" on the Path of the Coyote. If you are not certain that you are ready, then you are in the Refusal of the Call stage of the Hero's Journey, and are not ready for ecospirituality.

The way out of this Refusal of the Call is to trust the process. Trust your own instinct, and trust your own Supernatural Aid. Trust in your connections to others, to nature, and to self. Meditate on what your own inner voice may be trying to tell you. The way to know if you are ready to take the call is to know with certainty that it can be no other way.

When you achieved this sense of certainty, you will be ready to die to your old way of being and to be reborn as a follower of the Way of the Coyote.

2.1 Choosing to Answer the Call

Like Coyote in the story, a person who refuses the Call to Adventure has no confidence in himself/herself. When you have received the call, you stand at a crossroads. You have a choice. You can take the red pill or the blue pill. You are free to choose to continue to refuse the Call to Adventure. Such a refusal means staying in the familiar, but it also means accepting the status quo. It means surrendering to life as it is without considering possibilities of future growth.

If you find yourself stuck here but wishing to answer the Call to Adventure, the first step is to ask yourself, "If nothing changed from now on, could I live the rest of my life this way?"

If the answer to that question is, "No," then obviously something has to change.

To begin making this change is to begin trusting yourself. Out of the billions of people on this planet, the only person who is a true expert on you is you. You already have within you everything you need to know to begin the quest. All you have to do is to learn to trust your inner wisdom.

The path of ecospirituality involves following the Way of the Coyote. It is a spiritual journey...a hero's journey with many signposts and crossings. Each one of these crossings represents a phase along the way to becoming a seeker and a seer of visions. When you have arrived at the end of this journey you will have discovered a new way of being in the world. The first crossing is to answer the Call to Adventure.

At this first crossing we have to forge our will to commit to the path. When a vision seeker sets out on the path such a decision requires a firm and resolute will. The life of a shaman is not to be approached with an attitude of "I guess so," or "I'll do it when I have the time," or "this looks like fun if nothing else is going on." Such a path requires a complete commitment to the quest. Once you cross the threshold there is no turning back. The journey of the vision seeker is one of lifetime dedication. If you're saying to yourself, "I don't have the time or the energy," what you're really saying is, "It's not a priority for me." If it's not a priority, then you're not going to put forth your best efforts, so it's probably not the right path...or the right choice...for you at this time in your life. If that is the case, it's better to set aside the path and return to it with a firm resolve when you are ready to commit to do the work.

2.2 Conquering Your Fears

In many indigenous traditions throughout the world, the path of the shaman begins with a rebirthing ceremony in which the initiate is given a new spiritual name. This renaming signifies a person's birth to the spirit world. The naming ceremony is the vision seeker's announcement to the world that he or she has taken up the quest. Such a commitment is a death to the former way of being, and rebirth as a seer and a seeker of visions.

This rebirth depends upon conquering your own fears. Conquering fear doesn't mean never being afraid. It means rising to meet the challenges of the Way of the Coyote in spite of the fear. It is the first landmark in the decision to become the person you were meant to be by embracing your True Self. To overcome your own Refusal of the Call, complete the worksheet on the following page to help you determine what fears might be standing in your way as you prepare to undertake your own journey of discovery.

WORKSHEET 2.2 CONQUERING YOUR FEARS

Name _____ Date _____

As you contemplate answering your own personal Call to Adventure, do any fears rise up in your spirit? If so, what is the nature of these fears? If you feel ready and unafraid to begin the journey, then think about what things might stand in your way in the future and use those things instead to answer the questions that follow.

What are your greatest fears?

_____
_____
_____
_____
_____

How might you conquer these fears?

_____
_____
_____
_____
_____

How might you forge your will so that you may take up the path of the vision seeker with a firm and steadfast commitment? What Supernatural Aid might you require to help you succeed?

_____
_____
_____
_____
_____
_____
_____
_____
_____

WORKSHEET 2.2 CONQUERING YOUR FEARS

Name _____ Date _____

How might you strengthen your resolve to commit to the journey?

_____
_____
_____
_____
_____
_____

Which thoughts, feelings, and habits will you have to sacrifice in order to be reborn into the life of a seer/shaman?

_____
_____
_____
_____
_____
_____

What is your reason for seeking the path that leads to ecospirituality?

_____
_____
_____
_____
_____
_____
_____
_____
_____

2.3 Mindful Awareness and Ecospirituality

"You have noticed that everything as Indian does is in a circle, and that is because the Power of the World always works in circles, and everything tries to be round. The sky is round, and I have heard that the earth is round like a ball, and so are all the stars. The wind, in its greatest power, whirls. Birds make their nest in circles, for theirs is the same religion as ours. Even the seasons form a great circle in their changing, and always come back again to where they were. The life of a man is a circle from childhood to childhood, and so it is in everything where power moves."

–Black Elk, Oglala Shaman (1853-1950)

For hundreds of centuries prior to the Industrial Revolution, people lived together in small tribes, whether in nomadic bands or geographically fixed in location in villages or towns. Evolution wired our brains for nature. But with the advent of agriculture, we settled down more and more, and built cities. With cities came modernization. First we built mechanical machines, then, with the discovery of electricity, we began to build electric machines. Thomas Edison's invention of electric light forever robbed the night of its power to evoke mystery and terror by creating a perpetual electric twilight in our towns and cities, making more hours available to labor in the factories. The more domesticated we became, the more the wilderness retreated beyond the city limits. We ceased to mark time by the cycles of the seasons and began to keep time by the factory whistle.

Our minds retreated from nature, but our bodies did not. Evolution programmed us to need nature, and our bodies and minds still respond to it.

Our modern, mechanized lifestyle has brought about many changes for the better. We live longer and more productive lives, but our hearts still long for the cry of nature.

Ecopsychology studies the relationship between mental health and the environment. This field of research views the mental health of humankind as a part of the geo-ecosystem that is the living planet we call Earth. If all life on Earth is interrelated, and human beings certainly are a type of life on Earth, then what happens to the rest of the planet affects us all. Ecopsychology recognizes that not only does the environment impact our physical health, but it also has a direct influence on our mental health. While artificial, stressful, polluted environments have the power to harm, nature has the power to heal, both physically and mentally.

From the perspective of ecopsychology, everything is connected to everything else. According to this paradigm, people don't exist in a vacuum. They are part of the larger system of their neighborhood, and of the even larger system of their particular societies, and ultimately the system of all life on Earth, circles-within-circles. Each of these systems communicates to us in different ways, and we interact with each of these systems. The individual is not only a part of a system of interacting human beings, but also as a part of an ecosystem. We interact with the environment, and the environment interacts with us. For those who know how to listen, the wind in the trees can sing. The view of a mountain range or a moonlit ocean can tell a story. The smell of the first flowers of spring can speak just as clearly as a loved one's voice can. The touch of a ray of sun can be as powerful as a lover's caress.

On the other hand, a crowded, polluted city street can communicate as well. The messages we get from our environment have an impact on us, whether or not we are consciously aware of that impact. This environmental impact changes our sense of self, and our sense of wellbeing. If we could make a paradigm shift to a lifestyle that makes room for nature, what would that do to our sense of wellbeing?

Such a paradigm shift involves seeking inspiration (or spirituality) from the natural world. It is a solution-focused approach. It's easy to go into panic mode when we realize what we're doing to the environment, but such stress and anxiety doesn't do anything to solve the problem. A solution-focused approach helps us to find positive solutions rather than getting stuck in ruminations about the negative effects we're having on the environment. It's easy to get caught up in the doom and gloom, but that doesn't solve anything. What's needed is an intentional approach that works.

Such an approach to saving the environment means a grassroots, bottom-up approach. It starts with the individual. The most effective way to change a society or a culture is mindfully, one person at a time, through ecospirituality.

2.4 Doing Mode vs. Being Mode

One way mindfulness can help in this situation is by moving from *doing mode* to *being mode*. When problems arise, they cause stress. When we experience stress the natural tendency is to try to do something about it. The problem with this is that if you could do something about the stress you would have already done so, and you would no longer be stressed.

In *being mode*, we are able to just accept what we feel, without feeling obligated to do anything about it. Stress is a natural feeling. To expect not to feel stress from time to time is not a realistic expectation, and telling yourself not to stress out is stressful in itself. Think of it this way: Suppose I expect the weather to be sunny all the time. I complain whenever it rains, and my mood becomes irritable because of the cloudy weather. If I have such an expectation, I've set myself up to be disappointed, because rain is a natural part of the weather. So by grumbling every time it rains, I'm complaining about something that's a perfectly natural part of existence.

Now suppose I complain every time I stress out. Stress is also a perfectly normal part of existence, so expecting never to be stressed out is unrealistic.

The more I tell myself not to stress out, the more stressed out I become. Instead, if I learn to welcome the stress and simply allow myself to be with it until it passes it no longer has a hold on me. Note also that telling myself not to stress out is *doing* something, and not just *being* with the stress.

If I notice stressful events with the goal of "trying to relax" or "trying to calm down," trying is doing, and not being. My goal is to be and not to do.

In being mode, we recognize that when we are having strong feelings we don't have to do anything about them. So if we find ourselves having thoughts of refusing the Call to Adventure, such thoughts are just thoughts. However, if we find ourselves wanting to act on those thoughts by refusing the call, we are engaging in doing mode. One way to escape the Refusal of the Call is to merely shift to being mode and out of doing mode.

The first step to leaving doing mode is to become aware of the ways in which we engage in it. To explore this idea, go to the exercise on the next page.

WORKSHEET 2.4 WAYS I ENGAGE IN DOING MODE   PAGE 1 OF 1

Name: _____ Date: _____

Think about the ways in which you slip into Doing Mode throughout your day. Doing Mode involves solving problems, figuring things out, and participating in day-to-day activities. List a few of the ways you engage in Doing Mode below:

1. _____
2. _____
3. _____
4. _____
5. _____
6. _____
7. _____
8. _____
9. _____
10. _____
11. _____
12. _____
13. _____
14. _____
15. _____
16. _____
17. _____
18. _____
19. _____
20. _____
21. _____
22. _____
23. _____
24. _____
25. _____

2.5 Engaging in Being Mode

We sometimes create unrealistic expectations for ourselves by assuming that stressful or depressing thoughts and feelings are somehow not "natural." In fact, just the opposite is true. It is perfectly natural to have stressful or depressing thoughts and feelings from time to time.

Try this sometime: Ask everyone you know if they've never in their entire lives had a depressing or stressful thought. I'm willing to bet that you won't be able to find anyone who would say that they've never been depressed or anxious. That's because, like cloudy days, stressful and depressing feelings are a natural part of being alive.

If we can accept that we don't have to do anything to fix cloudy days, we can accept that we don't have to do anything to fix negative thoughts and feelings as well. In fact, sometimes our attempts to fix such thought cycles could be the very thing that makes them worse. Here's an example of how this process works:

Suppose I am prone to panic attacks. One day I find myself feeling anxious. I can tell by the way my thoughts are racing and by the way my body feels that my anxiety is rising. I know from previous experience that rising anxiety has led to panic attacks in the past. As I realize this, my anxiety increases even more because I'm afraid that I'm about to have yet another panic attack. So I try to do something to stop it by trying to force myself to calm down. But "trying to calm down" is doing mode. The harder I try to calm down, the more I stress out about the fact that I can't calm down. The more I stress out about the fact that I can't seem to calm down, the more my anxiety rises, because I'm trying to do something to fix it, and what I'm doing isn't working. The more I fail at fixing it, the more I stress out and try even harder to fix it. This cycle builds and builds until I have another full-blown panic attack.

What if, when I felt my anxiety rising, I was able to say, "Oh, that's another panic attack that's about to happen. I've had them before. Yes, they're unpleasant, but I've managed to survive them. No need to try to do anything to stop it."

In this case, I'm not trying to do anything. I'm not trying to stop the attack. I've consciously chosen to sit with it and be in the moment with the natural experience, paying attention to and describing the sensations to myself. Because I'm not engaging in doing mode by trying to fix something, I'm not adding to the anxiety. I'm just allowing things to happen in their own time, while I observe with my senses. From this perspective, even if I do have another panic attack, I'm being still with it and observing it rather than interacting with it. I know from previous experience that it won't kill me, however unpleasant the experience might be. I'm engaging my internal observer to be with the experience.

This ability to pay attention to the present moment is the essence of being mode. To gain some insight into how to explore Being Mode, go on to the next page and complete the exercise on *Ways to Engage in Being Mode*.

WORKSHEET 2.5 WAYS TO ENGAGE IN BEING MODE PAGE 1 OF 1

Name: _____ Date: _____

One of the most basic ways to engage in Being Mode is to simply start paying attention to the sensations you experience in the world around you. One thing you can always focus on is your breath. This is because your breath is always with you. Try this now by going outside and taking a few deep breaths while noticing the sensations you're experiencing. What did you feel in your body? Did you notice any smells in the air? Were you able to taste anything on the air as you exhaled? What does your breathing sound like? What physical sensations are you experiencing?

Leaving Doing Mode and entering Being Mode can be as simple as paying attention to what your senses are telling you in the present moment. Think about some ways you can engage all of your senses and write them in the appropriate sections below. For example, for "smell," you might write, "Light a scented candle," or, "Go outside and smell the flowers."

SMELL

1. _____
2. _____
3. _____

TASTE

1. _____
2. _____
3. _____

TOUCH

1. _____
2. _____
3. _____

HEARING

1. _____
2. _____
3. _____

SIGHT

1. _____
2. _____
3. _____

2.6 Being Mode and Answering the Call

Now that you have a list of activities you can engage in when feeling tempted to engage in doing mode, you can choose to be with these activities instead.

As noted earlier in this session's materials, the Refusal of the Call often manifests in a temptation to return to the way things have always been. Change is difficult, and setting out on a path of personal and permanent change for the better can sometimes be the most difficult life-changing experience of all. We feel tempted to tell ourselves, "change is too hard," or "I've always been this way, why change now?" or "people won't like me if I change."

We're very good at coming up with excuses because if we don't then we have to take responsibility for our lives. That can be a scary place to be for those of us who have never done it before. When we take responsibility for our own lives we have nobody else to blame if we fail. What we sometimes forget, though, is that if we take responsibility for our own lives, then we are the only ones who can take credit for our successes.

Taking the leap of faith required to trust ourselves is a major step in answering the Call to Adventure. Sometimes it helps to have a little Supernatural Aid.

Session 3 Supernatural Aid

As he arrived at his den, Brother Coyote thought about what Brother Eagle and Sister Cougar had said. He thought about how it had been getting colder with each passing day. He remembered their words that the People and Chief Buffalo did not know if the Sun would ever come back. He thought about how disappointed Chief Buffalo had been with him. The more he thought about it, the angrier he became.

"Why should this be my responsibility?" he cried, "I didn't ask for this burden! I just want to play in the forest! I don't want to go on any journey!"

As he thought about it, he grew angrier and angrier. He became so mad that he began to chase his tail. He ran around and around in circles on the ground. The faster he chased his tail, the faster it ran away from him, and the more frustrated he became.

Thus preoccupied, he didn't notice at first that a mysterious white substance had begun falling from the sky. It fell thicker and thicker around him until finally he could not help but notice. Puzzled, he caught a flake of this stuff on his tongue, and found that it was cold and tasteless. As he watched, the snow covered the ground, obliterating the dying plants as it fell. The air around him grew colder and colder.

Shivering, Coyote curled himself up into a ball to stay warm as the snow continued to fall.

As lay there on the ground tucked into a ball, watching the snow, Coyote began to think that it would never stop.

"Truly this is the end of all things!" he thought to himself, "I might as well just lie here and freeze to death!"

Soon the strange white stuff completely covered Coyote. Lying there buried in the snow, he had begun to compose his Death Song when he saw a faint light shining in the distance. As he watched, it grew closer and closer. He eventually saw that the light shone from atop a stick being held by a woman dressed in the color of the snow that surrounded her. The light on her stick looked like a miniature sun, and she was bringing it towards him. He was frightened, but also cold. If that miniature sun gave off heat as well as light, how he wanted to be near it! So he did not run away, but waited patiently as the woman dressed in white approached and sat next to him.

"Greetings, Brother Coyote," she said, "I am White Buffalo Woman."

Coyote was usually wary of strangers, but something about White Buffalo Woman put him at ease. She seemed wise and kind, so he greeted her and began to tell her his story. He told her that the People were frightened because of the cold, and that they were worried that it might never be warm again. He told her that the People wanted him to go on a quest to find a new place for the Tribe to live, but that he was afraid to go.

"It is wise that you are afraid," she told him, "Only fools are fearless in the face of the unknown. But that does not mean you shouldn't go."

As they talked, White Buffalo Woman gathered sticks and twigs and began arranging them in a pile in front of Coyote. When the pile was big enough, she touched her glowing stick to the pile, and it blossomed into heat and light. Almost instantly, Brother Coyote felt himself begin to thaw. The heat spreading across his body was almost magical.

"What is this strange thing?" he asked.

"It is called 'fire,'" said White Buffalo Woman, "If you have its secret, your People will not have to move away to a new place. With fire, you may stay warm through the winter until the spring comes again."

"What is 'winter'?" asked Coyote, "and 'spring?'"

"Winter is the reason it is cold now. It is a time known as a 'season.' Spring is also a season. Winter is a time of cold, decay, and death, and springe is a time of warmth and rebirth. Seasons come and seasons go, but when the time of winter has passed, the spring will return again. Fire will help you make it through the cold and dark of winter. Until then, you must be vigilant and wait for spring's return."

Coyote was amazed at the magical power of the fire. He was also glad to know that spring would come again, but if the People did not have this magical thing to help them through the winter, they may not live to see it.

Coyote and White Buffalo Woman sat warming themselves by the fire and talking. White Buffalo Woman told Coyote that the fire had come from a sacred village in the mountains to the North, where it was guarded by a greedy witch who wanted to keep it for herself. She told Coyote that if he followed the North Star he could find this village, and claim some of the fire to call his own.

"But why can't I just have some of your fire?" Brother Coyote asked.

"Because each person must find his own fire, and this fire is mine," replied White Buffalo Woman, smiling enigmatically. "It would not work for you because it is my fire. You could not make it burn."

They talked for half of the night until White Buffalo Woman lay down in front of the fire to sleep. Coyote tried to sleep himself, but after hearing of the village of the Fire Tribe, the fire, and the witch who guarded it, he was more frightened than ever. Yet he knew that he was the only one who could make this journey. When he had resolved for himself that he must be the one to go, he finally fell asleep just before dawn. When he awoke the next morning, White Buffalo Woman was gone, and the fire had gone out.

3.0 Supernatural Aid and Your Fears

Just as Coyote began to grow cold and numb in the snow, when we deny our emotions we open ourselves up to the process of emotional numbing. We kid ourselves into believing that certain emotions are "wrong" or "bad," and we hide them away. We don't want to own these parts of ourselves. Sometimes emotional injuries can lead to this state of numbing as well. The feelings are so powerful that they become overwhelming, so we learn to stuff them down and pretend they don't exist so we don't have to go through the pain of feeling them. Over time this denial of what we feel can make it difficult, if not impossible, to acknowledge our feelings at all. When this emotional numbing occurs, we have to actively work to "thaw out" our feelings. Sometimes we may do this by relying on our own Supernatural Aid.

To find your own Supernatural Aid, first ask yourself if there are there any fears that might have led to your own emotional numbing in life. Like Coyote, do you need to "thaw out" those feelings? How might the characteristics of a shaman help you to do so?

It can be difficult to answer the Call to Adventure. When our emotions freeze us into inaction out of habit, it sometimes becomes hard to choose a different path. When faced with the opportunity (or challenge) to discover new ways of being, our fight or flight response often takes over, and we remain stuck in the familiar. It can be scary to journey off into unknown territory, simply because it is unknown. But using mindful awareness in the present moment we can become aware that the unknown is just that…unknown. Dangers may lie ahead, but great rewards may lie ahead as well.

We only change when the pain of staying the same becomes greater than the pain of changing. Every action has a consequence, and answering the Call to Adventure is an action with unknown consequences. Answering the call means facing our fears. It means facing our pain. It is an acknowledgement that with great risk comes great reward. It is a willingness to risk it all in order to gain ourselves.

Ultimately, the Call to Adventure is about inspiration. Ecospirituality is all about finding that which is awe-inspiring in our own lives. When we find that source of inspiration, then the "fire" of our own Supernatural Aid comes to warm us. Your own Supernatural Aid will come to assist you when you realize that there are no other options but the path you're on. All other doors have been closed to you, and from that point on the only choice is to heed the call.

3.1 Finding Your Own Fire

At the end of your journey on the Way of the Coyote you will be able to live according to your own true nature, in True Self. You are a unique individual, with your own needs, wants, talents and skills. Because of this, you can never walk another's path. There are similarities along the journey that we all share. We all need basic necessities like food, clothing, and shelter. We all need to love and to be loved. We all search for a deeper meaning to give our lives purpose.

On the other hand, there are things that are true only of you. Your "fire" cannot be someone else's fire. Your journey is unique, and the things you will experience on the way will be yours and yours alone. Remember that when you seek your own Supernatural Aid, it will come to you in a form that only you may understand.

We all have inner voices that guide us along the way. We also have other voices that may have shaped our walk. These voices may have come from parents, or from partners, or from friends, or from teachers, or even from strangers.

When seeking the path of ecospirituality, the ultimate destination is your own True Self. This means that at the end of the journey we have learned to live according to our own true nature, and not according to expectations or life goals that others have implanted in our consciousness. It means learning to listen to the voice of your own inner wisdom, and learning to be able to distinguish that voice from all of the other voices that may have guided us through the years.

When your own Supernatural Aid helps you to find your own fire, that fire will be yours and yours alone, and not the fire of your parents, your mate, your friends, your children, or of anyone else.

3.2 Nature as Supernatural Aid

"If you really think that the environment is less important than the economy, try holding your breath while you count your money."

-Dr. Guy McPherson, University of Arizona

I grew up on a 400 acre farm in the 1960s and 1970s. Back then there were no video games, and the television only got three channels, and that was if the wind was blowing in the right direction. My best friend lived five miles away, and if we wanted to visit each other we had to ride our bikes or walk. Our afterschool entertainment consisted of building forts in the woods, taking hikes, fishing, or collecting plants and animals. Growing up this way not only allowed me an opportunity for fresh air, it also stimulated my imagination and curiosity. The mythology of my time consisted of stories from my Irish great-grandmother about Native Americans, faeries and Celtic lore, and Christian tales from my Scottish grandmother about the biblical patriarchs.

I was never much interested in the Christian mythology, as it mostly seemed to consist of people getting zapped by God for doing things in a way that displeased him. And he seemed to be displeased quite a bit. The Native American and Celtic lore were much more alive to me. Those stories were not black-and-white moral tales, but puzzlers where the right answer was often difficult to find. The more I studied these stories, the more I gained insight into myself and the world around me.

As I became much more acquainted with mythology and learned to interpret it not as literal stories, but as teaching metaphors, fables, and parables, I returned to some of those Bible stories and got a lot more out of them the second time around. If you look at those stories as teaching tools and not as literal textbook descriptions of actual places and people, they become useful again. They come alive again. The secret is to focus on the message and not on the messenger.

This poetical use of story and myth can also extend to nature. It is possible to use the wilderness as a metaphor for spiritual growth. In fact, many religious mythologies do just that. When Jesus asks us to, "Consider the lilies of the field' which don't toil or spin, yet they're complete," or when Buddha tells us that, "The Way lies in the nature that surrounds us," these spiritual teachers are using nature as a training manual.

A lot of the great enlightened teachers began their spiritual journeys by going off into the woods. Buddha did it, Jesus did it, Mohammed did it, Moses did it, the Native Americans did it, and so did most of the great spiritual masters throughout history. There is something about seeing the wild places firsthand that awakens our deeper, more intimate and more personal levels of awareness. It is a rite of passage that uses nature to give meaning to our lives while returning to our most primal instincts.

Science in recent years has begun studying the psychological aspects of wilderness experiences. In a 2005 study, van den Berg & Heijne researched some of these characteristics. The study, *Fear versus fascination: An exploration of emotional responses to natural threats*, explains that there are two basic types of attention: *focus* and *fascination*.

Focus is the type of attention we experience most often in artificial environments. Human hands make most, if not all, of the things we see indoors. Since we evolved in the wilderness, but have only been living in increasingly artificial environments for a few thousand years, our brains are wired to be on guard in unfamiliar surroundings. The more primitive parts of our brains recognize artificial places as somehow alien. Because of this, we tend to use more energy to focus our attention while indoors in order to avoid these man-made distractions.

Fascination is the type of attention we experience more outdoors. The deeper, older parts of our brains recognize natural environments as something familiar, so we tend to use less mental resources for focusing attention. This means that more mental energy is available to generate more meditative states. So unless a bear is chasing you, you're calmer and more relaxed in the woods or on a beach than in an office or classroom. Such serenity is a prerequisite to spiritual events, so experiences in nature are highly conducive to developing more spiritual awareness.

Such ecospiritual awareness, enhanced and induced by nature, is not about a particular religion. All religions contain aspects of nature, and all religions, when understood properly, hold a deep reverence for the natural environment. The Way of the Coyote is about fostering a spiritual connection by using nature as a tool to experience those awe-inspiring moments that make life worthwhile. When nature is experienced in this way, it is a Supernatural Aid to the seeker. Sitting or hiking quietly in the woods or in another natural environment will allow your own inner wisdom to come forth. This Supernatural Aid will help you to find your own fire of inspiration.

3.3 Animal Wisdom

At the start of Coyote's journey, he has answered the Call to Adventure and has overcome the Refusal of the Call. Like Coyote, at this point in the journey you are about to undertake a new, sometimes dangerous, quest through unfamiliar territory. It's as if you are about to go into an uncharted, deep, dark forest without a map. It is dangerous because it is leaving the familiar behind and venturing off into unknown territory. Such a challenge can be quite daunting. This is why, in most legends and on most spiritual quests, some sort of Supernatural Aid is required to begin.

If you have a belief in any supernatural entity, then by all means feel free to call upon your own higher power for assistance. But such a belief is not necessary in order to tap into the supernatural powers of nature for guidance. There are several ways to do this, and all of these ways involve using nature as a teaching metaphor. Any metaphor will work, but for our purposes in the ecospirituality program, my favorite type of supernatural assistance is Animal Wisdom.

If you're a sports fan, you're no stranger to the fact that many professional sports teams are named after animals. There's the Chicago Bears, the Carolina Panthers, the Atlanta Falcons, the Philadelphia Eagles, etc. We also use animal names as terms of endearment (for example, "Teddy Bear") or as nicknames (Richard the Lionhearted, or King Arthur, whose name means "The Bear"). This tendency is a vestige of a time when we lived closer to nature. We choose these nicknames because certain animals have specific characteristics. In using these names for ourselves, our loved ones, and our sports teams, we are either consciously or unconsciously invoking the characteristics of those animals. We are using the archetypal energy of animals to make changes in ourselves.

Animal wisdom is the wisdom our totem animals give to us. A totem animal is an animal soul that functions as a teacher, companion and helper. Some consider the practice of taking a totem animal as the practice of drawing the archetypal energy of that animal into yourself, while others believe that animal spirits are real and assist us in our endeavors. Regardless of what you may personally believe about the actual existence of animal totems or spirit animals, you may call upon the archetypal energy of your animal totems to help you begin your journey. You may also call upon them at any time during the quest, should the going become difficult.

Do you have an affinity for a certain animal? My wife and I both love cats, and she collects cat figurines and pictures. Other friends I know collect cows, pigs, bears, etc. When I ask people about their reasons for collecting a particular animal, the usual response is, "I don't know, I just like cats (or dogs, or whatever)."

If you have a favorite animal, have you ever stopped to think about why? What is it about that particular animal that attracts you? There is an almost universal tradition in indigenous spiritual paths of taking a totem animal. Sometimes even whole tribes took on the name of a particular animal (The Wolf Clan of the Cherokee people would be an example). Obviously, such connections with the animal world are important. But why are they important? Think about your favorite animal for a moment. You may have more than one favorite animal. If that is the case, pick the one that first comes to mind. Picture that animal clearly in your mind. It may help to do a mindful meditation while focusing only on your chosen animal. When you feel that you have established a connection in your mind with your animal, go on to the *My Animal Totem* exercise at the end of this section.

You may have more than one animal helper, but most of us have a primary power animal who serves as a helper. If you have answered the Call of the Coyote, it is safe to say that Coyote is probably one of your totem animals. In order to call upon your own supernatural aid to begin the quest, you must first find your own spirit animal. You may already have at least one. If so, that's okay. But if not, here are some ways of finding out what your totem animal is. Begin by asking yourself the following questions:

1. Is there a particular animal that you find yourself drawn to? Is there something about the energy of this animal that you could use in your own life?
2. When alone in the woods, is there a certain animal you find yourself looking for? When you find this particular animal, do you study its behaviors to see what it might be telling you?

3. What animal do you enjoy learning about? Have you studied a certain animal enough to be an expert on it? This animal could be a cherished pet, or a wild animal that calls to you.
4. Does a particular animal keep showing up in your dreams? If so, what is this animal doing? Pay particular attention to animals that might attack or devour you in dreams. When this happens, the animal is symbolically killing the old you so that you may be reborn to partake in your spiritual journey.
5. Have you ever been bitten, chased or attacked by a particular animal? Again, this doesn't necessarily mean that this animal is your enemy. It could mean that this is the only way your totem animal can get your attention.
6. Do you collect paintings, statues, stuffed animals or trinkets of a particular animal? Have you thought about why you do this? What does this animal mean to you?
7. If you've ever gone hiking, were you followed by a particular animal? If this happens to you, pay particular attention if the animal seems to be trying to tell you something.

If you're still uncertain about your totem animal after reading this list, then do a brief meditation before bedtime, and ask your power animal to reveal itself to you. Make a note of your dreams that night. Did any animal show up? If not, keep doing a meditation and recording your dreams until your spirit animal reveals itself to you.

Worksheet 3.3 My Animal Totem

Name _____ Date _____

Think about your favorite animal. Hold the picture of that animal clearly in your mind as you complete the questions below.

What is your favorite animal? Why?

_____
_____
_____
_____
_____
_____
_____

What are the characteristics of your favorite animal (for example, if your favorite animal is a lion, you might include 'fierce' or 'independent')?

_____
_____
_____
_____
_____
_____
_____

In what ways are you like your favorite animal (what personal traits do you share in common with your favorite animal)?

_____
_____
_____
_____
_____
_____
_____

WORKSHEET 3.3 MY ANIMAL TOTEM PAGE 2 OF 2

Name _____ Date _____

In what ways are you different from your favorite animal (what are some personal traits that you do *not* share in common with your favorite animal)?

_____
_____
_____
_____
_____
_____

Of those ways that you are different from your favorite animal, are there any characteristics you would like to have, but don't? For example, if your animal is a lion, and you see the lion as independent, and you don't see that quality in yourself but would like to possess it, list it below.

_____
_____
_____
_____
_____
_____

How might your totem animal bring these qualities into your life? How could you draw upon the energy of the archetype of your totem animal as a supernatural aid to help you to live more fully in your True Self?

_____
_____
_____
_____
_____
_____
_____
_____

3.4 Talismans

"Feathers are messages from the Ancestors. If you find one, pick it up and keep it."

-Cherokee Wisdom

Another form of supernatural aid is the talisman. These talismans can be anything from good luck charms to special magical items blessed by a shaman or healer. The only rule for talismans is that they mean something significant to the owner. I've found my best and most potent talismans in the woods while walking and just paying attention. When you're open to the Universe, there's no telling what she might reward you with, so keep your eyes open!

If you wish, you might make a medicine bag for carrying your talismans. Making your own bag out of cloth or leather adds a special touch and makes it even more powerful to you. While you could purchase one from a store, making it yourself lends a power to it that buying one could not. When you've made your medicine bag, you may place your talismans in it and keep them with you, especially when engaging in spiritual pursuits. Some people have small medicine bags to hang around their necks, while others make larger bags that may be worn around the waist. It's all a matter of personal preference. There is no right or wrong way to carry your talismans. The "right" way is the way that seems best to you, and you alone.

Talismans are any objects that have significance to the owner. They are spiritual and symbolic reminders of ideas, ideals, or events that we wish to recall. Talismans may also be messages from our own supernatural aid. If you are seeking a message from a talisman, these questions may help you to decipher what your supernatural aid may be trying to tell you:

- How did your talisman present itself to you? What was the context? What were you doing at the time? How did it catch your attention?
- What supernatural aid do you need from your talisman? What do you hope it will tell you?
- When did you find it? Was it morning, afternoon, evening, or at night? Could there be any significance to the time of day in which you found it? What about the season and time of year?
- Where did you find your talisman? Be specific. Was there anything in particular about the location that contains a message?
- Why do you suppose your talisman chose this particular time and place to present itself to you?

3.5 Seeking Supernatural Aid

Whether you choose to seek supernatural aid from talismans, or animal totems, or nature herself, or from some other means, it may help to know how to go about it. Whether you see your own supernatural aid as coming from a divine source, or as coming from your own unconscious archetypes, or from some other source, one of the best ways to commune with that supernatural aid is through meditation.

Meditation stills the mind and quiets your thoughts and emotions so that your own inner voice may come through. When practiced for the purpose of seeking Supernatural Aid, the goal of meditation is not to find answers to questions. The goal of meditation for this purpose is to allow your soul and spirit to become quiet enough to hear the answers when they come from your own supernatural source.

When practicing meditation for the purpose of seeking Supernatural Aid, first formulate the question you're seeking an answer to. Be as specific as possible in framing the question, so that when the answer comes, you will recognize it.

Next, do grounding and centering meditation, but don't try to seek an answer to your question while meditating. Just focus on the stillness. After you have meditated, remain open to the nature around you for the rest of the day. Don't actively seek Supernatural Aid; just allow yourself to receive it should it arrive. Be there, in the moment, with nature, and allow nature to speak to you in its own time.

If you've had little experience with meditation, the terms "grounding" and "centering" may be unfamiliar to you. *Centering* means directing your attention inward by letting go of distractions in the environment and focusing only on your own inner state of being. *Grounding* means rooting yourself to the earth so that you are not relying on your own energy. You are actually drawing energy out of the Earth herself.

One of my favorite grounding and centering meditations is the Tree of Life meditation. The instructions for this particular meditation follow below.

3.6 Tree of Life Meditation

Begin this grounding and centering meditation by finding a comfortable place to practice. If at all possible, this place should be outdoors. If you have a sacred space that you use for your spiritual practice, go to it. If your sacred space contains a tree, sit comfortably underneath it, with your back resting against the tree. By resting your back against the tree you are able to draw energy from the tree, so the tree chosen for this meditation should be a tree whose spirit is friendly to your own spirit.

If you must do this meditation indoors, sit comfortably in a quiet area that is familiar to you. Before beginning this meditation, center yourself by emptying your mind of all distractions. Start with a few cleansing breaths, making sure that your exhalations are longer than your inhalations. As you breathe, direct your attention inward. Do not proceed until you feel that you are centered. When you feel centered, go on to complete the meditation by following the steps outlined below.

1. Begin the Tree of Life meditation by thinking of a color that gives you peace and serenity. This should be a color that brings you happiness, joy, and relaxation.
2. Now visualize a small sphere of light in this color, radiating from your solar plexus, just above your navel. Picture this light flowing downward, out of the tip of your spine, into the earth below you.
3. See the light branching off like the roots of a tree, drawing strength and energy from the earth. With each breath, you are drawing more energy out of the earth and into your spirit body.
4. Your spine is becoming the trunk of a tree. The energy channeled within your spine is becoming the Tree of Life. Feel the energy rising from the ground to become part of your being. Feel the energy rise through the trunk of your spine into the crown of your head. See the energy as colored light, bursting forth from the top of your head. The light energy emerging from your head is branching off in all directions, reaching out to touch the heavens above with each exhaled breath.
5. Watch the energy rise far above you, like the branches and leaves of the Tree of Life. Feel yourself becoming a part of all that is. You are merging with the life force of all existence.

6. The energy beneath you is reaching deeply into the center of the Earth, drawing upon the life force of Gaia herself. The energy branching out above your head is reaching beyond the Earth. It is reaching to the stars. It is expanding into eternity.
7. Now that you are completely grounded, seek your own supernatural aid by sitting quietly upon the Earth. You are not trying to go anywhere. You are not trying to do anything. You are simply enjoying the bliss of being. You are waiting quietly in the silence for your supernatural aid to present itself and to speak to you in its own way.
8. Meditate on the silence, allowing your own supernatural aid to speak to you when and if it will.
9. When you feel you are ready, you may close the Tree of Life meditation. To close this meditation, see the roots and branches of energy slowly returning to the center of your being. The energy of the life force is not leaving you, it is simply concentrating itself into your center of being.

When you have returned to this world, open your eyes, and open your spirit to the world that surrounds you. Be ready to receive your supernatural aid in whatever form it chooses to manifest itself to you. If your supernatural aid did not make itself known to you during this meditation, then the meditation itself and the stillness it brings is its own reward. You may try again on another day to seek wisdom from your supernatural aid.

3.7 Walking the Path

With visible breath I am walking.
A voice I am sending as I walk.
In a sacred manner I am walking.
With visible tracks I am walking.
In a sacred manner I walk.

--Prayer for Bringing the Sacred Pipe, White Buffalo Woman

As you walk the Way of the Coyote, realize that you are not alone. When you set out to fulfill your destiny, things have a way of working in your favor. The stars align to assist you. Doors open. The Universe puts things in your pathway to assist you in your travels. Jung called this process "synchronicity."

When you set out on your path, it is easy to get discouraged when things don't always go as planned. The purpose of supernatural aid is to give you an otherworldly confidence in your ability to complete the tasks that lie ahead. Remember that as the trials appear, their purpose is to teach you what you're capable of. Don't be afraid to make mistakes along the journey. Mistakes are learning opportunities. If you never made a mistake, you'd never learn anything, because you'd be doing what you already know. Learning involves risk, and that is why your supernatural aid is there…to help you manage the risks along the way so that you may learn from them and not be overwhelmed by them.

As you set off on your own personal journey in the footsteps of Coyote, rest assured that this is the path chosen for you. All the events in your life up until now have led to this moment. When things are difficult, keep this in mind. This is your destiny, so you will succeed. How could it be any other way?

Session 4 Crossing the First Threshold

Since the fire had gone out sometime before dawn, Coyote had begun to get cold again, so he leapt up and set out on his journey. Following the directions White Buffalo Woman had given him, he ran north towards the mountains.

Coyote ran all day and most of the night, stopping to rest only when he was too exhausted to go on. After three days he had journeyed further than he had ever been before. He came to the river that marked the boundary of the tribal lands of his people. The snow was thick on the ground here in the north, but the river had not yet frozen, and he could not cross. So Coyote ran up and down the river bank looking for a way to get to the other side. The more he ran the more frantic he became. He could not find a shallow spot or a place with rocks that he could cross.

As he ran up and down the riverbank, Sister Beaver sat on a log by the river watching him. Amused at his antics, she called out, "Are you trying to cross the river?"

"Yes! I must get to the other side!" shouted Coyote, "Do you know of a way?"

Sister Beaver was wary of Coyote. He had played pranks on many members of her family, and in the spirit of vengeance, she was eager to do the same to him. So she said to him, "Continue on downstream and you will eventually come to a huge beaver dam. It's old, and a bit rickety, but I'm sure one as agile as you could cross it with no problem!"

"Thank you very much!" shouted Coyote as he ran down the river bank in search of the dam.

Sister Beaver knew that the dam was too old and rotten to support Coyote's weight for his river crossing, but she was out for revenge for his many tricks at the expense of her and her family. Anxious to see what happened next, Sister Beaver swam downstream silently, out of sight. When she arrived at the rickety old dam ahead of Coyote, she climbed out of the river and hid behind a tree to watch.

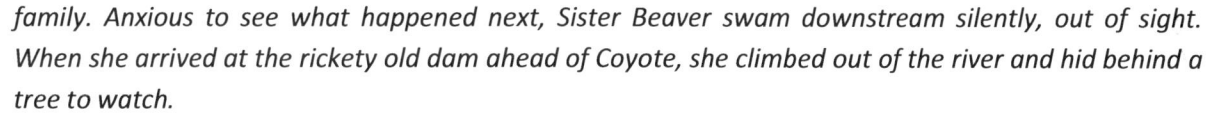

Coyote eventually arrived at the dam and began to make his way across, stepping gingerly on the rotting twigs that made up the dam. Things were going well, but about halfway across he stepped on a twig that gave way, plunging him into the icy water. The water was so cold that it took his breath away when he fell in. Gasping, he grabbed for a twig to keep from being swept downstream by the swift current. He managed to fight his way back to the shore. Shivering, he climbed onto the river bank, shook the icy water off his coat, and began again. Meanwhile, Sister Beaver stood behind her tree laughing at him.

Once again Coyote made his way about halfway across the dam, and once again he stepped on a twig that snapped beneath his paws. Once again he plunged into the icy river, and once again he barely managed to rescue himself before he drowned. All the while Sister Beaver gleefully watched his predicament, trying hard not to laugh out loud. She tried to giggle quietly while hiding and watching, but Coyote's keen ears heard her snickering. Quick-witted Coyote soon deduced what must be going on here. Needing to cross the river, but not wanting to spend the day plunging again and again into its freezing depths, Coyote quickly formulated a plan.

As he stepped onto the dam for his third attempt, he said aloud, "Oh woe is me! I just can't seem to find the right path across the river! If I do not succeed this time, I'm surely doomed, for Sister Cougar is hot on my heels, and she appears to be so hungry that even my scrawny carcass might look like a meal to her!"

Just as he expected, he heard a rustling from behind the tree where Sister Beaver was hiding. He knew what she was thinking; that if scrawny Brother Coyote would make a good meal for Sister Cougar, how much finer a meal would Sister Beaver's plump, well-fed body make!

Sister Beaver hesitated for only a moment before bounding out from behind her tree and onto the dam. Leaping from twig to branch, she made it all the way to the other side of the river. Coyote watched where she stepped, and careful to place his paws only where Sister Beaver had stepped, he followed her path across, making it safely to the other side without falling in again.

4.0 The Power of Intention

"In the universe there is an immeasurable, indescribable force which shamans call intent, and absolutely everything that exists in the entire cosmos is attached to intent by a connecting link."
--Carlos Castaneda

For every journey there is a first step. For those of us who seek the path of the Vision Seeker on the Way of the Coyote, the Crossing of the First Threshold is that first step to a wider world. The significance of that first step is that it indicates a commitment to the journey. The reluctance and refusal are over, and the intention of the seeker has been set. Once your intention has been determined, and you announce your intention to the Universe, there is no turning back. Crossing the First Threshold means that we can never return to the way things were before, because our world has changed.

In our story of the Way of the Coyote, Coyote has learned that if he sits still long enough, the fire goes out. This coldness before the dawn is a reminder that spiritual practice is a daily practice. If we don't tend the fire daily the fire grows cold. So Crossing the First Threshold is an acknowledgement that we are accepting a new way of seeing and being in the world. With that new way of being comes a new responsibility of living intentionally.

As we talked about in an earlier session, the *Hua Hu Ching*, by Lao Tzu, says this about living intentionally,

"Those who want to know the truth of the universe should practice the four cardinal virtues. The first is reverence for all of life. This manifests as unconditional love and respect for oneself and all other beings. The second is natural sincerity. This manifests as honesty, simplicity and faithfulness. The third is gentleness, which manifests as kindness, consideration for others and sensitivity to spiritual truth. The fourth is supportiveness. This manifests as service to others without expectation of reward."

As you set forth on the Way of the Coyote, make it a daily habit to intentionally practice these four virtues. Do so and see how your interactions with others, self, and nature improve.

4.1 Thought Streams - The River

Setting out on the path by Crossing the First Threshold means being open to new ways of thinking and new ways of being. One way to do this is to change your thoughts by learning to live in the present moment, with intention.

Imagine that your thoughts and feelings are like a river. The river is always flowing, ever changing. In this river of the mind, sometimes positive thoughts float to the top, and sometimes negative thoughts float to the top. If we find ourselves in a spot on the river where those negative thoughts are floating to the top, our goal isn't to stop the river by trying to dam it up. If we try to dam up the river, the water will only continue to back up behind the dam until either the dam bursts or the water overflows.

This is what happens when people have panic attacks or "nervous breakdowns." The water behind the dam has no place to go, and it eventually builds up until a catastrophe happens.

Trying to stop negative thoughts and feelings by damming up the river isn't the answer, since it could lead to catastrophe. So how do we deal with such thoughts?

What if there was an alternative to trying to stop the river by building a dam across it?

If we find ourselves at a place on the river where those negative thoughts are flowing to the top, we can consciously decide not to drown in the river by choosing instead to get out of the river, sit on the riverbank, and watch those thoughts and feelings flow by.

When we make this choice, the river is still flowing. We haven't tried to dam it up. We're just not swimming in it. From our viewpoint on the banks of the river, we can watch those thoughts and feelings flow by without being carried downstream. Using our intentional powers of observing and describing our own internal states, we can acknowledge the river's presence without being at the river's mercy.

4.2 Upstream and Downstream Thoughts

In our analogy of the river, the thing that makes it flow from Point A to Point B is the presence of time. The sage has said, "You can't step twice on the same piece of water." This is because the water is always changing from moment to moment.

If you have the opportunity, find a gently flowing river near you. This should be a river where the water isn't flowing too rapidly, and where the water isn't too deep. Remember, safety first! This should be a river you know well, and it's best not to do this activity alone.

Once you have found your river, go out into it. Don't go any deeper than your waist. It's preferable to find a spot on the river where nature surrounds you.

Now stand in the river and do a little deep breathing. Inhale and exhale deeply for at least three breaths. Ground and center yourself. You may wish to do a brief meditation before continuing.

Now call upon your own Supernatural Aid. You may call upon the archetypal energy of your spirit animal, or it may help to hold a talisman in your hands. When you are ready, contemplate the river.

This is a river of the mind. Upstream, the past spreads out behind you. Downstream, the river flows into the future. To return to the past would involve wading upstream against the current. To visit the future would require swimming downstream with the tide.

Suppose you tried to wade upstream or swim downstream. Once you got to your new location, the past would still lie behind you upstream relative to where you are now. Likewise, the future would still lie downstream ahead of you.

No matter which direction you move, you will always find yourself right here, right now, in the river.

Imagine yourself turning now to face upstream, towards the past. You already know what lies behind you. There may be rocky shoals and rapids behind you. There may even be high waterfalls and boulders. But the fact that you are standing right now at this place and this time in the river means that you survived the journey. Regardless of what lies behind you on the river, you have made it this far. This means that you are a survivor! You have met the challenges on the river and have gotten to where you are today.

Now turn to face downstream. This part of the river is unknown to you. You haven't ventured there yet. There is no way of knowing whether more rapids lie ahead, or whether there is smooth sailing for the rest of the journey. You might try to make educated guesses as to what the downstream journey might be, based on the parts of the river you have already traveled, but there is no way to know with any certainty whether or not those guesses are correct. Rivers can suddenly change, and if you spend all your time worrying about what lies downstream, you miss the moment in which you find yourself. Worrying too much about what might lie downstream takes energy away from enjoying the pleasant experience of the river here and now.

Even if the worst happens, and we encounter catastrophes downstream, the choice to remain in the river is still ours. We can, at any time, make the conscious choice to step outside of the river for a while to watch it flow by.

We can't know what lies downstream, but we can prepare ourselves for it. We can't change the river, but we can change ourselves in order to increase the likelihood of a safe journey.

Life is like a river. When we learn to go with the flow, we decrease our chances of running aground.

Now cultivate an open and accepting attitude towards everything you are experiencing. What do you see? What do you hear? Can you feel the river's currents with your body? Are there pleasant aromas on the breeze? Enjoy the experience of being in the river right here, and right now.

When you feel at peace with your surroundings, take a mental snapshot of all you have experienced here in the river. Mentally record the river in as much detail as possible. When you have done so, you may recall and retrieve this experience the next time you are feeling stressed out.

When you are ready, leave the river and sit on the riverbank while thinking over these questions:

1. Once you were grounded and centered, did you find yourself thinking about what lies upstream or what lies downstream, or neither?

2. Once you were grounded and centered, did you find your mind wandering to your mental "to do" list of daily activities?

3. What was it about the river that made this experience different than your day-to-day life?

4. Is there a way to carry this experience with you into your day-to-day life?

5. How might this experience help you to see things in new ways that will lead you to your True Self?

6. How might this teaching metaphor help you to cross the first threshold on your own Call to Adventure?

4.3 Crossing the River

So here we are, in the middle of the river. On one riverbank is the life we are leaving behind. On that other, unknown shore is the new life we're moving towards. Crossing this river of the mind is consciously making the spiritual quest that is the Way of the Coyote the first and foremost quest in our lives. Rather than making pleasures of the flesh and the accumulation of material goods our goal and ambition in life we are is seeking a higher calling.

Seeking True Self doesn't mean that we're leaving our loved ones behind. It's just the opposite. The more we are able to live according to our own true nature, the more we are able to help others. This is because when we are able to be the person we were born to be, we set aside the obligations that others have placed on us against our will. When we learn to do this, we learn to act for others because it is what we have chosen to do for ourselves, and not out of a sense of guilt, or shame, or self-blaming. This frees us to fully act for others of our own free will and to set aside resentments.

As we cross the river into the realm of the shaman, it's not that we are leaving the material world behind either. We are instead learning a new way of seeing and being in the world. That way of seeing shows us that there is more to life than the trinkets and baubles of material possessions and status symbols. It is the path of true wealth that leads to love, connection, and ecospirituality.

This phase of the quest that is the Way of the Coyote involves emptying your cup. In order to be reborn as a seer, one must leave behind the former life. This means setting aside a life of pursuing material wealth just for the sake of owning things and instead seeking a life that makes room for nature and the spirit.

It's very easy to get caught up in the idea that material things are the key to happiness, and a certain amount of material goods are necessary to survive. But if that is the sole motivation for life, our lives become meaningless and empty. The vision seeker instead searches for, and finds, things of spiritual significance. These spiritual things guide and enhance the quest. It is the path of true success and personal power.

Crossing the First Threshold, or crossing the river, involves announcing to the world and to yourself that the old ways have passed away. From this moment on, now and forever, a new journey begins. By announcing your intent to yourself and to others, you hold yourself accountable to staying on the path until the journey's end. It is an acknowledgement that things will never again be as they were before.

To begin crossing the river, go on to the next page and complete the worksheet, *Crossing the First Threshold*.

WORKSHEET 4.3 CROSSING THE FIRST THRESHOLD

Name _____ Date _____

Meditate on your answers to the questions that follow as you prepare to leave your old life behind to set out on the sacred journey of the seeker.

What ancient wisdom do you seek on your journey?

_____
_____
_____
_____
_____
_____
_____

What is your initiation into the sacred path of the vision seeker? What do you need to begin the journey?

_____
_____
_____
_____
_____
_____
_____

How might you call upon your own inner wisdom to make the spiritual quest of the sacred seeker the first and foremost thing in your life?

_____
_____
_____
_____
_____
_____

WORKSHEET 4.3 CROSSING THE FIRST THRESHOLD

Name _____ Date _____

What gives your life meaning?

_____
_____
_____
_____

Being a seer is not about refusing to own things. It's about refusing to let things own you. In what ways can you set aside the material world when seeking spiritual enlightenment? How might you seek nature instead of goods and possessions?

_____
_____
_____
_____

What things of spiritual significance can assist you in finding happiness and enlightenment?

_____
_____
_____
_____

How might these sacred things of spiritual significance assist you on the way of the Seeker?

_____
_____
_____
_____

Contemplate your answers to these questions. Call upon your own inner resolve to resist the temptation of material pleasures as you seek the pleasures of the spirit. Conclude this exercise in the spirit of peace and serenity, knowing that you already possess everything you need to achieve enlightenment: Mind, body, emotion and spirit.

4.4 Spiritual Power

At this point in the seeker's journey, reluctance has been overcome, the decision has been made, and the purpose and intention have been set. Supernatural Aid has been found, and the quest can begin.

A journey of a thousand miles begins with a single step, and the Crossing of the First Threshold is the first step on the journey. Although there is still a long way to go, at least the quest has begun. At times when you feel overwhelmed at how much still remains, just remember to focus on one step at a time. If you are walking a thousand miles, and you focus on the fact that you have a thousand miles to go, you'll get so discouraged that you'll never take the first step. But if you just focus on the first step, and nothing but the first step, then focus on the next step, and only on the next step, and so on, the thousand miles will be over before you know it. It may help to remember that life is a journey, and not a destination. The key to walking in the Way of the Coyote is to enjoy the trip, in the present moment.

The whole purpose of setting out to answer the Call of the Coyote is to partake in a process of self-discovery that leads to the ability to live fully according to your own true nature. To answer the Call and to follow the Way means learning who you are, and what your place in the world might be. It is a quest to seek power of a spiritual nature.

The Way of the Coyote is the way of personal spiritual power. Such power is not power in the way the world conceives of power. It is not power that is involved in the accumulation of material possessions, or power that seeks to dominate and destroy other people. It is power that operates in the spiritual realm. Such energy is the power to master the self, to heal, to nurture, and to gain wisdom.

As you set out on the Way of the Coyote, you are leaving your old life behind. This means that you have already learned everything your old way of being in the world could teach you. Sometimes the baggage we carry from this older life as we cross the threshold can hinder us. Sometimes it can help us. In either case, the old way of being is part of your own personal mythology. At some point, this personal mythology has either failed you, or no longer satisfies you. If it did, there would be no reason to answer the Call of the Coyote, and you would have never begun this journey.

As you look back on the story of your life up until this point, consider why you find yourself now on a new path. What did your personal mythology teach you about the path you now seek to walk? If you are like many others, you may have been told that the Way of the Coyote is a dark and dangerous path. You may have been warned against following such a path. It may go against your religious upbringing, or it may seem too "weird" to some people in your life. People in your life may have actively discouraged you from answering the Call of the Coyote. Perhaps you were told that life is about the accumulation of material possessions, and not about answering a spiritual calling. Maybe you learned this from people whose idea of success is the accumulation of property rather than the accumulation of personal power. Maybe it's just frightening to contemplate going off on a path you know little or nothing about. If these or any other reasons are conspiring to keep you from crossing the first threshold, don't despair. With much risk comes much reward. As Mark Twain said, *"Why not go out on a limb? That's where the fruit is."*

4.5 Time is an Illusion

By the time you finish reading this sentence, the experience of reading it will lie in the past. At which point does the present become the past? Now? How about now?

How about never?

Where exactly does the past lie, anyway? Once you have finished reading this sentence, the only place it will exist is in your memory. This means that all of your past experiences, all of those journeys you have already taken, only exist in what you remember about them. The past is a product of the mind.

Let's turn to the future now.

Without turning the page, do you know what lies ahead in this book? You may have read the table of contents, so you might have a general idea of what is to come, but can you, without turning the page, tell me what the fifth word of the second paragraph on the next page is?

Of course not, because you haven't experienced it yet.

The problem with catastrophizing about what may come is that such thinking tries to predict the future. We are quite good at negative thinking. This is because negative thinking helps us to plan for the future. We look towards what might go wrong as a means of being prepared for any contingency. Without a little planning and prediction, we would never make any progress. If I don't plan to make the house payment, I may not have a house in the future. If I don't plan to eat today, and the next day, and the next, I might eventually starve to death.

But there is a difference between planning and catastrophizing. Catastrophizing involves focusing our attention only on the bad things that might happen in the future. I sometimes refer to it as *musturbating*, because it often takes the form of phrases like, "I must do this," or "I must not do this."

The difference between planning and catastrophizing is that planning involves setting concrete, measurable goals for the future while catastrophizing often ends in a storm of musterbation. Planning is a way of relieving anxiety, not of causing it. So if you're feeling anxious while planning, you're probably musturbating.

When you find yourself anxious while planning for the future, check to see if you are indeed catastrophizing or musterbating. Planning for the future is a way of anticipating negative outcomes and preparing for them so they don't catch you unprepared further down the river. It is a way of relieving anxiety by minimizing future catastrophes. When planning for the future, watch out for statements that focus on negative outcomes rather than positive ones. This doesn't mean that you cannot anticipate and plan for negative outcomes. If it did, nobody would ever buy health insurance! What it means is that you're planning for negative outcomes in order to prevent or guard against them. When discussing possible negative outcomes during planning, it is as a means of having positive outcomes at a later time.

What if we do find ourselves catastrophizing? How do we escape it?

It's called "catastrophizing" for a reason. It focuses only on potential future catastrophes. But unless you have a crystal ball, you cannot know the future with any certainty. This can be a scary proposition for people who have experienced catastrophes in the past, but if I find myself anticipating further disasters in the future, that possible future only exists in my mind. It is just as likely that something good might happen in the future. But if I've set my perception filter to only anticipate and look for bad outcomes, will I see a positive opportunity even if it presents itself?

Our perception filters only exist in our minds. The good news is that we are in charge of how those filters are set. We can choose which events in our lives to pay attention to.

The past only exists in memory, and the future is just an educated guess about what may or may not happen further downstream. Both past and future are nothing but products of the mind. We can consciously choose in the now which thoughts and feelings about past or future to give our energy to. When we do so, we are living in the now.

When we have anxiety, stress or depression, it is almost inevitably because we are dwelling on the past or on the future. As you read this sentence, are you having any stressful thoughts or feelings? If so, how many of those stressful thoughts or feelings are about what is going on right now, as you read this? How many of them are the result of things that happened in the past, or how many may or may not happen in the future?

To dwell on memories of the past, or projections of memory onto the future, is to be trapped by the mind. In the now, we can escape the mind trap and make conscious decisions on how much attention to give to those thoughts and memories. When we escape the mind trap, we step outside of time to the now. Here in the now, the past and the future cannot touch us unless we choose to let them.

In the now, we recognize that time is just the mind's way of keeping everything from happening at once. Once we grasp the concept that time is just an illusion, we are free to connect with our True Self, in nature, and in the present moment.

4.6 Reality and the Now

"Reality is that which, when you stop believing in it, doesn't go away."

-Phillip K. Dick

As we discussed in the previous section, the past only exists in memory, and the future is just a projection of our memories. This means that both the past and the future only exist in our minds. The present moment is always becoming the past as we continue to move forward in time, and the future is always becoming the now as we continue to move forward in time.

Is time real? If the past and the future are products of memory and projections of the mind, do they have any real existence outside of this present moment? If so, how? Can a thing exist only in memory? If the past and the future are just imagined experiences created by the mind, then we are free in the now to create different experiences.

If there is any such thing as real time, then it can only exist right here, right now. If there is any such thing as free will, then it too can only exist right here and right now. This is because the past is gone, and the future is not here yet. We cannot travel back in time and exercise our free will about conscious choices in the past, because it no longer exists. Likewise, we cannot travel forward in time to choices that have not presented themselves yet because the future isn't here yet.

But here in the now, we can make choices. Here we may exercise our free will to believe anything we want about the future…or the past. That is because this present moment is all that is real.

4.7 On the Nature of Fear

We've often heard the saying that the only thing to fear is fear itself. Our brain can conjure up scarier monsters than actually exist in real life. When our brains do this to us, we sometimes do well to prepare ourselves for the worst case scenario. Supposed a battered wife needs to leave her abusive husband. If she doesn't think about the possible things he could do to drag her back, she may find herself in a dangerous situation. In such a case, fear of the unknown has a basis in reality.

But much of what our imagination doles out when facing the unknown can get in the way of progress unless we deal head-on with it. This is what crossing the first threshold, psychologically, is about. Until we look closely at the dark stuff that stands in our way, we may not realize exactly why we can't progress. We may make excuses of limited time, money, energy, or choices when really we're suppressing our will to overcome all odds and make things better for ourselves.

We have to cross thresholds into the darkness of the mind throughout our lives. Does it get any easier? I think it does because we learn to surrender. "Here we go again," or, "Get ready to feel crappy." In such a scenario, we are not acting out of personal power, but out of learned helplessness. We've grown so accustomed to the way things are that we no longer believe we have a right to something better.

Of course, we all have dark times, and we all feel like giving up from time to time. But the passage through the dark places always brings light and strength if we have the patience to endure. Without darkness, you could not know the light. Without the bad times, you could not acknowledge the good times. Although sometimes we must walk through the darkness, as long as we keep sight of the path, we may emerge on the other side wiser and stronger. If we can remember to trust the path in spite of our fears, we will have crossed the first threshold into the Belly of the Whale.

Session 5 The Belly of the Whale

Once Coyote crossed the river to the other side, he was further from his home village than he had ever been. The terrain looked strange and unfamiliar, and the sights and smells were confusing to him. He walked on and on throughout the rest of the afternoon. Near twilight, he came upon a cave entrance.

From deep within the cave he could hear the distant sound of drumming and singing. The sound was so faint that for a moment he wondered if he'd heard it at all, or if he'd simply imagined it. He strained his ears to listen.

Yes, it was definitely the sound of chanting from deep within the cave.

Although the thought of journeying into an unknown cave this late in the day filled him with trepidation, the idea of sleeping out in the open in unknown territory with this strange, cold, white substance falling from the sky frightened him even more. He took a deep breath and entered the cave.

As he made his way down the tunnel, he gradually became aware of a faint light in the distance, coming from the direction of the music. He descended down the narrow passageway towards it.

When he arrived at the source of the light, he found himself in a large inner chamber. At the center of the chamber was a fire. The heat from the fire instantly warmed him to the point that he was almost uncomfortably hot. Its light reflected off the crystals that adorned the cavern walls, making shadows and bits of light bounce throughout the chamber. He had never seen anything like this. It was as if the stars of the heavens had come down to the earth and were dancing to the music. And what music it was! It was at once soothing and invigorating; calming, yet disturbing.

As he entered the main chamber he saw a tribe of two-leggeds dancing around the fire. They were all adorned in paint and feathers, and each wore a mask designed to mimic one of the creatures of the earth. There were masks of four-legged creatures like Brother Wolf and Sister Cougar, and masks of the creatures of the air like Brother Eagle and Sister Wren. There were also masks in the likeness of the fishes, like Sister Salmon and Brother Trout. All the creatures of the three realms of earth, air, and water were represented.

As Coyote watched the dance, he noticed something unusual: All of the dancers were circling the fire backwards. They danced in a spiral, moving in the direction opposite of the way their masks were facing.

"This is very strange!" thought Coyote. He settled down to watch the dance so that he might glean from the performance what his next move might be.

He lay down on the cavern floor to watch. He tried his best to stay awake, but the warmth of the fire and the surreal quality of the music, combined with the rhythmic motions of the dancers, soon conspired to lull him into a trance, and he fell fast asleep.

As he dreamed, he pondered the quest. He was full of self-doubt. "I'm just a Coyote. I can't do this," he kept saying to himself. "I haven't the skills or the strength to complete this mission!"

As he lay dreaming and thinking about these things, he was startled by the sound of screaming. The two-leggeds had stopped dancing, and they were all rushing towards him! One grabbed his hind legs, another grabbed his forepaws, another seized his tail, and yet another grabbed him firmly about the neck. They began to pull, still screaming at him, until he came apart and his body was ripped to pieces!

He awoke on the cold ground with a start. He quickly checked himself to discover that he was still in one piece. It was only a dream, but it had seemed so real! He had thought himself dying. The illusion was so complete that upon waking he was actually puzzled to find himself still alive.

5.0 Who are You? Centering Yourself

Why are you, you? What are the things that make you the person that you are today? Why do the inner work required by ecospirituality in the first place?

Many of us carry a vision of who we would like to be. We also carry a vision of who we perceive ourselves to be at this moment in time. The Humanist Psychologist Carl Rogers called these two visions the *Ideal Self* and the *Perceived Self*. At the times when we do not feel at peace with ourselves because of some anxiety, stress or depression, it is most often due to a conflict between our vision of who we would want to be, and who we actually perceive ourselves to be. In other words, we experience a conflict between the Ideal Self and the Perceived Self.

The act of centering involves striking a balance between the powers of chaos and order in our lives. From this perspective, the Ideal Self represents the power of order, and the Perceived Self represents the power of chaos. The way to strike a balance between these two powers is to introduce a little chaos into the order, or introduce a little order to the chaos.

If conflict and inner turmoil are arising within you because of the gap between your Ideal Self and your Perceived Self, then the way to achieve balance would be to narrow that gap or to close it completely. Suppose for example that your Ideal Self is a person who is organized, punctual and capable of completing multiple tasks at once during the day. On the other hand, your Perceived Self (the person you see yourself as) is not very organized, always late, and incapable of meeting all the goals you set for yourself in a day. The conflict within you has arisen in this case because you have set impossible standards for yourself, yet you feel you should be able to meet those standards anyway. One way to find balance in this situation would be to realize that your Ideal Self doesn't have to be perfectly organized and punctual all the time, thereby allowing a little chaos to enter into the "perfect'" order established in your vision of your Ideal Self. Another way to introduce balance is to impose a little more order upon the chaos of your Perceived Self by taking the time to plan better so that you are more able to meet the schedule set by your Ideal Self.

The ultimate goal of the inner journey that is the Way of the Coyote is to strike a balance between the Ideal Self (or the life of perfect order) and the Perceived Self (or the life of perfect chaos). The more we learn about our own inner wants, needs and desires, and the reasons for them, the more we will draw closer to achieving the balance of individuation. In short, if we can change our thoughts and feelings, we can change the world. But in order to change our thoughts and feelings, we must first know what those thoughts and feelings are. *Centering* is a way to learn about your thoughts and feelings so that you may change them if you so desire.

There are many things we may wish to change about ourselves and about the world. We may even be able to change many of them. But there are also things that are beyond our power to change. Those things we cannot change, we must learn to accept. If we do not, then we will be endlessly frustrated by attempting the impossible. Of course, it can be very difficult to tell which things we can change, and which things we cannot. This is where wisdom enters the picture. One purpose of centering is to gain enough inner wisdom to be able to know the difference between the things we can change, and the things we must accept.

Think for a moment about the last time you were anxious or stressed out. Do you remember what caused your anxiety? Did that cause of your worry have something to do with an event that happened in the past, or an event that might happen in the future? Until someone invents a time machine, there is no way to go back and change the past. So worrying about something that happened in the past is counterproductive. Likewise, if you are worrying about something that may or may not happen in the future, you are wasting energy that could be put to better use in the here and now. Unless you have a crystal ball, there's no way of knowing for certain what may happen in the future. By worrying about it, you are expending energy that could be used to prevent the possible future disaster from happening in the first place.

When stress arises within us due to conflicts between our Ideal Self and our Perceived Self, we can restore balance and eliminate or reduce that conflict by seeking wisdom through acceptance and change. If there is something we cannot accept, then we must change it. If there is something we cannot change, we must learn to accept it. These are the only two choices we have. The wisdom comes in knowing whether a thing is something that can be changed, or if it's something we have to accept.

If the conflict between our Ideal Self and our Perceived Self has to do with something that happened in the past or something that might happen in the future, then that is something we will have to learn to accept, since it is impossible to change the past, and it is impossible to predict the future with any degree of certainty. The only changes we may make involve things that are happening right now, in the present moment.

Remember, as you set out on the path of making changes in your life, that you cannot change anyone but yourself. If problems arise in your life because of the actions of another person, you cannot force that person to do anything. All you can do is to accept that they are who they are. Knowing this, you may then be able to change yourself so that you can accept others more easily. This acceptance can occur more readily if you learn to let go of the past and the future and focus only on the present moment.

5.1 Dying to the Old Ways of Being

The problem with crossing the first threshold is that it is stepping into the unknown. The unknown is unfamiliar. We don't know the rules. We don't know what's expected. We don't know how to act. We don't know the dangers. We don't know what to assume about the way the world works now.

In order to learn new ways of being, we must first cast off our assumptions about the way things worked before. Our assumptions create our perceptions, and our perceptions create our reality. If we're journeying to new realities, our old perceptions and assumptions have to be discarded. This can be an especially difficult task, since many of our assumptions and perceptions are involved in our own sense of identity. If we cast them off, we might lose who we are. But in order to become someone new, we *must* lose who we were before. We must die to our old ways of being. We must be willing to bury old ways of doing. We must cast off old assumptions and perceptions so that we may gain a new reality.

Jonah spent three days in the Belly of the Whale after his Refusal of the Call. This was Jonah's casting off of his former identity so that he could step into his new role as a spiritual leader. This time in the whale's belly is a time of reflection and of challenging preconceived notions before initiation into a wider world. It is the preparation for the death of the old in order that the new may be born.

5.2 Finding a New Truth

"Your vision will become clear only when you can look into your own heart. Who looks outside, dreams; who looks inside, awakes."

-Carl Jung

"The truth will set you free, but first it will piss you off."

-Gloria Steinem

There is a Zen koan about a student who came to a Zen Master for training. The student wanted to impress the master with his knowledge, so he talked non-stop for several minutes about the previous masters he had studied with, and all the knowledge he had accumulated. As the student talked, the Master offered him a cup of tea. The Master, still listening intently, placed the cup before the student and began to fill it. When the cup was filled, the Master continued pouring until the tea ran out of the cup, onto the table, and into the student's lap. The student yelled for the Master to stop pouring the tea, "Can't you see that the cup is full? There's no room for any more tea!"

"Yes," the Master replied, "Once the cup is full, it cannot be filled any further. You come to me to learn, but I cannot teach you. Your cup is already full. You must first go and empty your cup. When you have done this, then I can fill it again."

In Phase One of the Hero's Journey, the Departure, we learned what it means to seek a new spiritual path by leaving the familiar behind. In Phase Two, the Initiation, we will learn what it means to die to the old ways of being and to be reborn as a spiritual seeker and a follower of the Way of the Coyote. Like the student with the full cup, a seeker on the Way of the Coyote must first empty her cup of all other teachings. This means forgetting old ways of being. It means casting aside any assumptions or perceptions about what may lie ahead on the path. To die to the old ways of being means to erase the past, letting go of any preconceived notions about the way the world worked in the past. It means starting over in every sense of the word.

There are three components of this rebirth: Assumptions, Intentions, and Motivations (think of the word *AIM* to help you to remember these three components). Before you can be reborn to the Way of the Coyote, you must address all three of these components in the following ways:

Assumptions – What assumptions were you living by before answering the Call of the Coyote? How are these assumptions different from the assumptions you would need to live by in order to answer the call? What assumptions might you have been making about your old life that were leading to problems? What new assumptions, if any, would you need to make in order to be reborn? In order to follow the Way of the Coyote?

Intentions – What was your intention in living the way you did prior to answering the Call of the Coyote? What were you trying to accomplish? What were your goals then, and how will your goals be different when you answer the Call of the Coyote? What is your intention in seeking the Way of the Coyote? What do you hope to accomplish?

Motivations – What were your motivations for living the way you did prior to answering the Call of the Coyote? What were the rewards for your old way of living? Were those rewards spiritual or material? What will be the rewards (motivations) for answering the Call of the Coyote? Will these motivations be spiritual or material? Are you prepared to make the sacrifices necessary to follow the Call of the Coyote? If so, what will the rewards be? If not, what's standing in your way?

When you are able to answer all of these questions honestly you will be ready to leave the cave. You will have found a new truth to live by, and this new truth shall be your road map on the Way of the Coyote.

5.3 Katabasis

"The word 'ashes' contains in it a dark feeling for death; ashes when put on the face whiten it as death does...some men around thirty-five or forty will begin to experience ashes privately, without ritual, even without old men. They begin to notice how many of their dreams have turned to ashes."

–Robert Bly, *Iron John: A Book about Men*

Katabasis is Greek for "to go down" or "to descend." To be in the Belly of the Whale is to engage in your own personal katabasis. It is a realization that the way you have lived your life up to this moment is not in accordance with your own true nature. If this were not so, you wouldn't have taken up the Way of the Coyote in the first place. Katabasis means asking yourself, "If nothing changed from this day forward, could I live the rest of my life this way?" If the answer to that question is, "no," then obviously something must change. In katabasis, change happens when the fear of staying the same forever becomes greater than the fear of changing forever by taking the journey into the unknown.

The way to escape the Belly of the Whale is by completing the process of katabasis. To explore one possible way of doing this, complete the exercise on the next page.

Katabasis can be a dance with death, or challenging our greatest fears

WORKSHEET 5.3 BELLY OF THE WHALE: YOUR OWN PERSONAL KATABASIS   PAGE 1 OF 4

Name _____ Date _____

Katabasis is Greek for "to go down" or "to descend." To be in the Belly of the Whale is to engage in your own personal katabasis. It is what the poet Robert Bly referred to as *"spending time in the ashes."* When our old ways of being in the world burn down around us, we cannot go on anymore the way things were. We must start over by finding a new path. The way to escape the Belly of the Whale is by reversing this process of katabasis. To explore one possible way of doing this, complete the exercises on this worksheet.

What is your own personal katabasis? What past thoughts, feelings, words and deeds have led you to descend into the ashes? What sameness can you not allow to continue for the rest of your life?

_____
_____
_____
_____
_____
_____
_____

As of this very moment, what is your own true nature?

_____
_____
_____
_____
_____
_____

As you spend ashes time in the Belly of the Whale, what are you casting aside about the way your life has been in the past?

_____
_____
_____
_____
_____
_____

WORKSHEET 5.3 BELLY OF THE WHALE: YOUR OWN PERSONAL KATABASIS   PAGE 2 OF 4

Name _____ Date _____

What new thoughts, words, deeds, and feelings would you need to embrace in order to live more fully according to your own true nature in the future?

_____
_____
_____
_____
_____
_____
_____
_____

What about your currently reality needs to change in order to live according to your own true nature?

_____
_____
_____
_____
_____
_____
_____
_____

For the questions that follow on the next page, use the definitions below to formulate your answers:

> *Assumptions* – Guesses we make, often without supporting evidence, about the way the world works
>
> *Perceptions* – The "filter" through which we view the world, based on our assumptions about how the world works
>
> *Intentions* – What we are trying to accomplish with our lives
>
> *Motivations* – What we hope to be rewarded with if we accomplish our intentions

WORKSHEET 5.3 BELLY OF THE WHALE: YOUR OWN PERSONAL KATABASIS   PAGE 3 OF 4

Name _____ Date _____

What assumptions about the way the world works would you have to change in order to re-create your present reality so you may live according to your own true nature?

_____
_____
_____
_____
_____

What perceptions about the way the world works would you have to change in order to re-create your present reality so you may live according to your own true nature?

_____
_____
_____
_____
_____

What intentions would you have to change in order to re-create your present reality so you may live according to your own true nature?

_____
_____
_____
_____
_____

What motivations would you have to change in order to re-create your present reality so you may live according to your own true nature?

_____
_____
_____
_____
_____

WORKSHEET 5.3 BELLY OF THE WHALE: YOUR OWN PERSONAL KATABASIS

Name _____ Date _____

Use the information from the previous questions on this worksheet to make a list of all the thoughts, feelings, actions, and beliefs you would like to leave behind in the ashes as you prepare to leave the Belly of the Whale. This list should consist of things you never hope to return to; the things you cannot allow to continue. The list represents the old self that you are "dying" to in preparation of being reborn in your new ecospiritual True Self.

_____
_____
_____
_____
_____
_____
_____
_____
_____
_____
_____
_____
_____
_____
_____
_____

Now that you have completed your list, go to an outdoor space, preferably during the evening, and build a small fire if possible, being sure to follow all fire safety precautions as you do so. Once you have built your fire, take the list you created above. Hold the list in your hands and make an announcement to the Universe that you are dying to your old way of being and that the old you is being symbolically cremated. Now throw this list on the fire. As it burns your old self is melting away into the ashes, in preparation for the birth of the new you.

If you are doing this as part of an ecospirituality group or program, your coach may go around the fire and have each participant say something meaningful about their list before throwing it on the fire. At the end of the ceremony you may finalize the death of the old self by burying the ashes in the earth.

5.4 Death and Rebirth in the Belly of the Whale

Throughout the world at various times and in various cultures, there have been shamanic traditions. One of the tasks of the shaman is to commune with the dead. Another is to journey to the Otherworld (or the Underworld) and to bring back knowledge. Most, if not all, shamanic traditions have some sort of initiation rite in which the candidate "dies" to his former life and is reborn to the life of the shaman.

These rites usually took place in some sort of representation of the womb of the Earth Mother. The Hopi tribe used kivas for this purpose. In ancient Europe there were many earth mounds. One of the largest of these is Brú na Bóinne in Newgrange, Ireland.

Some Celtic tribes engaged in a ritual called "bull sleep," in which the shaman ingested psychoactive substances and wrapped himself in the hide of a bull while seeking visions. Many Native American tribes used sweat lodges for such a purpose.

No matter the form the rites took, they were symbolic of the rebirth of the shaman into his new role. Such a rebirth followed a phase of preparation and purification, then a period of sensory deprivation involving an earth mound, tent, leather hide, sweat lodge, or other representation of the womb, and finally a re-birth into a new life.

There is usually a feast prior to the rite. The candidates do not eat at the feast, nor will they eat for the entire period of their initiation, although it is possible that they may ingest plants or herbs to enhance their visions. This practice of fasting is common among many shamanic traditions.

Ancient Mesopotamian god Dumuzid (Tammuz) imprisoned in the Underworld

Amid dancing and the drumming, the candidates are admitted to the central chamber of the mound. There are no torches or other light sources, so the candidates await the journey in total darkness. The journey into the darkness of the mound symbolizes death and burial. This is consistent with the technique of sensory deprivation used by many cultures throughout the world. When used in this manner, the senses are deprived of stimulation in order to achieve a state receptive to visions and dreams. Lacking any outside stimuli, the mind turns inward. When turned inward in this manner, freed of distractions, the mind makes contact with the collective unconscious shared by all. It is a time where the candidate may call upon his or her Supernatural Aid for guidance.

Many shamanic practices use a period of three days and three nights for such initiations.

So the petitioner finds himself (or herself...there is also a large history of female shamans) in the center of a burial mound, in total darkness, calling upon her Supernatural Aid to guide her to the Otherworld. The petitioner may spend up to three days and three nights communing with the spirits of the Sacred Ancestors present with her there in the womb of the Earth Goddess. On the third day, at dawn, the candidate emerges into the sunlight, marking the first time in three days that she has seen any light whatsoever. This also marks the first time she has seen the Sun with her new, shamanic eyes. She leaves the chamber, sometimes crawling through a narrow earthen passage like an infant struggling to be born, so that she may share the sacred wisdom of the vision with the rest of the tribe.

5.5 Reborn to the New

This rebirthing exercise will allow you to experience your own katabasis in the Belly of the Whale by engaging in your own ritual death and rebirth. The idea of sensory deprivation, or of stimulating certain senses while repressing others, is a useful technique when engaging in vision quests of this nature. Music is one of the tools used most often for this purpose. Anything from rhythmic drumming to flutes to symphonies may be used when seeking visions. To employ this method, lie comfortably, preferably in darkness, while allowing the music to take you. Allow the notes and the rhythms to create landscapes in your mind. If you are doing this workbook as part of an Ecospirituality group, your instructor may hold a drum circle or other rite for such a purpose. If doing this workbook on your own, you may select or play your own music.

Prior to your own rebirthing rite, you may experiment with isolating and stimulating merely one sense at a time. For example, try shamanic meditation while sitting in a dark room with incense burning, or gaze at a single lit candle, or lie in a warm bath. Another influence on shamanic journeying is the position of your body. Try this: Sit cross-legged on the floor or the ground with your hands resting on your knees. Notice what the energy in your hands feels like. Now try the same thing with your hands palm-up in your lap. Finally, place your hands, palm together, in front of your heart. Do you sense any difference in energy in these various positions? Likewise, the position of your body during vision seeking can determine the quality and flavor of your vision. Experiment until you find a position suitable for your needs.

5.6 The Journey to the Otherworld

When traveling to the Otherworld, first find a place where you will be undisturbed for the duration of your journey. The journey itself may be as long or as short as you like. If you're participating in an Ecospirituality group, your instructor may have a specified time for the journey. If doing it on your own, you may do it for whatever length of time seems appropriate.

Such a journey is best undertaken outdoors. I've had some powerful visions while camping alone in the woods, for example. But you may also engage in spirit journeys from the privacy of your own bedroom if you're not able to be in a natural space. If you have to be indoors to do this, it may help to have recordings of nature sounds to play during the meditation. You may also bring in some plants and place them in the area where you plan to engage in the meditation.

It may also help to make the journey more authentic and true to what our ancestors may have practiced if you are able to create some sort of representation of the womb of the Earth Mother. This could be a tent, or a blanket over your head, or even a sweat lodge if one is available. A word of caution first: Don't attempt to build a sweat lodge of your own without instruction from an expert! People have died in improperly constructed sweat lodges!

When you've selected your space and determined the length of time for your journey, follow the steps below.

1. Begin by grounding and centering. Do not go any further until you are fully relaxed and clear of purpose, with a firm and fixed intention.
2. When you are grounded and centered, meditate on what parts of you are "dying" and what parts of

you are being "reborn." What of your old life do you wish to leave behind? What areas of your new life as a shaman do you wish to grow in? What does this symbolic rebirth mean to you?

3. In order to access the Otherworld, you must first cross the waters. Water symbolizes the mind, and the depths of the sea represent the vast depths of the unconscious mind. When crossing the waters, I find it helpful to visualize myself in a boat upon a calm sea. Gradually the boat moves into a fog that becomes thicker and thicker. I then will the mists to part, granting me access to the Otherworld that lies within my unconscious mind.

4. The way to enter the Otherworld is to begin by knowing you are already there. Picture each and every life consciousness in the Universe as a silver thread. See the silver threads stretching out to infinity, forming a web of infinite probability. This Silver Web represents all possibilities in all worlds and in all universes. Consider the purpose of your journey here, and ask your own Supernatural Aid to guide you to the proper thread to find the answers you seek. Take the thread that stands out to you and follow it until it leads you to the purpose of your journey.

5. When you have arrived at the knowledge you seek, follow the silver thread back to your body. As you return, allow yourself to gradually become aware of re-entering your body. As your body comes back to you, breathe deeply and slowly become aware of your surroundings. When you are ready, open your eyes, remembering the knowledge you have gained.

When you have completed your journey, go on to the next page and fill in the worksheet that follows.

5.6 REFLECTIONS ON THE JOURNEY TO THE OTHERWORLD

Name _____ Date _____

After you have completed your own death and rebirth rite and meditation, go on to answer the reflection questions on this worksheet.

What were you dying to or leaving behind of your old life when taking this rebirthing journey?

_____
_____
_____
_____
_____
_____

What was being born in you in your new ecospiritual life when taking this rebirthing journey?

_____
_____
_____
_____
_____
_____

Assuming you conducted this rebirthing rite in an outdoor space, what elements of nature assisted you in completing the journey? Were there any signs or omens in the natural space in which you conducted your meditation? Examples of such "omens" might include animals behaving in ways that attracted your attention, or any other sights, sounds, aromas, textures or unusual experiences that seemed to call to you?

_____
_____
_____
_____
_____
_____
_____

5.6 Reflections on the Journey to the Otherworld

Name _____ Date _____

Did you use any sort of music while undertaking this journey? If so, what did the music add to the meditation? If not, what did the absence of music add to the meditation?

_____
_____
_____
_____
_____
_____
_____
_____

In what ways are you a new person now that you have been reborn to your new ecospiritual life?

_____
_____
_____
_____
_____
_____
_____
_____
_____
_____
_____
_____
_____
_____
_____
_____
_____

5.7 Seeing the Road of Trials with New Eyes

Now that you have completed your time in the ashes, you are able to be reborn with new spiritual eyes. You are no longer seeing the world through your old assumptions and perceptions. You've learned a new way of seeing and a new way of being in the world.

This newfound vision will help you as you continue on the Road of Trials that leads you to your new, ecospiritual self.

Phase Two: Initiation

In the Initiation phase, the hero must "die to herself." Many religious and shamanic rituals involve a symbolic death and rebirth to a new way of being. Initiation is an emptying of your cup so that it may be refilled with new knowledge. For a spiritual seeker, Initiation means being open to new experiences and being willing to experiment with new ways of being.

Session 6 The Road of Trials

Glad to find that he was not dead, Coyote looked up to see what had become of the dancers. The cavern was empty. All that remained of the fire were the dying embers. The tribe of two-leggeds was gone, and with them the haunting music. Not knowing what to do next, he decided to leave the cave, but as he turned to go back the way he came, he saw that the path behind him was blocked. The opening was no longer there!

In a panic, he ran around the chamber looking for a way out. As his eyes adjusted to the dim light of the embers, he spied an opening on the other side of the embers, and he made his way towards it.

The passage was narrow, and he had to crawl to make his way down. It seemed to go on forever. Just when he was at the point of thinking that coming into the narrow tunnel had been a mistake, he saw a faint glow at the other end of the passage. Steeling himself for what might lie ahead, he continued to crawl towards the light. It grew brighter and brighter, until he found himself outside of the cave, standing in a valley.

There in front of him was White Buffalo Woman. Her right hand held the torch of magical fire. She greeted him once again, and they both sat down on the snow-covered ground while she kindled a fire with her torch. The fire was bright. The snow reflected the light of the flames, giving the landscape a beautiful yet ghostly appearance. Coyote watched the light of the fire twinkling and reflecting off the new-fallen snow. As the fires blazed, she began to teach him about the road ahead.

6.0 Control

"He who angers you conquers you."

-Elizabeth Kenny

The Road of Trials begins with what the poet Robert Bly calls "Time in the Ashes," or "Ashes Time." Spending time in the ashes leads one to realize that sometimes things get worse before they get better. As the spiritual seeker's old identity is stripped way in the Belly of the Whale, there is nothing yet with which to replace it. To a spiritual seeker, this katabasis may feel like the end of the world. Sometimes it manifests as a sense that one's entire life has been meaningless up until this point. Author Richard Bach, in his bestseller *Jonathan Livingston Seagull*, describes this feeling best:

"I gave my life to become the person I am right now. Was it worth it?"

This knowledge leads to the feeling that one's life is out of control. Feeling out of control can lead to anger, especially regarding our relationships with other people. When we feel out of control we most often take it out on the people we care the most about.

We often forget, however, that if someone has the ability to anger you, then that person just controlled you. If you allow others to "make" you feel angry, you have relinquished control over your own emotional well-being. Similarly, anger is often the result of failed attempts to control others. By analyzing our beliefs about control, we learn to manage our moods so that control is no longer an issue.

Once there was a sculptor who was famous for his carvings of animals. Of all the animals he carved, his elephants were the most lifelike and inspiring. One day an art student came to him and asked him the secret to creating such beautiful elephants.

"The answer," he said, "Is simple. You just get a block of marble and chip away anything that doesn't look like an elephant."

When difficulties arise in our relationships, it's usually because we've set out to carve an elephant, but we suddenly find ourselves carving a bear or a donkey or some other animal instead. When this happens, we've gotten caught up in the details of living, and we have lost sight of our original goal, the elephant. The way to get back to carving the elephant is to realize that we cannot control others. We also cannot control what life throws at us. What we *can* control is what we *believe* about what life throws at us. That ability to change our beliefs to get the results we want is the secret to escaping the cave.

6.1 Escaping the Cave

In our Coyote story, Coyote symbolically died to his old way of being by being ritually torn apart by the dancers in the cave. His spiritual death to the old way of being was a metaphorical emptying of his cup so that it might be refilled when he is re-born to his new spiritual self. Once the symbolic death to the old way of being has occurred, the cave has fulfilled its purpose. The time in the ashes is over. It is time to escape the Belly of the Whale and to take up the Road of Trials.

The cave in our Coyote story that represents the Belly of the Whale may be a symbol for many things on the path of the Coyote. At the threshold to the cave the Seeker may once again face some of the doubts and fears that first surfaced upon his Call to Adventure and his subsequent Refusal of the Call. He may need some time to reflect and meditate upon his journey and the treacherous Road of Trials ahead in order to find the courage to continue. It is also a time for ritual purification as the Seeker casts aside any remnants of the old ways of being, burning them in the sacred fire of enlightenment.

It is also a time for casting away any lingering self-doubts, regrets and recriminations. This ritual process of elimination and purification is necessary so that the Seeker may step out of the cave and into the light as an empty vessel for the journey to fill with wisdom.

6.2 Heal Thyself

At this point on the journey of the vision seeker, the transition to the Road of Trials involves caring for others by caring for yourself. Healers love to help people. It's what we do. Just remember when you are healing people to include yourself in the people being healed. Those of us who nurture and care for others sometimes think it is selfish to take time to care for ourselves. In fact, just the opposite is true. If we never care for ourselves we will eventually have nothing left to give others. If others depend on us and we allow ourselves to become exhausted, or burned out, we won't be able to do them any good either, so it is highly important to take time out once in a while to recharge our own batteries. One of the best ways to do this is to spend time in nature. So crawl out of that cave and get out into the sunlight!

As the Seeker climbs out of the cave onto the Road of Trials, she is face-to-face with the portion of the path that will test her to the limits of her endurance. It is as if the Universe wishes to evaluate our sincerity and commitment by throwing everything it can at us. The wisdom of the healer on this portion of the journey allows us to care for our own needs as well as the needs of others. It is also a reminder to know when to lead and when to follow. We don't have to do it all. We can sometimes delegate and let others take charge for a while, relaxing and following their lead.

As you cross onto the Road of Trials, it may be helpful meditate on your answers to the questions on the next worksheet.

WORKSHEET 6.2 HEALING ON THE ROAD OF TRIALS   PAGE 1 OF 2

Name _____ Date _____

The Road of Trials in the Way of the Coyote involves learning a new way of being in the world. It is a journey into the unknown, and a setting aside of old patterns of thought and behavior. It involves an element of trial and error as we learn to do things in new ways without falling back into old habits. As you contemplate your own Road of Trials, meditate on your answers to the questions below.

What rules did you follow in your life before and after your Belly of the Whale experience?

_____
_____
_____
_____
_____
_____

Who do you follow in your life now? Who did you follow prior to your time in the ashes?

_____
_____
_____
_____
_____
_____

What things that you have followed in the past might be hindering your walk on the Way of the Coyote? What is the key to letting them go and leaving them behind?

_____
_____
_____
_____
_____
_____
_____

WORKSHEET 6.2 HEALING ON THE ROAD OF TRIALS　　　　PAGE 2 OF 2

Name _____ Date _____

What things that you plan to follow in the future might be helping you to walk on the Way of the Coyote?

_____
_____
_____
_____

In what ways can you follow a healing path rather than a path of harm?

_____
_____
_____
_____

In what ways may you use the wisdom of the Coyote to heal others? If you need a refresher on Coyote medicine, return to section 1.2 of this workbook.

_____
_____
_____
_____

In what ways may you use the wisdom of the Coyote to heal yourself? If you need a refresher on Coyote medicine, return to section 1.2 of this workbook.

_____
_____
_____

As you meditate on your answers to these questions, call upon your own inner healer so that you may heal yourself by healing others. If it helps, you may draw on the archetypal energy of your totem animal's supernatural aid. You may also wish to burn a bit of healing herb or incense in thanks for the healing you have received while completing this exercise. Conclude this worksheet with a spirit of health and wholeness, knowing that you have already received the healing you need to live in the Way of the Coyote.

6.3 Coyote Walk

When we picture someone engaged in meditation we usually think of someone sitting quietly, legs crossed, while focusing on the breath. While this is one way of meditating, it is not the only way. One of the lessons of ecospirituality is that we may meditate anywhere, at any time. As long as we are living in the now by paying attention to what our senses are telling us in the moment, we can be said to be engaged in mindful meditation.

This means that we may engage in any activity in a mindful way.

A common exercise to perform in a mindful manner is an activity called *mindful walking*. The basic process of mindful walking is to walk while focusing on the physical sensations of the process of walking by shifting energy from the thinking cycle to the cycle of sensations. What do my leg muscles feel like as I walk? Can I feel my diaphragm as I breathe? What sights do I see as I walk? What do I hear? What aromas are in the air?

The Coyote Walk is a way to practice mindful walking. To use this technique, first picture how a coyote walks. She places her paws one in front of the other so that she makes as little noise as possible. She experiences here environment largely through her sense of smell, pausing here and there to read her environment before moving on. If she spots something of interest, she stops for a while to investigate. She is open to what her senses tell her, but at the same time she approaches life with a playful attitude.

The way to perform the Coyote Walk is to allow yourself to become the Coyote by drawing her archetypal energy into yourself. Shamans from around the world are credited with the ability to shape-shift. What if this shape-shifting is not a physical transformation, but a transformation of the mind? Imagine yourself becoming a Coyote and you will be halfway there.

- To perform the Coyote Walk, first go to an outdoor place, weather permitting, and find a spot where you may walk undisturbed for at least thirty minutes.

- When you have found your place, stand with your feet about shoulder-width apart. Now ground and center yourself while contemplating the energy in the archetype of the coyote described above.

- Feel yourself becoming the coyote. Take the coyote energy into yourself and begin to walk, placing one foot in front of the other as quietly as possible. To do this, it may help to visualize a straight line drawn on the ground. Imagine your feet touching that line with every step.

- Continue to walk, remaining open to the sensations of your feet as they rise and fall, to the sensations of your breathing, and to all of the information your senses are giving you about the immediate environment.

- Don't stare at your feet, but instead look around you so that you may experience the environment to the fullest.

When you have completed this exercise, go on to answer the questions on the Coyote Walk worksheet on the next page.

WORKSHEET 6.3 THE COYOTE WALK

Name _____ Date _____

Complete the Coyote Walk exercise from Section 6.3 of the *Ecospirituality Workbook* before answering the questions below.

When you took the coyote energy into yourself by getting in touch with your coyote archetype, what did you notice about yourself? Did you feel any differently? If so, how?

_____
_____
_____
_____

During your walk, did coyote hold up a mirror to you? If so, what did you see in it?

_____
_____
_____
_____
_____

Did you like what you saw in the mirror? If so, describe it. If not, how might you change it?

_____
_____
_____
_____
_____

Did coyote show you any ways you might be tricking or fooling yourself? If so, what were they?

_____
_____
_____
_____
_____

WORKSHEET 6.3 THE COYOTE WALK

Name _____ Date _____

Did coyote show you any ways you might be tricking or fooling others? If so, what were they?

_____
_____
_____
_____
_____
_____

Did coyote show you anything you might like to change about yourself? If so, what was it, and how might you change it?

_____
_____
_____
_____
_____
_____

Did the Coyote Walk change your perception of time? If so, how?

_____
_____
_____
_____
_____
_____

Would the Coyote Walk be a useful tool to help you live more fully in True Self, according to your own true nature? If so, how? If not, why not?

_____
_____
_____
_____
_____

6.4 Coyote Walk on the Road of Trials

One of the lessons of Coyote is that we cannot escape ourselves. We all have a dark side. We cannot escape this dark side because it is a part of us. Coyote teaches us that if we ignore our darker natures and try to pretend they don't exist, we will be consumed by our darker natures. But if we are able to acknowledge our darker and more chaotic tendencies, we have taken the first step towards channeling their energy for creative purposes. When coyote places us before the mirror, it's up to us what to do with what the mirror shows us.

We all contain both light and dark, order and chaos. This lesson is reflected in nature as well. If you are a frequent hiker, you have probably come upon the carcasses of dead animals in the wild. If you live in a place where there are seasonal changes, you're probably intimately acquainted with the leaves changing color and eventually falling to the ground as they die before winter. Even the seasons themselves are divided into a darker part of the year and a lighter part of the year. These cycles of darkness and light, birth and death are not "bad" or "good." They simply are.

Coyote's lesson on the Road of Trials is that there is no such thing as a "bad" feeling or a "wrong" feeling. Just as the seasons change, our emotions run in cycles. These cycles and the feelings they generate are not "bad" in themselves. What may or may not be "bad" is the behavior that comes after the feeling. By acknowledging our more chaotic feelings we learn that just because we are having feelings, we don't have to act on them. By living in the now, we learn that feelings are just feelings.

So suppose I am angry at my wife and I yell at her. She's probably very likely to become angry in return. Now suppose instead that I'm angry at my wife and I go to her and say, "I'm angry with you, and I don't want to be. Can we work this out?" In either of these scenarios, the feeling, anger, is the same. What is different is the way I chose to respond to the anger. If I respond badly by yelling, the behavior, and not the feeling, is the problem.

Here on the Road of Trials, Coyote will teach us a new way to walk, if we are willing to be open to the lessons. These lessons will help us to walk more fully in our own true nature.

6.5 Supernatural Aid on the Road of Trials

The Road of Trials is where our mettle is tested to see how committed we are to the path, and to the quest of living according to our true nature. Sometimes we may need Supernatural Aid to accomplish this so that we don't have to rely solely on our own energy. In ecospirituality we can rely on Supernatural Aid from our totem animals.

Could you draw on the power and energy from your own spirit animal to help you to succeed on the Road of Trials? Shamanistic cultures throughout the world use animals as metaphors for emotions, or as teaching tools. We even do this in our own culture. People can be "as hungry as a bear" or as "quiet as a mouse" or as "gentle as a lamb" Animals and their traits are deeply rooted in our psychology. We tend to separate ourselves from nature, and to forget that people are animals too. We are part of nature, and we cannot change that, no matter how much we might try to deny it. We even use animals in our research labs, from the white mice in the psychology lab to the often horrible conditions in animal testing labs. If humans don't have traits in common with our animal brothers and sisters, then why do we consider research on animals to be helpful at all to humans?

As human animals, our psyches are rooted in the natural world. Each of us contains within us archetypes of various animals. We instinctively know that snakes can be dangerous, just as we know we have nothing to fear from the timid rabbit. When using animals as metaphors for our own personal lives, we can draw upon the strength of these archetypes when walking the Road of Trials.

You don't have to be a shaman in order to use animals as teaching tools, or as tools of learning. You already have within you volumes of knowledge on animals and their characteristics. You can draw on these traits to create your own personal stories and legends. We understand the world through metaphor, and animal stories are just one of the many metaphors from nature that we may use on our own personal ecospiritual journeys. Watch the animals and learn from them. See what they have to teach you.

6.6 Who are You?

Who are you really? Who is this internal observer known as your True Self? Let's do a thought experiment to discover the nature of this entity. Think about what makes you, you. Right now you are looking at this page through your own eyes. Right now your senses are experiencing the sights, sounds, smells, and other sensations of your immediate environment. You are observing the world through your own perspective. The sum total of everything you have experienced up until this moment is contained within your head and body.

Now let's suppose it were possible to make an exact clone of you. This clone is your age and has all of your memories and experiences. For all practical purposes this clone is identical to you in every way. Once this clone is created, would you continue to see the world through your own eyes, or would you begin to see the world through the clone's eyes? Where is your point of view? Would it be with you or the clone?

Obviously you would continue to see the world from your own perspective, even though the clone was an exact, identical copy of you.

So what is it that makes you unique? The clone is an exact copy of you in every way except one: The way in which your clone views the world. The clone has his or her own point of view, their own perspective, on the world, just as you have your own.

What does this mean? It means you have your own unique perspective on the world, and that perspective is not a product of blood, bone, sinew, or neurons. Since your clone would be an exact replica of all of your biological and neurological functions, yet you would still see the world from your own head and not your clone's head, this True Self cannot be solely a product of biology and material existence. It is something different. It is something eternal. It is something that is not dependent on time or matter.

It is your own internal observer. It is your own True Self.

When you encounter difficulties on the Road of Trials, it may help to remember that you are a unique child of the Universe, and that you were meant to be here, doing what you're doing right at this moment, in this place, and in this time. When you can come to fully accept this, you will have completed the Road of Trials, and you will be ready for your Meeting with the Goddess.

Session 7 Meeting with the Goddess

"Tell me what you saw in the cavern," White Buffalo Woman began.

Coyote described what he had seen. As he spoke, a smile spread on her face while the firelight danced in her eyes.

He told her of the fire with the mysterious backwards-facing dancers. He described the masks they wore. He told her of the dream of being dismembered by the two-leggeds. He told her that when he had tried to escape, the opening was no longer there, but a new way had opened on the other side of the cave. When he had finished speaking, she stirred the fire with a sharp stick as she spoke in reply.

"The two-legged tribe is called the "People of the Ashes." They went on a quest to find fire for themselves, and they were able to find it. But in their greed, they wanted to keep it for themselves. They forgot to return and share it with the rest of their tribe. They jealously guard the secret of their fire. When they teach one of their tribe to make the fire, that person is sworn to secrecy on pain of death. They only teach other members of the tribe how to make the fire in secret rites and rituals, and they are not allowed to talk about it with people outside of their own tribe. That is why, when they saw you, they sought to tear you to shreds. They prize the fire, but they burn with jealousy at the thought of anyone else ever learning its secret. Because of this, their fire contains more heat than light."

"They wear the masks because in their hearts they remember their other brothers and sisters that they left behind, and they secretly long to re-connect with them. The masks remind them of what they lost when they became greedy and wanted to keep the fire to themselves. Yet the masks also blind them, so that they cannot see the way out of the cavern. It has been sealed to them forever out of their own blindness. The masks they wear to remind themselves of their four-legged brothers and sisters are the very things that keep them from finding their way back."

"When first they saw that they could not escape the cavern, they began to dance backwards, trying to re-trace their steps in order to find a way out. They forgot that the way forward does not lie in the past. By walking backwards, they are merely re-living their past mistakes. They are caught in a spiral dance with no end, and they shall never escape until they are able to sacrifice their selfishness. When they are able to do so, they will cast aside their masks and the way will be open to them again."

As she spoke, she leaned over and began to stroke the fur on Coyote's head.

"You were sent this vision of your own death to remind you not to tread the path that they have chosen. When you entered the cave, you were full of self-doubt. You did not think that you would ever be able to complete your journey. The vision of your death has changed that about you, for once you have faced your own death, what else can stand in your way?"

Coyote puzzled over her words. She watched him struggling with these new ideas.

"Do you not yet understand?" She motioned for him to stand, *"If you think you cannot complete your journey, you will be correct. But if you think you can complete your quest, then that wisdom will be the very thing that allows you to succeed."*

She guided him to a still pond nearby. Although the snow was falling all around, the pond's surface had not yet frozen. She watched the sparkling moonlight reflecting from its surface, and motioned for him to look into the water. "What do you see?" she asked.

He gazed into the glistening pool and saw a reflection of himself. His face was familiar to him, and yet not familiar. In that face he saw newfound wisdom. In his face he saw knowledge and confidence, and he knew that her words were true. With a renewed sense of purpose, he determined to go on. He was now willing to face whatever might come.

He looked up as White Buffalo Woman bid him farewell, and he continued on his journey.

7.0 The Goddess on the Road

"For she is the incarnation of the promise of perfection, the soul's assurance that, at the conclusion of the exile in a world of organized inadequacies, the bliss that once was known will be known again…"

– Joseph Campbell, *The Hero's Journey*

The Road of Trials is harsh. Even with the ability to call on our Supernatural Aid for assistance, conquering unknown lands can be taxing. It is the portion of the journey where we are leaving our old selves behind and discovering who our new selves might be. The difficult part of the Road of Trials is that while we already know from experience what doesn't work, we may not yet know what *does* work. This trial-and-error process can lead to second-guessing and self-doubt on the road to spiritual enlightenment. This is why it is a perfect time for a little extra help from the supernatural in the form of the Meeting with the Goddess.

The Goddess here isn't necessarily an actual divine entity, although she can be. Since the heroes in most of the myths Campbell studied were heterosexual males, the Meeting with the Goddess represents the ideal partner for a heterosexual male. Since we're talking about a spiritual and metaphorical level here, the Meeting with the Goddess symbolizes the idea of completeness and perfection, and not some actual physical entity. After having our former identities stripped away in the Belly of the Whale, and after our Initiation in the Road of Trials, the Goddess appears to us in ideal form with the promise of what could be, if we persevere. The Goddess represents perfect love. It is a love that is truly unconditional; a love that applies not only to others, bur to self as well.

7.1 Completeness and Perfection

Every human being on the planet has experienced occasional feelings of shame, guilt, blame, or inferiority. Such feelings are a natural part of the human condition. They are the source of many of the problems we experience with our relationships, careers, spiritual endeavors, and day-to-day living.

As human beings we're conditioned to disown certain parts of ourselves. We don't like to admit our feelings of shame or guilt, because doing so might mean that we are less than perfect. But how do we define "perfect?"

Try this sometime. Ask three of your closest friends or family members what their idea of the "perfect day" is. I'm willing to bet you'll get at least three different answers. So if you do get three different answers to the question, "Describe your perfect day," what does "perfect" really mean?

The obvious answer to this is that the term "perfect" is defined by the individual. This means that your idea of perfect might be completely different from my idea of perfect. Each of us is in charge of defining what "perfect" means to us.

The good news about this is that if "perfect" is self-defined, and if my own personal idea of what "perfect" means is causing me stress, then I am free to change it at any time. The way to do this is to realize that all of us have feelings of depression, stress or anxiety from time to time. All of us fail to live up to our own expectations for ourselves from time to time. We all have our moments of self-doubt. When this happens, we may choose to beat ourselves up for failing to be "perfect," or we may choose to realize that as human beings, failing to be "perfect" is a natural part of existence.

By learning to love ourselves "warts and all," we learn the art of radical acceptance of the True Self.

7.2 Shadow and Persona

The psychotherapist Carl Jung believed that all human beings contain within them the potential for all behaviors, both "good" and "bad." According to Jung, the *Persona* is the mask we wear in our everyday lives. It is the face we present to others. The Persona represents who we think we are, and who we would like to be. The *Shadow*, on the other hand, represents all those traits we wish to suppress in ourselves. All our anger, fears, and negative emotions and behaviors are pushed down into the unconscious world of the Shadow and denied expression in the Persona.

Jung believed that the key to mental health was a process called *individuation*. Individuation involves striking a balance between the Shadow and the Persona. The Shadow represents the forces of chaos and darkness within an individual, and the Persona represents the forces of order and light. While the Shadow contains all of our darker and more negative emotions, it is also the seat of creativity. To deny the existence of one's Shadow is to deny one's own ability to be creative. However, allowing the Shadow to rule one's life creates a situation where the individual is ruled by the forces of chaos and darkness. Jung saw psychoanalysis as the process by which we balance light and darkness within ourselves, thus achieving individuation.

Some moral, religious and ethical systems try to deny the existence of our darker impulses. These systems focus solely on the Persona. This is the face we present to others. The more such systems of thought and belief suppress the darker impulses in the Shadow, the more unbalanced the individual becomes. In such a case, the Shadow becomes a pressure cooker with no means to release the pressure. In extreme cases, the pressure cooker blows, leading to dysfunction and even psychosis.

Ecospirituality recognizes the need to balance Persona and Shadow. By acknowledging our darker impulses, we open the door to creating this balance, leading to individuation. Many people think that acknowledging our darker impulses means having to act on these impulses. Nothing could be further from the truth.

Suppose someone has done something that leads you to be angry with that person. Your first impulse might be the desire to retaliate in some way by returning anger for anger, or by hurting that individual in some way. Those who focus only on the Persona would attempt to suppress and deny this impulse, even though the desire to retaliate is a perfectly normal reaction to being angered. The angrier such a person becomes, the more he tries to suppress that anger, until he reaches boiling point and reacts explosively to the situation.

In Ecospirituality we seek to restore balance by acknowledging this impulse. Instead of swallowing our anger, we would recognize it as a darker impulse. But instead of returning anger for anger, we strive to express that anger in positive ways; perhaps by confronting the source of the anger and saying to the person, "You know, I really felt angry when you _____. I don't want to be angry with you. What can we do to resolve this situation?"

In this way we are able to acknowledge the anger in constructive, rather than destructive, ways. The anger itself is not "bad;" it is merely a catalyst. It's up to us to choose what to do with it.

7.3 Connecting with the Goddess

When we meet the Goddess on the road, it is symbolic of our own meeting with our own concept of perfection. In Ecospirituality, "perfection" means the ability to accept our darker impulses from the Shadow without feeling obligated to act on them. By recognizing and accepting these parts of ourselves without feeling obligated to do anything about them, we create the capacity to just be with those darker impulses, without acting on them, until they pass. When we are able to do so, we are able to integrate the Shadow and the Persona into a perfect, whole True Self. These integrative experiences are of the awe-inspiring variety that is the goal of ecospirituality.

Sometimes these experiences are described as *reconnecting*. The idea of reconnecting implies that we are connecting again to something that we somehow became disconnected with in the first place. How we became disconnected isn't really as important as finding out how to reconnect ourselves. If there are barriers between ourselves and the things we wish to be connected to, we have the ability to remove those barriers. Ecospirituality allows connectedness by eliminating the barriers that keep us separate from our concept of the divine, from each other, and from our true selves.

So the way to have truly meaningful spiritual experiences (meetings with the Goddess) is to remove those things that keep us from connecting.

Take some time right now to think about the things that keep you from feeling connected. Make a list of these on the next page. Complete the exercise on the next page before reading any further.

7.3 Things that Keep Me from Feeling Connected   Page 1 of 1

Name: _____ Date: _____

Write down some of the things that in the past have kept you from feeling connected to others, to nature, to the divine (or your concept of "perfection"), and to your own True Self. Try to think of at least three.

1. _____
2. _____
3. _____
4. _____
5. _____
6. _____
7. _____
8. _____
9. _____
10. _____
11. _____
12. _____
13. _____
14. _____
15. _____

Now that you've completed your list, look at it again. Of all the things you've listed, how many of those things on your list have to do with barriers within yourself? How many of them have to do with barriers from other people? How many of them have to do with barriers due to your circumstances or the environment in which you live?

What would it take to remove those barriers? Remember, you can't change others, you can only change yourself. So focus on things that would involve activities and actions that are within your power to change about yourself. For example, you may have a person in your life who has a talent for making you angry. This anger keeps you from feeling connected to this person. Since you can't change the other person, is there something you could change about yourself that would make dealing with this person easier and less stressful?

Brainstorm a number of solutions to removing the barriers you've listed above. If the answers are too difficult for now, don't be discouraged. Set this list aside and come back to it when you've completed this entire section of the handbook.

7.4 Faces and Masks

Now that we've thought a bit about the barriers to connectedness we find in our own lives, how do we go about changing those barriers so that we can achieve connection to others? To nature? To our True Selves?

Think for a moment about the different faces we wear each day. If you're interacting with people at work, do they see the same person that your family at home sees, or do you wear a different face in work situations? When you're at school, do you interact with people in the same way that you would interact with someone on a date? If you are at church, mosque, or temple, do you act in the same way you would act if you were out for a night on the town?

If you're like most people, you probably have different masks that you wear for different social situations.

Now look back on your list on Worksheet 7.3 above. Are there any people on your list who prevent you from feeling connected?

Think about those people for a moment. Be totally honest with yourself. Do you think that those people act the same way in all social situations, or do they wear masks as well? Pick out one individual with whom you have difficulty feeling connected. Think of the mask they wear that seems to act as a barrier to your ability to connect with them. How much of that mask is their natural inclination, and how much of it is their response to the mask that you wear when you are with them?

This is not to say that you are responsible for the rude or reprehensible behavior of others. Each individual is responsible for his or her own behavior. The idea here is to evaluate your own responses to such behavior. Is there anything you can change that might make it easier to connect with them? If so, try it and see if their behavior improves. If, after changing the way you respond, you still find the person difficult to connect with, or even to be around, then you've done all you can do to correct the situation. At that point, your part in the problem interaction is over and done with, and you will have to practice mindful awareness. If you've done everything you can to try to get along with a difficult person, and they're still being difficult, then this is usually a good indication that the problem lies with the other person and not with yourself. You are not obligated to change other people's behavior.

With this idea in mind, you can also try to see beyond the mask that the other person is wearing. Masks are often worn to hide a person's true identity. Is the other person trying to hide something? Could it be that they wear the mask out of fear of letting someone see who they really are? What could you do to help them change their mask? Even if you can't get them to put on a different face with you or with others, you may come to understand that their mask hides a deep hurt, and their mask is their way of protecting themselves from further hurt.

Going back to Jung's ideas of the Shadow and the Persona, the Persona is the mask we wear in our day-to-day lives, possibly to hide those darker impulses in the Shadow. Think about your Persona mask. What sort of mask do you wear with the world? What sort of mask would you like to wear?

Now imagine the person you are becoming as you walk the Way of the Coyote. If your True Self were a mask, what would it look like? Go on to the Faces and Masks exercise on the next page to find out.

7.4 Faces and Masks Exercise

Name:_____ Date:_____

We all have different faces (masks) that we present to others. These masks sometimes change depending on the person and/or the situation. The psychoanalyst Carl Jung called these masks the *Persona*. *Persona* is Latin for *"mask."* In ancient Rome actors often wore masks that portrayed the characters they were playing.

We all have characters, or masks, that we like to put on from time to time. For this exercise, we're going to create a mask for the character of your own True Self.

To begin this exercise, meditate for a while on the nature and character of your own True Self. The True Self, for the purposes of this exercise, is the person you are if you are living up to your own highest aspirations for yourself.

When you have a good image of your own True Self in mind, answer the following questions before going on to the next page:

What is the nature of your True Self? Are you a lover, a warrior, a sage, a teacher, a trickster, a peacemaker, or something else? What word best describes who you are?

_____
_____
_____
_____

What are the elements of nature that might reflect your own True Self? Are you patient like a mountain? Strong like an oak? Wise like an owl? Playful like a coyote? What elements best describe who you are?

_____
_____
_____
_____

How might these elements of nature assist you in finding your True Self? When you create your mask, how might you incorporate these elements into its design?

_____
_____
_____
_____
_____

7.4 FACES AND MASKS EXERCISE

Name: _____ Date: _____

CREATING YOUR MASK

Now that you have a good idea of which elements to incorporate into your mask, gather the materials to make it. Try to focus on natural materials as much as possible, using wood, feathers, twigs, leaves, leather, etc. Some Native American tribes used dried gourds for this purpose. You may also use a plaster cast of your face, or a carved wooden mask, or papier mache, or even paper plates or brown bags.

When you create your mask, hold the idea in mind that it is a representation of your True Self; the person you are in the process of becoming. As such, when finished the mask should tell your own story in such a way that anyone looking at it would have a good idea of who you are.

When you have finished constructing your mask, go on to the next section of this worksheet and answer the questions below. Do not attempt to answer these questions until you have completed your mask. It may help, before answering the questions below, to meditate or take a walk in the woods first.

REFLECTIONS ON THE "TRUE SELF" MASK

Now that you have completed your mask, what did the exercise teach you about your own true nature and how you relate to it? Be as specific as possible when answering.

_____
_____
_____
_____
_____
_____
_____
_____
_____
_____
_____

7.4 FACES AND MASKS EXERCISE

Name: _____ Date: _____

Now that you have completed your mask, what did the exercise teach you about the way you think about your own true nature as manifested in your own True Self? Be as specific as possible when answering.

_____
_____
_____

Now that you have completed your mask, what did the exercise teach you about your own sense of "perfection?" This sense of perfection is about what you really care about, and what gives your life meaning. In other words, it tells you how to become the perfect "you" and to live according to your own true nature, so be as specific as possible when answering.

_____
_____
_____
_____

Now that you have completed your mask, what did the exercise teach you about your own spiritual development? In other words, what did it tell you about your growing ability to connect to nature, to others, and to your own True Self? Be as specific as possible when answering.

_____
_____
_____
_____

Imagine an archaeologist digs up your mask a thousand years in the future. What might this archaeologist conclude about the person who wore it? Would the mask be a good representation of who you are? If so, why? If not, why not? Be as specific as possible when answering.

_____
_____
_____
_____
_____

7.5 Omens and the Unconscious Mind

One of the activities for this session is a pilgrimage. On the pilgrimage you will undertake for this session, be especially aware of any omens that might appear to you on your journey.

Dictionary.com defines "omen" as:

omen (noun)
1. anything perceived or happening that is believed to portend a good or evil event or circumstance in the future; portent.
2. a prognostic.
3. prophetic significance; presage: a bird of ill omen.

So omens may be used to predict the future or to determine a future course of action.

The psychodynamic therapist Carl Jung believed that some parts of our unconscious mind were hardwired to recognize certain symbols, just like birds are born with a migratory instinct without having to learn how to migrate. This hardwiring causes us all to recognize things he called *archetypes*. Archetypes are symbols that have special significance and meaning. This group of archetypes he called the *collective unconscious* because it was common to all the cultures he observed everywhere on Earth. These themes occurred again and again in their mythologies, legends and histories. Since these symbols occurred worldwide in all cultures, Jung believed that they had to be inborn rather than learned.

An example of one of these Jungian archetypes would be the Sacred Tree. The Bible speaks of the Tree of Knowledge, Judaism talks about the Tree of Life, Norse and Celtic myths talk about the World Tree, Buddhists believe that Buddha received enlightenment under the Lotus Tree, and many Native American cultures have a Sacred Tree. In fact, all cultures Jung observed have some legend or myth of the Sacred Tree.

For me personally, when I speak of omens I recognize them as getting in contact with the archetypes in my unconscious mind in order to allow my unconscious motivations to have a say in my actions. By exploring these aspects of myself, I allow my unconscious motivations to come to the surface. I come into contact with my deeper, inner and hidden motivations for my actions and feelings and become a conscious co-creator with the energy of the universe.

For example, Raven is one of my totem animals. So if I'm out walking in the woods and I see a raven, I pay particular attention to what I was thinking prior to sighting it, and what the raven is doing. Because ravens are already sacred to me, my attention is naturally drawn to them. But if another person has no spiritual connection to ravens, they might walk in the same woods, have the same experience as I, and get an entirely different message. This is because the omen came from my own unconscious and not necessarily from the raven itself.

You may consider your own experiences with omens and animal totems as archetypes or as real entities. In the end, what matters is how you are able to commune with them. The magical thing about such workings is that any message you receive is yours, and yours alone. So how you choose to interpret these experiences is totally up to you.

While on your pilgrimage, you may use the opportunity to practice with omens. Note what you see, hear, smell, and come into contact with on the trail. What were you thinking just before you noticed it? How did your omen make its presence known? What about it attracted your attention? If you feel that nothing happened during your pilgrimage, is it possible that you may have missed something? Even the smallest events can be omens.

When omens come, they should be omens of special significance to you. If ravens held no special significance for me, I wouldn't expect to see an omen in the flight of a raven. Look at it this way…if you spoke Latin, and had a friend who didn't speak Latin, would you send your friend a message in Latin? What would be the point? Likewise, omens come in forms that have special significance to you, from your own unconscious. They should be in your "language."

7.6 Pilgrimage

Pilgrimages are probably as old as the human race. A pilgrimage is just a journey undertaken for a sacred or spiritual purpose. If you are participating in an ecospirituality workshop series, or just completing this workbook on your own, you are on a pilgrimage of a sort. Such a pilgrimage is a way of meeting with your concept of divinity. It is an encounter with your own conception of "perfection." This Meeting with the Goddess can also be a spiritual journey to your True Self. Such a journey is one more step along the way to living according to your own true nature.

This pilgrimage activity is a way to "meet with the Goddess" in your own life. It means traveling the road to perfection, but it can also mean changing your idea of what "perfection" means. Such a Meeting with the Goddess is awareness that perfection in a spiritual sense is an attainable goal. How does this work?

Everyone has two images of self; the Perceived Self and the True Self. The Perceived Self is how you see yourself now, at this part of the journey. The True Self is how you wish to be. True Self is what you would be if you were able to live fully according to your own true nature. Your True Self is your own personal idea of what "perfect" looks like for you.

A Meeting with the Goddess means being able to accept even your perceived "flaws." It is an acknowledgement that change is only possible if you first accept who you are. It's saying to yourself, "You're perfect just the way you are. Now change, if you must." The pilgrimage is a walking meditation that allows you to integrate your separate visions of Perceived Self and True Self.

Worksheet 7.6 – *Pilgrimage Reflections* has two sets of questions. The questions are identical, but one set is to be completed prior to beginning your pilgrimage, and the other set is to be completed after you have done your pilgrimage. It's recommended that you don't do the second set immediately after completing your pilgrimage, as you will need some time to process and digest the experience. Go ahead and do the first set of questions now, prior to beginning the pilgrimage. After your pilgrimage, complete the second set. Did you notice any change in your answers? What could these changes, if any, tell you about your journey towards living according to your own true nature?

In order to complete the pilgrimage, you must first have access to some sort of hiking trail or other outdoor space. If you are completing this workbook as part of an ecospirituality group, your instructor will have pre-selected such a trail for you. If participating in a group, make sure your facilitator knows if you have any physical limitations that might restrict your participation in the activity. This might include physical limitations on your mobility but it could also include things like allergies to local flora and fauna.

The place selected for your pilgrimage should be a trail that you can walk comfortably in a half-day or less, unless you feel ambitious enough to make it a weekend or week-long backpacking and camping trip.

The purpose of this pilgrimage is to spend at least a morning or an afternoon journeying in a natural setting while contemplating your own spiritual path. Be sure to take enough food and water for the journey! If possible, set out at dawn and return no earlier than noon. If this is not possible, or if you are participating in a group that requires a different meeting time, adhere to the chosen schedule. If you are doing it alone and have the option of setting out at dawn, there's something magical about watching the world come alive around you in the morning as you set off on a pilgrimage towards your own Meeting with the Goddess.

As you walk the trail, engage in mindful breathing and mindful walking (e.g. the Coyote Walk) as much as possible while remaining open to everything the trail has to show you and tell you. In addition to contemplating the questions on Worksheet 7.6, your one additional task for your pilgrimage is to find a *power object* to remind you of the journey. This object or talisman should be something small enough to fit into your pocket. It should be something that seems to call to you on the journey. It could be a stone, a plant, a twig, a feather, or any other small object that could serve as a reminder of your Meeting with the Goddess on the trail. When you have found your power object, place it in your pocket as a constant reminder of this day on your spiritual quest.

Prior to beginning your pilgrimage, complete the questions in Part A of Worksheet 7.6. As you walk on your pilgrimage, contemplate the questions that appear on Worksheet 7.6 and the answers you gave to them. Practice the Coyote Walk or some other walking meditation in a mindful manner, with an open and trusting attitude, focusing on the present moment and all the information your senses are giving you about the hike. What do you see? What do you smell? What do you hear? What sensations are you feeling on your skin? Is there any taste to the air as you walk? What is this journey telling you about your own sense of perfection? How is this pilgrimage helping you to draw closer to living your true nature in your own True Self?

As you walk, look for a power object that seems to call to you. It should have some special power or significance related to your own emerging sense of self. When you have found your power object, place it in your pocket for safekeeping. When you have completed your pilgrimage, meditate on the experience for the rest of the day. When you wake on the day after your pilgrimage, read Section 7.7 then go back and answer the questions on Part B of Worksheet 7.6.

Note: Some of your answers from Part A to Part B may not change, and that's okay too, as long as you're being honest with yourself and remaining open to what you may have learned during your pilgrimage during your Meeting with the Goddess.

Worksheet 7.6 Part A: Pilgrimage Reflections

Name _____ Date _____

The questions on this worksheet are to be completed twice. The first questions, in Part A, are to be completed prior to your pilgrimage. The next set of questions, in Part B, are to be completed the day after your pilgrimage. Focus on your own Meeting with the Goddess when answering. In other words, focus on what your own idea of "perfection" is for yourself. How might the pilgrimage help you to live in True Self according to your own true nature?

Who am I?

_____
_____
_____
_____
_____
_____

Who do I want to be?

_____
_____
_____
_____
_____
_____

What is my mission or purpose in life?

_____
_____
_____
_____
_____
_____

WORKSHEET 7.6 PART A: PILGRIMAGE REFLECTIONS

Name _____ Date _____

How am I living that purpose?

_____
_____
_____
_____
_____

How am I not living that purpose?

_____
_____
_____
_____

What would I have to change about myself in order to accomplish my life's mission?

_____
_____
_____
_____

How might my own Meeting with the Goddess during my pilgrimage help me to accomplish my life's mission?

_____
_____
_____
_____
_____

WORKSHEET 7.6 PART B: PILGRIMAGE REFLECTIONS

Name _____ Date _____

You should have completed the Part A questions and conducted your pilgrimage prior to answering the same questions in Part B. You should also have read Section 9.6 and slept at least one night before answering the questions in Part B, so both your conscious and unconscious minds have had time to process the experience. Focus on your own *Meeting with the Goddess* that you experienced during your own pilgrimage when answering. In other words, focus on what your own idea of "perfection" is for yourself. How might the pilgrimage help you to live in True Self according to your own true nature?

Who am I?

_____
_____
_____
_____
_____
_____

Who do I want to be?

_____
_____
_____
_____
_____
_____

What is my mission or purpose in life?

_____
_____
_____
_____
_____
_____

WORKSHEET 7.6 PART B: PILGRIMAGE REFLECTIONS

Name _____ Date _____

How am I living that purpose?

_____
_____
_____
_____
_____

How am I not living that purpose?

_____
_____
_____
_____
_____

What would I have to change about myself in order to accomplish my life's mission?

_____
_____
_____
_____
_____

How might my own Meeting with the Goddess during my pilgrimage help me to accomplish my life's mission?

_____
_____
_____
_____
_____

7.7 The Womb of the Goddess

Think for a moment about the power object you found on your pilgrimage. Take it out and look at it for a moment. Is it "perfect?" Can any natural object ever truly *not* be perfect? Are you a "natural object?" If so, how can you ever not be perfect?

Coyote energy is reflected in the phrase, "Simplicity is perfection." She teaches us to learn to distinguish what we need from what we want. Coyote won't give us everything we want, but she will lead us to everything we need. If we need to find a path to our True Selves, Coyote will help us find the way.

In many legends from many lands, the hero accessed the Otherworld, that world that lies on the other side of the veil, through earth mounds or round houses with sodded roofs. These hollow earthen mounds hint at some sort of ritual preparation for the journey. They symbolize the womb of the earth mother. A seeker enters into one of these round mountains and emerges reborn after a vigil or other rite. A person reborn in this way is a child of the Earth Goddess.

This stage of the Way of the Coyote requires developing the skill of pattern finding. Such a skill means seeing connections in ways that others may not. It is a method of stepping back and seeing the bigger picture while still being able to focus on the details. Such ability transcends space and time and the barriers of life and death. Making connections that others cannot see is the heart of the poet's art. One who masters this crossing has achieved the ability to channel divine wisdom through the art of the poet. Such a one has become a bard, able to walk between the worlds of the living and the dead. Such a one has met the Goddess and has learned to be "perfect" by being the person they were born to be.

Contemplate your own Meeting with the Goddess. What did you learn about yourself on your pilgrimage? What did you learn about your relationship to others? What did you learn about your relationship to nature? What did you learn about your own idea of perfection? Did any omens present themselves to you on your journey? When you have contemplated these things, go on and complete Part B of *Worksheet 7.5 Pilgrimage Reflections.*

After completing your pilgrimage and answering Part B of Worksheet 7.5, did your answers change? How? What does "perfection" look like for you? If you're living in your own true nature, is that "perfect?" If you're not, is that "perfect?" Remember, as always, that you're the only person who gets to decide what "perfect" means for you. This is the lesson of the Meeting with the Goddess.

Session 8 The Tempter

Coyote walked on for many days and many nights, always following the North Star. As he journeyed, it got colder and colder. He spent his nights curled up in hollow places, shivering against the night winds. There were many times when he was tempted to give up, turn around, and go home, but whenever he got into these moods, he remembered the teachings of White Buffalo Woman.

Still, it was lonely on the trail. He often longed for a companion on the journey.

Then one day, as the north wind was blowing particularly hard and the snow was falling so rapidly that he could barely see the trail, he heard the voice of someone singing up ahead in the distance. His curiosity got the better of him and he left the path to see where this music was coming from.

The trail he was on had been running between two hills. He climbed a snow-covered hill to his left so that he could follow the sound of the music. As he crested the hill he saw the glow of a fire in the valley below. The music was coming from the direction of the fire, so he descended the hill into the valley. When he got close to the source of the fire, he saw a figure in the shadows. He drew even closer towards the figure, who stepped out of the shadows at his approach.

He watched as the shadows resolved themselves into the most beautiful creature he had ever seen! She was a Coyote, like he. Her voice was melodious and welcoming as she invited him to warm himself by her fire.

But as he joined her by the fire, he noticed something strange. Her fire glowed with a sickly greenish hue, and it barely contained any warmth at all. The paltry heat from her fire was just enough to take the chill from his bones, but no more. Nonetheless, a little heat was better than no heat at all, so he settled down to join her beside her fire.

She told him her name was Coyote Woman, and asked what brought him to this place, so far from home. Coyote told her the story of his journey, and about how Chief Buffalo had sent him on this quest to bring back fire for the People.

She listened to his story, and then told him about herself. Like Coyote, she enjoyed playing tricks on her tribe. Like Coyote, she was a lover of practical jokes and pranks. But one day her tribe grew weary of her games, and they banished her. Since that time she had been wandering alone. In her wanderings she had met many witches and sorcerers from the North, and one of them had taught her how to capture fire from the fireflies. The fire they were sitting beside now had been kindled with such magic.

They sat by Coyote Woman's magical fire and talked well into the night. They awoke the next morning all wrapped up in each other.

Coyote Woman smiled at Coyote and said, "I know you are on a quest, but stay a while with me and rest before you continue your journey. My fire is warm, and I enjoy your company."

So Coyote agreed to stay with her for a time.

They laughed and played together, but as days stretched into weeks, and the days grew shorter and the nights grew colder, Coyote began to think of the People at home, and how maybe it was time for him to be on his way so that he could continue to seek the fire. He tried to tell Coyote Woman this, and as he spoke, she grew angry.

"Why should you care so much about your precious People, when they have sent you out alone into the cold and dark to fend for yourself?" she cried. "Stay here with me, and forget about your tribe!"

Coyote thought about this, but had no answer. So he said nothing.

A few days later, he again thought about the People, and about how they were depending on him. Again he told Coyote Woman that he needed to be on his way. This time she grew even angrier.

"If you really care so much about the people who sent you out into the wilderness to die, then why not take some of my fire to them? There's no need to go out into the unknown when there is fire right here. You have no way of even knowing if you might find what you seek!"

Coyote thought about her words. He had to agree that there was some wisdom in what she was saying, but somehow such a course of action just didn't feel right. He thought about what White Buffalo Woman had said, and how she had told him that every seeker must find his own fire. So he said nothing to Coyote Woman.

Time passed. The days continued to grow colder, and the world changed around him. Everything was covered in snow. Even the stars in the sky looked different. A sense of urgency about his journey overtook him. Finally, he came up with a plan, and went to Coyote Woman.

"I feel myself torn between my duty to the quest and my loyalty to you," he began, "But I think I have found a way to resolve this problem. Come with me on my journey. If I do not find what I am looking for, then we can return to this place and to your magical fire. If I do find what I am looking for, I can take the sacred fire back to my People. I am sure that you would be welcome among them."

Coyote Woman hesitated at first, but eventually she agreed to go with Coyote. Coyote breathed a sigh of relief and they snuggled together by the fire to fall asleep.

Coyote woke the next morning, shivering. When he opened his eyes, Coyote Woman's magical fire was gone. As he sprung to full alertness, he looked around the fire circle to discover that Coyote Woman herself was also gone! He frantically searched the woods near where the fire had been, but there was no trace of her. She had left no paw prints in the snow. There wasn't even a scent to mark her passing.

Heartbroken, Coyote decided that there was nothing left to do but to continue the quest, so he took his bearings and headed north.

As he walked, he thought about how Coyote Woman had tricked him into believing that she would come along with him. The more he thought about it, the angrier he became. The angrier he became, the more he thought about her betrayal. He began to think about how he might seek vengeance on her.

As he trotted along, plotting his revenge, a thought occurred to him.

One of the reasons he had been so attracted to her was that she was just like him in so many ways. And like her, he loved playing tricks on others. But now that the shoe was on the other foot, Coyote knew exactly how the victims of his pranks felt. How could he be angry at her for doing to him what he had done to so many others?

With this realization, the anger began to melt away, and he was able to continue on his journey with a clear conscience.

8.0 The Tempter's Supreme Ordeal

At this point in the quest, Coyote has encountered the Tempter in the form of an attractive female partner who tries to lure him away from his intentions. Campbell originally referred to this phase as "Woman as Temptress." The gender bias of referring to the Temptress as a woman is a by-product of centuries of the male bias in mythology from around the world. The Temptress can just as easily be a Tempter, as when Lucifer tempted Jesus with all the wealth of the world if he would give up his seeker's journey. In any case, the Tempter/Temptress is anything which might try to distract you from your goal of living in True Self.

Whichever sex you choose to picture the Tempter, its purpose is to entice you with the easy way out. The Tempter manifests in shortcuts, laziness, and leaving things half-done. The lesson to be learned by an encounter with the Tempter is that if we cheat by taking a shortcut on the road to enlightenment, we are ultimately only cheating ourselves.

The Tempter will tax your integrity and character, but there is a purpose in this trial. By testing your character, the Tempter gives you an opportunity to display your honor and commitment to the path. True honor is how we act when nobody is watching, and the Tempter gives us the opportunity to practice that honor. He will attempt to sway us from the path and try to prevent us from owning the darker parts of ourselves. If the Tempter is successful at this aim, we will fail to achieve Atonement with the Father on the next leg of the journey.

When we meet face-to-face with the Tempter, we must encounter the Supreme Ordeal. This Supreme Ordeal manifests as a deep inner spiritual, emotional or mental challenge that the Seeker must face and defeat. It signals its arrival when the Seeker realizes that things cannot go on as they are now. The Tempter must be defeated before any further progress can be made. It may mean facing our greatest fears or defeating our deadliest foes.

The Supreme Ordeal will require us to draw upon all of our skills and energy to conquer the challenge. After being reborn as a spiritual seeker on the path of ecospirituality, we can never return to the old life. The Tempter will challenge our commitment to the new path by insisting that we retreat to the comfort of the known rather than to face the challenges of the unknown. Only supreme commitment to the quest can gain a victory against the Supreme Ordeal.

8.1 Acceptance

Think back for a moment to a time in your life when you knew exactly who you were, and what you wanted to be. It may have been a time in your childhood, or a time later on in your life. Or it may be that you've never thought about exactly who you were and who you wanted to be. That's okay too. Perhaps you've never just learned how to acknowledge your own motivations in this way. If this is the case, close your eyes and think for a moment about who you would be if there were no barriers keeping you from living up to your own potential. Imagine your own Supernatural Aid has showed up and offered you the power to transform yourself. Who would you become?

The vision you have right now in your mind is your True Self.

Hold that vision firmly in your mind as you contemplate your own Supreme Ordeal.

Your True Self is that part of you that recognizes when you've done something in character for you. It is the part of you that is the internal observer; the part that holds your highest aspirations and your highest dreams for yourself. It is the part of you that holds your core values. The Humanist psychotherapist Carl Rogers called it your Ideal Self. According to Rogers, the Ideal Self is the person you would be if you could "get out of your own way" and dare to be who you were meant to be.

The ultimate goal of ecospirituality is to find the road to your own True Self, and to live more fully in it. If you're not living in your True Self, what is it that is keeping you from doing so? The Way of the Coyote may help you to answer this question.

8.2 The Supreme Ordeal

For purposes of ecospirituality, the Supreme Ordeal can be conceptualized as "anything that keeps us from living in True Self, according to our own true nature."

This could be thoughts like, "change is too hard, and I can't do this." It could also be any thoughts or beliefs that are encouraging us to go back to familiar, though unproductive, patterns of thinking and believing. These thoughts could come from ourselves, or they could come from friends or family who might be giving us messages that we can't change. Sometimes they might even mean well by giving us these messages, but ultimately we are responsible for our own lives, and we can never live by another's judgment of who we are and what we should be if we're going to live in True Self. True Self is, by definition, your own concept of self, and another can never know what it is like to be you, nor ultimately choose a life path for you.

Once we set out on the road to change that leads to ecospirituality, there can be no turning back. Anything that would have us re-trace our steps and go back on the promises we have made to ourselves can be seen as an element of the Tempter confronting us with the Supreme Ordeal. It is the fear of the unknown speaking to us. It may also be the fear of taking responsibility for our own lives and our own destinies. In whatever way the Tempter presents the Supreme Ordeal to you, it is up to you and you alone to accept the challenge.

8.3 Radical Acceptance

The way to conquer the Supreme Ordeal and to begin to live according to your own nature is through radical acceptance. One way of achieving radical acceptance is by living in the now. This is accomplished by focusing on the present moment. To illustrate how this works, think about something that has stressed you out. Now ask yourself, "Did the thing that stressed me out happen in the past, or am I worried about it happening in the future?" How many things that stress you have to do with right now, at this present moment, as you're reading this sentence? Radical acceptance means choosing right now, in the present moment, which thoughts and feelings about the past or the future to pay attention to.

You might be worried about something that happened in the past, and also worried that it might happen again in the future. Maybe you've had past arguments with a family member, and you're expecting a visit from them. Based on past performance, you're expecting a future argument. Or maybe you're stressed out right now about something that happened in the past or in the future. If so, the reason you're stressed out in the present about something about the past or the future is because you're choosing to lend your energy and your attention to it in the now.

Think about the nature of your own Supreme Ordeal. What is the Tempter showing you that might make you want to give up on the quest? How many of those things have to do with past or future events? How many have to do with right now, at this very moment? How might radical acceptance help you to survive the Supreme Ordeal and defeat the Tempter?

The point to this exercise is that most of the things that cause us stressful or depressing thoughts are things that involve past or future events. This means that we can consciously choose, right now in the present moment, which thoughts to give our energies to.

It has been said that if you are worried about the past you are depressed, and if you are worried about the future, you are anxious. We have all been hurt in the past, and we tend to make educated guesses about what the future holds for us based on past performance. In this way, the future is just the past projected forward. In either case, whether past or future, the stress or anxiety only exists in our minds. The present is the only moment that's real, and it's in the present that we may choose which thoughts and feelings about the past or the future to focus on.

A way to achieve radical acceptance of the things that stress us out is to realize that if we are victims of our circumstances, then we cannot control our lives. This is because we cannot control what goes on outside of ourselves. We cannot control what other people do, and we can rarely control what life throws at us. So if we are victims of our circumstances, we will always be victims. But if we are victims of our *beliefs* about our circumstances, then we are always free to change our beliefs. Doing so frees us from the tyranny of the past and the anxiety of the future.

We are very good at anticipating the thoughts, actions, and feelings of others and ourselves by placing judgments on motives and intentions. Theoretically, this has survival value. If you're around a dangerous person, it's probably a good idea to anticipate what they might do that could threaten your wellbeing. So we're good at it because we want to minimize danger to ourselves and to our loved ones. The problem comes when we try to guess what another person is feeling or thinking and we get it wrong. How often have you assumed what another person might be thinking or feeling? How often have you guessed incorrectly, and how did that person react?

The past gets brought up quite often between partners who are arguing. The reason for this is that when a partner has done something "wrong" in the past the other partner automatically assumes that this behavior will continue in the future, based on past performance. The problem, from the point of view of the partner being accused of wrongdoing, is that until someone invents a time machine he or she cannot go back in time and correct past mistakes. They can only promise to do better in the future. So if the other partner continues to bring up the past, this individual will be constantly battling the ghosts of previous behaviors.

By constantly bringing up the past, we forestall any opportunity for change in the future, because we judgmentally set up our perception filters only to look for evidence that confirms our assumptions. In this case, the assumption (or judgment) is that the past behavior will continue in the future. If we assume that this is true, then we're going to have a hard time seeing any evidence that confirms the opposite assumption: That this behavior will not continue in the future.

Likewise, a lot of arguments among family members come about because one family member guesses at what another family member is feeling at a given moment. Consider this conversation:

Jane: "What are you mad about?"

Joe: "I'm not mad about anything."

Jane: "Yes you are, I can tell. So what is it?"

Joe: "I told you, I'm not mad about anything."

Jane: "Come on, I know you. I can tell when you're mad!"

Joe: "I'M NOT MAD!"

In the above scenario, Jane's interpretation of Joe's emotional state became a self-fulfilling prophecy. Although Joe wasn't angry at the start of the conversation, by the end of it he most definitely was. In this case the Tempter presented Jane with the thought that she could read Joe's mind, and she believed it.

In this context, being accepting means not making assumptions about what the other person is feeling or thinking. The easiest way to tell what a person is thinking or feeling at any given time is to simply ask them, and not to try to guess what their motivations or emotions might be. If you feel tempted to anticipate what a person is thinking or feeling, you are engaging in what I call crystal ball thinking. The Tempter loves to hand us crystal balls and convinces us that we can predict the future with them.

But unless you have such a crystal ball, you cannot possibly know what another person's thoughts or feelings may be. Of course, if you ask them, they can always be deceptive in their answers, but if they are, then that's their responsibility, not yours. You've given them the opportunity to be truthful about their feelings. If they choose not to be, then you can't control their need to be emotionally distant. All you are responsible for is acting upon the information they give you, and how you choose to respond to that information.

Another type of crystal ball thinking occurs when we try to make predictions about our own behaviors based on past experience. We can tell when this happens because there's a tendency to use statements like the following:

"I always screw things up."

"I'll never find love."

"I'm just not good enough for this."

"I'll never understand."

Based on the examples above, you can probably come up with your own statements that reflect your own crystal ball thinking. Such thinking means that the Tempter's Supreme Ordeal in this case is causing you to view the future in negative ways, only seeing the bad things that could happen while ignoring potential good things.

Note that identifying such statements doesn't mean that we're going to try to make them go away. Trying is doing, and one of the objects of ecospirituality is to leave doing mode and enter being mode. So we're not trying to change this inner dialog the Tempter offers us. Instead, using the skill of mindful acceptance, we are just going to observe and describe these thought cycles to ourselves, without choosing to interact with them or to believe them to be true. Radical acceptance means, in part, that we accept that on occasion our minds are going to engage in these crystal ball thinking cycles, but that doesn't mean we have to believe what our minds are saying. Mindful acceptance is the knowledge that we are not our thoughts, and we are not our feelings. We are something else. That something else is what gives us the power to survive the Supreme Ordeal.

That something else is the True Self. The True Self accepts that minds occasionally generate thoughts that can be negative. But the True Self also recognizes that these thoughts are just thoughts, and they are neither true nor false unless we choose to believe that they are. True Self recognizes that our brains are going to do what they're good at, and that's generating thoughts and feelings. But when we're living in True Self, we can recognize that even though our brains are going to generate thoughts and feelings, we don't have to let those thoughts and feelings bully us or push us around. In this way the True Self defeats the Tempter.

The True Self also knows through past experience that if we can enter into being mode and sit quietly with these thoughts and feelings that they may eventually subside. And even if they don't, True Self knows that those crystal ball thoughts cannot touch us unless we choose to let them. They are only "true" if we decide to make them true by believing what the Tempter is telling us.

The way to escape crystal ball thinking and defeat the Tempter is to remember mindful awareness. Crystal ball thinking is just another type of thinking, and thinking is doing. The goal is to move from troublesome thoughts about the past or anxious thoughts about the future by shifting from doing mode to being mode. In the being mode, there is no past, and there is no future. There is only this present moment. If we are truly connected to the present moment, then we avoid the temptation to blame others or ourselves for our past mistakes, or to try to anticipate what our future mistakes might be.

In being mode, mindful acceptance becomes possible because we are not using our crystal balls to make educated guesses about our own motivations or the motivations of other people. Educated guesses are still guesses, and mindful acceptance is a way of setting such guesses aside while being present in the moment with self and others.

When we learn the art of acceptance, we also learn to accept that whatever other people may be feeling or thinking in the present moment is their responsibility, and not ours. The only responsibility we have to ourselves is to change ourselves in order to accommodate our own sense of wellbeing. When we are able to ground and center ourselves using mindful acceptance, we are able to share our own sense of wellbeing with others.

If this involves changing how we respond to difficult people, the choice is still ours, not the Tempter's. We get to decide whether such a change is worth it or not. Radical acceptance doesn't mean accepting any sort of abusive treatment from others. It means being able to set firm and consistent boundaries with abusive people. In some cases, mindful acceptance can mean accepting the fact that an abusive person isn't going to change, and in that case we will have to accept the loss of the relationship.

That's okay too. Living in True Self means accepting that you as a worthy child of the universe do not have to accept being abused, whether that abuse is physical, sexual, emotional, or verbal. When we learn this, we have survived the Supreme Ordeal and defeated the Tempter.

8.4 Mindful Acceptance

> *"Never underestimate your power to change yourself; never overestimate your power to change others."*
>
> - H. Jackson Brown, Jr.

One of the more difficult life lessons from the Supreme Ordeal and from life in general is that we cannot change the thoughts, feelings and behaviors of others, no matter how much the Tempter might tell us otherwise. We can only change our own thoughts, feelings and behaviors. The best we can do where others are concerned is to ask them to change. Then if they are willing to change, they will; however, if they are not willing to change, then at that point we've done all we can do. Further attempts to get them to conform to our expectations of them are doomed to failure because we are not in charge of how other people choose to live their lives.

If we are trying to change others to conform to our expectations of them, we are judging them to be less than perfect (by our standards, at least) as they are now. But what if we set aside attempts to change others? What if, using the power of being non-judgmental, we were able to recognize that people are doing the best they can in the only ways they know how? Would such a change in viewpoint allow us to accept them for who they are?

Mindful acceptance is the ability to set aside our expectations and assumptions about self and about others so that we may be more accepting of our own true selves and of the other people in our lives.

8.5 Basic Mindful Meditation

The Tempter will always manifest in the idea of doing something that is counter to the ultimate objective of the quest for ecospirituality, which is to live in True Self and to seek those moments of awe and wonder that make life worth living. The Supreme Ordeal is the Tempter's offer to take the easy way out by going back to the old way of doing things.

Mindful meditation is letting go of *doing mode*, and embracing *being mode* while focusing on the moment. We may recognize doing mode when we are attempting to problem-solve or when we are stuck in the feeling that we need to *do* something to fix a particular situation. This is the voice of the Tempter talking. Usually, if we find ourselves stressing out over the need to do something, it's because we've already done several things that didn't work. If we could do something to fix a particular problem, we'd have probably already done so. So if a lot of our anxiety comes from trying to figure out what to do, it may be a good time to just let go of the idea of *doing* something and just allow ourselves time for *being*. This act of letting go allows us to enter being mode because we are accepting ourselves and our thoughts and feelings in the present moment, free of expectations, judgments, or assumptions. It is an exercise in the mindful acceptance of self. It is a way to escape the Supreme Ordeal.

One of the simplest ways to do a mindful meditation is to focus on something in the environment and to allow ourselves to experience it through our senses, without expectations or assumptions. From the perspective of ecospirituality the best way to practice a mindful meditation is to find an outdoor space in which to do this.

This is because meditation is about letting go of thoughts and feelings and focusing on the information we get from our senses. Natural environments are rich in physical sensations, so such spaces afford us ample opportunity to move from thinking mode into sensing mode. When practicing mindful meditation outdoors, ask yourself what you see in your meditative space. What sounds do you hear there? What aromas might the space be revealing to you? How does the sun feel on your skin? If you're sitting or lying on the ground, how does the earth feel beneath you? Explore your meditation site with all of your senses as you let your thoughts and feelings retreat. Come out of your head and into the present moment.

Remember, when doing a meditation, you're not trying to stop thinking. Telling yourself not to think is just more thinking. Instead, just let your thoughts drift away on their own, like a leaf floating downstream, while focusing only on the information your senses are giving you.

For centuries, Buddhists who practice mindful meditation have focused on the breath. The reason for this is that our breath is always with us. By focusing on our breath we may engage in mindful meditation almost anywhere, at any time by directing our attention to the sensations of our breathing.

Once you have found a suitable outdoor place for meditations, read over the list of steps below at least once to gain an understanding of the process of basic mindful meditation before trying it:

1. To begin the basic mindful meditation, find a comfortable position, free of distractions, either sitting or lying down. Align your spine so that you are free of any stress points. If you are wearing any tight clothing, you may wish to loosen it. It is best to practice this meditation at least an hour after eating, as digestion tends to interfere with relaxation.

2. When you find your comfortable position, close your eyes.

3. Remember that at any time during this meditation, should you encounter thoughts or feelings that become overwhelming to you, it is best to cease the exercise until you can return to it in a calmer state.

4. To begin, first center yourself. To center yourself, let go of the cares of the day by turning your attention inward. Focus on nothing but the sensations of your breathing.

5. To allow yourself to just 'be,' gradually become aware of thoughts and feelings you may be experiencing.

6. In the 'being' mode, we realize that just because we are having thoughts and feelings, we do not have to act upon them.

7. Notice the sensations of your abdomen as it rises and falls with each breath. Turn your attention inward as you focus only on your breathing. You are not trying to go any place; you are not trying to do anything. You are simply present in this moment, observing your body as you breathe.

8. As you continue to focus only on your breathing, you may notice that from time to time your mind begins to wander. This is only natural. It's what minds do. Be aware that if your mind wanders, you don't have to follow it. Simply wait for your mind to return to you by continuing to focus on your breathing.

9. If you do notice your mind wandering, don't consider this to be a failure. If you start judging yourself

for allowing your mind to wander, such thoughts are simply more thoughts, and one of the objects of Mindful Meditation is to empty your mind of thoughts so that you can just 'be.' If you find yourself having such thoughts, just return to your breathing and allow your mind to come back to you by returning your attention only to your breathing.

10. As you continue to breathe, remember that there is no past, there is no future. There is only this present moment. Allow yourself to be in this moment…here and now. Any time your consciousness wanders, return to the 'now' of the present moment.

11. To end the meditation, gradually expand your awareness. If you are sitting, allow yourself to become aware of how your body makes contact with the chair. If you are lying down, allow yourself to feel how your body contacts the bed or the floor.

12. Continue to expand your consciousness outward until you become aware of your immediate surroundings.

13. When you feel you are ready, slowly open your eyes and return to yourself.

14. Conclude this mindful meditation by taking with you any insights, thoughts or feelings you may have gained in your practice. As you end this meditation, open your eyes while remaining calm, yet alert and relaxed.

8.6 Overcoming the Tempter

When preparing to defeat the Tempter and to gain victory over the Supreme Ordeal, you should first gain practice with mindful meditation. Practice for at least 20 minutes per day for at least a week. If you are completing this workbook as part of an ecospirituality program, practice a daily meditation until your group's next session. Many people say they don't have time to meditate, but when we say we don't have time what we're really saying is, "It's not a priority for me." This is the voice of the Tempter speaking. You don't have to make it 20 minutes in a row. If you're driving to work and find yourself waiting at a traffic light, that's a good time to do a brief meditation. If you're standing in line at the grocery store or waiting in your doctor's lobby, that's also a good time. You don't have to sit still and close your eyes in order to meditate. You can do it while walking, or while doing repetitive tasks, or while driving, or during any other daily activity. With enough practice, you can turn almost any activity into an exercise in mindful meditation. A few minutes here and a few minutes there, and you'll find that you have more than enough time for 20 minutes of meditation per day.

When you've had about a week's worth of practice with mindful meditation in natural environments, you will be ready to go on to exercise *8.6 Overcoming the Tempter*.

WORKSHEET 8.6 OVERCOMING THE TEMPTER　　　　　　　　　**PAGE 1 OF 3**

Name _____ Date _____

The Tempter will test our resolve to become the person we were meant to be. This test might manifest itself in thoughts like, *"I don't have the time for change,"* or, *"Change is too hard for me,"* or, *"This is the way I've always been."* When such thoughts appear in your consciousness, meditation may help to overcome the Tempter's Supreme Ordeal and to return to the path that leads to ecospirituality. You should already have practice with meditation before beginning this active meditation. To complete this exercise:

1. Read over the questions below on this worksheet.
2. Find a comfortable outdoor place where you will be undisturbed for the duration of the meditation.
3. Meditate on these questions.
4. When you have completed your meditation, come back to this worksheet and fill in your answers.

How did the Tempter present your Supreme Ordeal to you? What challenges are you currently facing that seem to be blocking your way to living according to your own true nature in your own True Self?

_____
_____
_____
_____
_____
_____
_____

What is the nature of your own Supreme Ordeal?

_____
_____
_____
_____
_____
_____
_____
_____

Worksheet 8.6 Overcoming the Tempter

Name _____ Date _____

What challenges do you face in overcoming your own Supreme Ordeal?

_____
_____
_____
_____
_____

How might the skills you have gained so far on your journey to ecospirituality help you when facing your own Supreme Ordeal?

_____
_____
_____
_____
_____
_____
_____
_____
_____
_____

How might radical (mindful) acceptance help you when facing your own Supreme Ordeal?

_____
_____
_____
_____
_____
_____
_____
_____
_____

WORKSHEET 8.6 OVERCOMING THE TEMPTER

Name _____ Date _____

How might meditating in nature help you when facing your own Supreme Ordeal?

_____
_____
_____
_____
_____
_____
_____

What have you learned so far from the Way of the Coyote that might help you to live more fully according to your own True Self?

_____
_____
_____
_____
_____
_____
_____
_____
_____
_____
_____
_____
_____
_____
_____
_____

Session 9 Atonement with the Father

That night Coyote dreamed of his homeland. In that dream, he was sitting before a fire. Across from that fire sat Chief Buffalo.

Coyote poured out his heart to Chief Buffalo. He apologized for his many pranks. He told Chief Buffalo the story of Coyote Woman, and how she had tricked him and betrayed him. He told his Chief exactly how he had felt being a victim of a prank so much like the ones he had pulled so many times on so many of his People. He begged for forgiveness from Chief Buffalo. He promised that he would never play another prank as long as he lived, so long as Chief Buffalo would accept him back into the tribe.

When Coyote had finished his tale, Chief Buffalo sat in silence for a long time before speaking.

"It is good that you know now how your actions have affected others," he said, "And that you are truly sorry for what you have done in the past. In the name of all the People, I forgive you. But I do not ask you to change. You cannot promise that you will never again play tricks on the People. You are a Trickster. That is your nature. That is what you are. Asking you to cease your pranks forever would be like asking Sister Salmon not to swim, or Brother Eagle not to fly."

"No, you cannot stop being a Trickster, for that would be death to you and to your spirit. To live in such a way would be to deny your own true nature. What I would ask of you instead is this: When you jest with others, your tricks must have a teaching purpose. You must use your trickster's art to make others look inside themselves and face the reality of what they are. Your tricks must reveal their true nature to them. If you can promise me that you can do this, then we will accept your gift of fire and you will be welcomed back into the tribe as a brother."

Coyote thought that this was a fair bargain indeed! Not only would he be welcomed back into the tribe, but he would still get to play the Trickster, as long as his tricks could accomplish some teaching purpose. In this way, he could still be himself, and at the same time serve a useful purpose among the People.

9.0 Injuries from the Father

> *"Our story...says that where a man's wound is, that is where his genius will be. Wherever the wound appears in our psyches, whether from alcoholic father, shaming mother, shaming father, abusing mother, whether it stems from isolation, disability, or disease, that is precisely the place for which we will give our major gift to the community."*
>
> — Robert Bly, *Iron John: A Book about Men*

The poet Robert Bly, in his book, *Iron John*, talks about the son receiving an injury from the father. Often it is this injury that sets the son off on a journey of self-discovery in the first place. In primal cultures this injury is sometimes ritualized. In some African cultures, the father knocks out one of the son's teeth in a rite of passage ritual. In some Native American cultures, the son receives some other form of injury, such as in the ritual tearing of the pectoral muscles practiced during the Sun Dance of the Lakotas. In other cultures it may manifest in other ways.

This dark aspect of fatherhood is reflected in the idea of the Shadow we previously discussed. Carl Jung believed that all human beings have the potential for all behaviors. The most moral among us have the potential to become evil, and the most immoral among us have the potential to redeem themselves and become saints. Since, according to Jung, all humans have the potential for all behaviors, the behaviors we choose not to express are suppressed. To recap, the unconscious part of the psyche in which these behaviors are repressed is what Jung called the *Shadow*. The behaviors we choose to express, the mask we wear in our daily lives, is what Jung called the *Persona*.

The Atonement with the Father in ecospirituality is the successful integration of the Shadow with the Persona. Although the Shadow is where our dark, "evil" impulses lie, it is also where our creativity lies. Without it, we can have no imagination, and no creativity. In order to tap into this creative power of the Shadow, we must integrate it into the Persona so that we may use its energy for positive and creative functions while avoiding or rechanneling its destructive aspects. So Atonement at this phase of the journey is literally "at-ONE-ment," meaning that the Shadow and the Persona become one. This does not mean that we consciously choose to act on those evil impulses from the Shadow. It means that by acknowledging their existence in the first place, we can move towards mastering them. When they are mastered, we can achieve the apotheosis that comes on the next leg of the journey.

In our Coyote story, Coyote incorrectly believed that Chief Buffalo was asking him to cast aside his true nature as a Trickster in order to be welcomed again by the tribe. Instead, what Chief Buffalo was asking was for Coyote to embrace his true nature and to use it for teaching rather than for pranks. By encouraging Coyote to embrace his true nature for creative purposes, Chief Buffalo was offering him an opportunity to achieve atonement by integrating his Shadow with his Persona.

Out own time in the ashes involves looking back on our lives up until this point and figuring out what to carry forward, and what to burn in the ashes. It's a time of casting off old, unproductive behaviors and a time for discovering who we really are. It is a time of fearless soul searching and brutal honesty with ourselves. In order to atone with the Father, we must be willing to own even the unpleasant parts of ourselves, because that's the only way we can change them and turn them towards the better.

While aboriginal cultures ritualize the injury from the father in coming of age rites of passage, in modern society the injuries we receive from our fathers may not be so obvious. They may be hidden within our psyches. Sometimes these deep emotional injuries prevent us from moving forward by choosing a path of our own. When this happens we may hear the Tempter's voice telling us that living according to our own true nature will disappoint the Father. Note again that Campbell's phases of the Hero's Journey are based on mostly male characters, so the "father" at the stage of Atonement with the Father doesn't necessarily have to be male. It could be a mother, or a grandparent, or a spouse, or a cherished family member, or any other mentor or teacher we may have encountered in our lives. The voice of the Father at this phase of the quest is any voice inside our heads other than our own; especially if that voice is trying to tell us who we are. In other words, Atonement with the Father means honestly asking ourselves what our true nature is, then asking if this is *really* our own true nature, or if it is the voice of another demanding that we live up to their expectations of who we are and what we should be. Atonement with the Father is the process of teasing out our own thoughts, feelings, and beliefs about the nature of our True Selves, away from the expectations of others.

Once we've discovered our own True Selves through this process of soul-searching, and weeding out demands placed on us by the Father (or the Mother, or the Grandmother, or the Grandfather, or whoever placed those expectations on us), we will have achieved Atonement with the Father.

9.1 Sacred Space

The original meaning of the word "sacred" was "set apart." A sacred thing is a thing that is set apart from ordinary everyday living. It is a place for quiet contemplation and meditation. Many aboriginal people believed that time and space are not separate things. This was and is especially true of sacred spaces. The stone circles in Europe were aligned to mark the passage of time. For the early Europeans time was measured in sacred places. The perception of time in sacred sites is therefore linked to space.

In the observation of many tribal rituals throughout the world, people believed that to enter sacred space was to step outside of time. This is the essence of living in the now. It is the ability to leave the time stream for a moment. Once inside sacred space, we may embrace the timelessness of simply being in the moment.

From a psychological perspective, setting aside a sacred space allows you to enter that space, step outside of time, and do your own work of contemplating the essence of being yourself. If you have a special place set aside for this activity, and only for this activity, then entering it puts you in a special state of mind. Psychologists call this *situation-specific learning*. If your sacred space becomes associated in your mind with relaxation, meditation and contemplation, then after a while simply entering your sacred space will put you into a meditative state.

9.2 Creating Sacred Space

If you are fortunate enough to have access to a natural place that calls to you, you may make it your own and yours alone by placing symbols and signs there that mean something to you. My own sacred space is marked by statuary and wind chimes. The gentle music of the chimes lends itself well to contemplation. When I am at home with the windows open, sometimes the wind blows through the trees, stirring the chimes. When this happens I am instantly reminded of my sacred space and the peace I find there. Even if I am busy working at the computer, the music of the chimes reminds me for a moment of the happy times I have spent in my sacred space in meditation.

If you don't have access to an outdoor place to create your own sacred space, you can create one indoors. Set up a small table somewhere in a corner of your home. Cover it with things that help you to achieve a meditative state. You may use candles, incense, house plants, or pictures of nature scenes or loved ones. You can use anything that might help you to connect with your True Self.

You may also find sacred spots on a hike. If you're out walking in the woods, you may come upon a place that calls to you. Stop there and meditate for a while. If this place is particularly meaningful for you, you may mark it for others by making a small pile of stones. This has been a tradition of mine for decades now, and when we do ecospirituality workshops, my students often do this. Coming upon a small pile of stones left by another can be a powerful way to connect yourself to others who have walked the path before you and enjoyed its peace and tranquility.

Whether your sacred space is indoors or outdoors, it can be a useful place for finding your center and connecting with your True Self.

9.3 Atonement with the Father through Sacred Space

Creating Sacred Space allows us to do deep inner contemplative work in a place that energizes us. This place belongs only to you, and you alone. This doesn't mean that others aren't allowed into your sacred space. It just means that it is a place that holds special spiritual significance to you, apart from the influences of others. Your own personal private Sacred Space should be an outer manifestation of your own inner journey. It should reflect who you are as a person, and who you are in the process of becoming.

The true way to be yourself by setting aside the voices of the Father and listening to your own inner voice is to return to a primal state in a natural environment. When you are able to cast off the trinkets and the baubles of material existence and get back to nature, you will create space that is much more conducive to hearing your own inner voice. You will know you have arrived at this moment and at this place when you can stand naked and alone in the wilderness, at peace with yourself and with the world.

As Robert Bly reminds us, the true source of our inner strength is the very wound that defines us. When striving for Atonement with the Father, look for those areas of your life where the voice of the Father has caused you the most pain. Where are those injuries you received from the Father? How do those injuries reveal your own hidden strengths, lurking there in your Shadow? What has the voice of the Father tried to get you to suppress about yourself?

Your own Sacred Space can help you to more readily identify the voices of the Father by placing you in an environment free of the distractions of the modern world. By escaping from man-made environments and seeking sanctuary in the natural world, all of the associations we make with those man-made environments disappear as the natural world of our Sacred Space seeps into our consciousness. When we leave our houses behind, we are not reminded of mortgage payments, utility bills, and household maintenance chores. When we leave our cars behind, we are not reminded that the car needs an oil change and the car payment is due. When we enter our Sacred Space, the natural world reminds us that we are children of nature, and we are therefore sacred by our very nature. In such a mindset and head space, Atonement with the Father becomes easy because we are in a place that makes it possible to cast aside those voices of the Father and to focus on our own true inner nature. Sacred space allows our own inner voices to speak.

To explore how Sacred Space can help you to achieve Atonement with the Father, try the Sacred Space Meditation.

9.4 Sacred Space Meditation

Prior to performing the Sacred Space meditation, you must first have your own Sacred Space. This should be a place that is fairly easy to access for you. It should be as free of man-made artifice as possible. This means that it should not be a place of manicured lawns and trimmed hedges if at all possible. It should be a pristine place, undisturbed by modifications dues to humankind. Of course, this is the ideal, and you may not have such a space readily available to you. If not, that's okay. Just try to get as close to a wild, untamed environment as you can. For the purposes of this meditation, the fewer reminders you have of the modern world, the more successful your meditation will be.

Once you have found your Sacred Space, make sure that you will be undisturbed her for the duration of the exercise. When you are ready to begin, follow the steps below. It may help to record these steps so that you may play them back to listen to as you engage in the Sacred Space Meditation.

1. Ground yourself by standing in your Sacred Space with your feet about shoulder-width apart, parallel to each other. Relax your shoulders while keeping your spine erect. Imagine a string going through the top of your head and holding you up, and adjust your spine accordingly.

2. Center yourself by first taking three deep breaths and then by letting go of any thoughts about the past or the future. You are bringing your awareness fully into the moment while focusing on the information your senses are giving you about this place. What do you see here? What do you smell here? What can you tell about this place by the sensations you feel on your skin? What sounds do you hear? Can you taste the air on your tongue as you inhale and exhale?

3. Now gradually become aware of your body. Feel the weight of your body distributed evenly on your feet. Notice any areas of tension or stress in your body, and will yourself to release them.

4. If you are experiencing any pain or tension in a particular part of your body, ask that part of your body what message it may have for you. Is tension manifesting anywhere in your body as you contemplate seeking Atonement with the Father by releasing the voices that tell you not to live according to your own true nature?

5. When your body feels at peace with itself, begin to walk by slowly raising your right foot and taking one step forward. Feel each muscle in your leg and your foot as you do so.

6. When your right foot touches the ground, notice which part of it first makes contact. Now notice the next, and the next, until your foot is completely at rest on the ground. Feel the weight shift as your foot comes to rest.

7. Now shift your attention to your left foot and do the same, noticing all the physical sensations your body is giving you as your shift your weight in preparation of taking a step with your left foot.

8. Continue to walk in this manner, placing one foot in front of the other. Focus your attention on the sensations of walking.

9. Now shift your attention to the rest of your senses. What do you see in this place? What do you smell? What do you hear? Move out of thinking mode and into sensing mode, allowing the environment of your Sacred Space to envelope you and to embrace you.

10. Continue to walk in this manner until you find something in the environment that calls out for your attention. It could be a plant, or an interesting rock, or a particular patch of ground, or even an animal. When you have found this thing, stop walking and direct your attention to it.

11. Explore the object with all of your senses. Observe it and describe it with your eyes. Now with your ears. Is it making any sound? Do you detect any aroma from it? If it is a safe object to touch, what is its texture? Be in the moment with your object.

12. Now expand your attention to your immediate surroundings. Observe and describe it to yourself in deep detail. Imagine you are a painter and you are about to paint the scene you see before you.

13. If there is a comfortable place to sit, do so now, and just spend a few moments at peace with your surroundings here in your Sacred Space.

14. Notice anything about your Sacred Space that might help you to connect to your True Self the next time you return here.

15. Now think about the voices of the Father and how they manifest in your mind and in your soul. What injuries have these voices given you?

16. How might the pain subside if you could let those voices of the Father go?

17. How might the nature of your injuries change if you could hear and acknowledge those voices of the Father without having to believe that what they tell you is true?

18. How might the strength and energy you find from your Sacred Space lead you to achieve Atonement with the Father by allowing you to focus on your own inner voice?

19. Contemplate these questions for as long as you need to.

20. When you are ready, conclude the meditation, remembering what you have experienced here.

Worksheet 9.4 Sacred Space Meditation

Page 1 of 3

Name _____ Date _____

Achieving Atonement with the Father requires meditation and self-reflection on your own true nature, with a special emphasis on setting aside the opinions of others as to who you are and what you should be. These inner voices that are not your own represent the Father. Although Campbell refers to "the Father," these voices could also be Mother, or Spouse, or Grandparent, or any other significant person in your life who may have tried to change who you are in order to get you to live up to their expectations of who you should be.

The goal of this Sacred Space meditation is to reach Atonement with the Father by setting aside any expectations or obligations put upon you by the Father. When the Father condemns something we think, feel or believe, the tendency is to deny it and suppress it by moving it into the realm of the Shadow. To integrate these suppressed thoughts, feelings and beliefs into the Persona, we must first become aware of their existence, then we must acknowledge it as a part of ourselves. This acknowledgement is the first step towards mastering it and using its power for creative rather than for destructive purposes.

To complete the Sacred Space Meditation, first read over the questions on this worksheet, then go to your own sacred space and contemplate your answers to the questions. When you feel you have reached a conclusion to the Sacred Space Meditation, remain in your Sacred Space with this worksheet, and write your answers in the spaces below.

What is the voice of the Father in your own life? What elements of your own true nature have you suppressed because you've been told by others you shouldn't express them? List a few of these below.

_____
_____
_____
_____
_____
_____
_____
_____
_____
_____
_____
_____

WORKSHEET 9.4 SACRED SPACE MEDITATION

Name _____ Date _____

If you have inner voices telling you that it's not safe to express some parts of yourself, or that you should be ashamed of these parts of yourself, who do these voices belong to? Are they yours, or someone else's?

_____
_____
_____
_____
_____

If any of these voices of the Father belong to you, and you are telling yourself not to express these suppressed parts of your own true nature, what are you afraid might happen if you do express them?

_____
_____
_____
_____
_____

What would you need to do in order to set aside these voices of the Father so that you can embrace your own true nature?

_____
_____
_____
_____
_____
_____
_____
_____
_____
_____

WORKSHEET 9.4 SACRED SPACE MEDITATION

Name _____ Date _____

Think about the object that you connected to during the Sacred Space Meditation. What was it about this object that attracted you to it?

_____
_____
_____
_____
_____

Think about some of the characteristics of this object. How might these characteristics help you to achieve Atonement with the Father by focusing on your own true inner voice? For example, if you were attracted to a stone, stones are hard and firm, so a stone might suggest being firm in your purpose of trusting your own True Self.

_____
_____
_____
_____
_____

How might your Sacred Space help you to achieve Atonement with the Father and connect to your own True Self?

_____
_____
_____
_____
_____
_____
_____
_____
_____
_____

Session 10 Apotheosis

Sometime later Coyote woke from his dream. The conversation he'd had with Chief Buffalo lingered in his mind and in his spirit as he stretched sleepily and rose to take a drink from the nearby creek. All this time he had though himself unworthy to take up this quest because of his nature, but the Chief Buffalo of the dream time had told him that it was his very nature that made him the perfect candidate for the quest in the first place!

Coyote had thought that he must somehow deny his true nature, the essence of his being, in order to complete the quest. But now he saw his nature as a Trickster was the very thing that would help him complete his quest. All he had to do was to trust his own inner wisdom.

He pondered the idea that it was strange that a dream should teach him this. After all, dreams come from within his own head, and because it was a dream, it meant that Chief Buffalo wasn't really there talking to him. Some part of his mind had imagined that conversation.

But the more he thought about it, the more he realized that this wasn't true. "What if we are all connected at some level?" He thought to himself, "What if a part of me is Chief Buffalo, and a part of Chief Buffalo is me? What if separation is an illusion, and we are all part of the same whole? What if there is only one Soul in the entire world, and we are all a part of it?"

The more he thought about this, the more it made sense.

"Chief Buffalo is holy, but so am I. White Buffalo Woman is sacred, but so am I. We are all part of the same whole. Whenever I need their assistance, all I need to do is remember that they are a part of me, and I am a part of them. With this knowing, I will always have their wisdom to call upon."

"We are all holy," thought Coyote. "We all are sacred. Everyone I look upon is holy, and whatever ground my paws touch, it is sacred ground. My eyes are holy, and everything I look upon is sacred. When I see my brothers and sisters, I am seeing them as aspects of myself, in love and wisdom. Every day and every night they will all be with me. No distance can separate me from their love. From this day forward I am walking in a sacred manner upon the Earth, and nothing and no one can ever take that from me. I can never go back to the old way of being, for I have been re-born into this sacred wisdom. Nothing…not even death…can separate me from this divine love. Knowing this, I will never doubt myself again. I will never be afraid again."

10.0 Apotheosis

"The only difference between you and God is that you have forgotten you are divine."

— Dan Brown, *The Lost Symbol*

The word *apotheosis* comes from the Greek. It means, "To become divine or godlike." For our purposes, apotheosis is the result of integrating the Shadow and the Persona. Divinity is usually associated with perfection, but in our version of apotheosis, this perfection doesn't apply to some unrealistic and dogmatic ideal defined by others (or defined by the voices of the Father). "Perfect" in this sense means acting in ways that are perfect for *you*, and not anyone else. The way to achieve apotheosis is to learn to accept all of your perceived shortcomings, weaknesses, and darker impulses that dwell in the Shadow as a part of you. By embracing your whole being, you are able to turn weaknesses into strengths.

The first step in apotheosis is to examine all the things about ourselves we have tried to suppress in the Shadow. Are there any hidden strengths in these suppressed things? Could these things become sources of strength if we learned to express them in creative, positive ways?

What's in your own Shadow? Just as Coyote attempted to suppress his own true nature as a Trickster, what impulses might you have been suppressing that are really a part of your own true nature? How might those feelings, thoughts, beliefs and behaviors be turned into allies and abilities on your seeker's journey to True Self?

Sometimes such repressed impulses manifest in anger. We're rarely taught to express anger in positive ways. Instead, when we feel angry, we're told to deny those feelings rather than to express them. The problem with this is that angry people are passionate people. We get upset because we feel passionate about something. If we try to suppress the anger, we also run the risk of emotionally numbing the passion.

What if, instead of suppressing it, we could find positive ways to channel the passion of that anger? The Founding Fathers were angry at the way the British Empire was treating them, and they channeled that anger into fighting for independence. Martin Luther King was angry at civil injustice, prejudice, and bigotry, and he channeled that anger into fighting for equal rights, as did Gandhi, Susan B. Anthony, Abraham Lincoln, and a host of other historical icons. In fact, I would go so far as to say that most, if not all, great movements for change in the world began because someone was angry about the status quo. So anger itself isn't the problem. It's how we choose to channel the energy of that anger.

Perhaps it's not anger that is suppressed in your Shadow, but some other emotion like sadness, fear, or anxiety. In such a case, the way to integrate those emotions from the Shadow is to ask yourself what your intention is in suppressing these emotions, and what might happen if you learned to express them in positive ways. If you wrestle with sadness and depression, could you support others who do the same? If your fears are being suppressed in the Shadow, could you learn to face your fears and channel that energy into positive resolutions? If you suffer from anxiety, could you confront it in ways that allow you to take advantages of the opportunity such stress brings?

Like Coyote, we can learn to use our Shadow energy for creative purposes. From Chief Buffalo, Coyote learned that he could use his gift of trickery as a teaching tool. In doing so, he would not have to go against his own true nature. Instead, he could channel his preference for pranks into positive activities that would help others learn.

To achieve apotheosis, first ask yourself what elements of your own Shadow you might have been suppressing. Next, ask yourself how these elements might be used in positive ways. When you are able to do this consistently, you will have learned how to accept who you are, warts and all. You will have learned that your own true nature is perfection. Nobody else can be a perfect "you" but you.

Once you have integrated Shadow with Persona, you will have come to the knowledge that all things are sacred. As Coyote realized in our story:

> *"We all are holy. We all are sacred. Everyone I look upon is holy, and whatever ground my paws touch, it is sacred ground. My eyes are holy, and everything I look upon is sacred. When I see my brothers and sisters, I am seeing them as aspects of myself, in love and wisdom. Every day and every night they will all be with me. No distance can separate me from their love. From this day forward I am walking in a sacred manner upon the Earth, and nothing and no one can ever take that from me. I can never go back to the old way of being, for I have been re-born into this sacred wisdom. Nothing...not even death...can separate me from this divine love. Knowing this, I will never doubt myself again. I will never be afraid again."*

When you come to understand this, you will have attained apotheosis.

10.1 Spirits in the Material World

> *"We are spirits in the material world."*
>
> --Gordon Sumner (aka "Sting" of the Police), *Spirits in the Material World*

In order to understand apotheosis, we must first understand our own true nature. As Sting reminds us, "We are spirits in the material world." The part of us that is divine is the part that is spirit. From the perspective of ecospirituality, we're not talking about anything supernatural when we say "spirit." We are talking about "that which inspires."

Inspiration comes from *Wise Mind*.

When we are being logical, rational, and devoid of emotion, we are in *Rational Mind*. When we are allowing our thoughts to be driven by our feelings, we are in *Emotional Mind*. A goal of apotheosis in ecospirituality is to achieve *Wise Mind*. Wise Mind is the joining of Rational Mind and Emotional Mind in perfect balance and harmony. It is a moving beyond opposites to a mindful state of acceptance.

We sometimes tend to think of things in black-and-white terms. When in this mode of thought, we tend to see experiences as "all good" or "all bad." But if we use our skills of mindful awareness to see what is really there, we may come to recognize that rarely are things all good or all bad. There is usually a little bit of bad in the best good things, but likewise there is usually a little bit of good even in the worst bad things. One of the skills of Wise Mind is seeing the gray areas of life for what they are instead of interpreting them as black or white.

Apotheosis in ecospirituality is about achieving balance. The way to gain this balance in our lives is through integrating our Shadow and our Persona, thus achieving Wise Mind. It is learning to live in the gray areas.

To look at an example of how this Wise Mind might appear in the real world, let's imagine that a woman has stolen a loaf of bread to feed her children, who are starving. A person who is totally cold, calculating and logical, devoid of emotion, and operating solely from Rational Mind, might say something like, "Yes, it's unfortunate that her children were starving, but the law is the law. She should be punished."

But a person who is operating from Wise Mind has the ability to use a rational mind tempered by emotion. In this case, such a person might say something like, "The law is the law, but we should also have compassion. Who among us wouldn't steal a loaf of bread if our children were starving?"

Let's look at another example, this time from Emotional Mind.

Suppose I'm in line at the grocery store. I only have a few items, so I'm in the "ten items or less" lane. The person in front of me has a cart completely full of groceries. It's obvious that she has far more than ten items.

If I'm operating from Emotional Mind, I might let my emotions get the better of me and make an angry comment to this person, causing a scene in the grocery store. But a person operating from Wise Mind in this situation might temper the emotional reaction with Rational Mind. Such a person might take the opportunity to say to himself, "This person is obviously going to be a while. I don't need to let the fact that she's breaking the rules ruin my day. Instead, I can take this opportunity to do a mini-meditation while I wait."

When operating from Wise Mind, we are able to gain the wisdom to know what we have the power to change, and what we must accept. Once we have achieved this state of acceptance, we are able to integrate Shadow into Persona. This is because Shadow and Persona are part of the same whole that is Self. If we were to graph out the idea that Wise Mind is a blend and balance of Emotional Mind and Rational Mind, the graph would look like the illustration below.

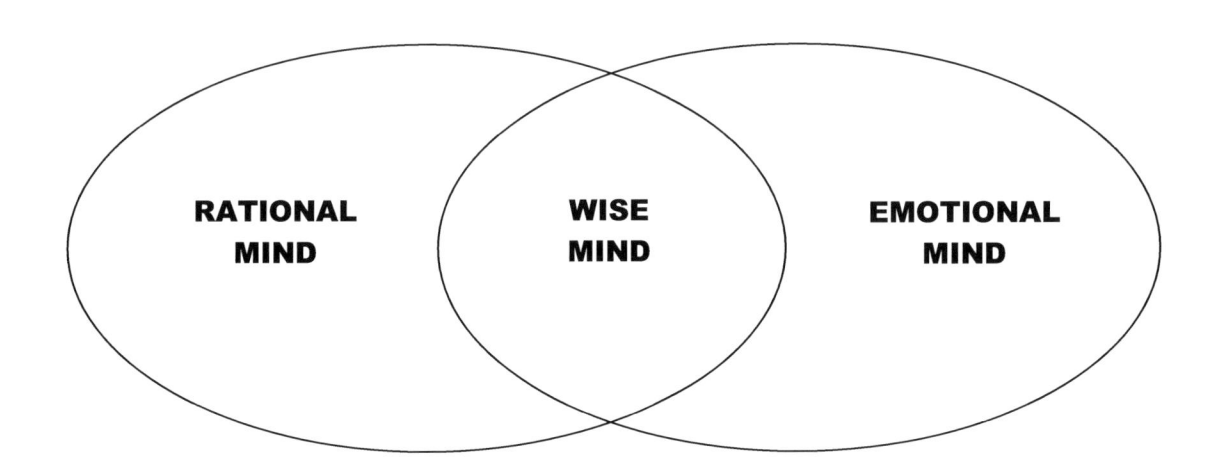

10.2 Wise Mind: Doing vs. Being

Imagine you could recognize the divinity in yourself by accepting *all* parts of your identity as perfect. What sort of life would that person have? How would that person relate to self? To nature? To others? How can ecospirituality and the Way of the Coyote help you to become that person?

So far on our journey we have answered the Call to Adventure by recognizing that life cannot go on as it is, and acknowledging that something has to change. We've avoided the Refusal of the Call by conquering our fears. We've called upon our own Supernatural Aid by selecting a spirit animal and talismans to assist us on the journey. We've crossed the First Threshold by committing to the journey. We've experienced time in the ashes and had our own personal katabasis and rebirth in the Belly of the Whale. We have "burned up" our former selves on the Road of Trials in preparation of becoming someone new. We've met with the Goddess/God on the road to request mentorship and guidance on this new ecospiritual path. We've avoided the temptation to take the easy way out by conquering the Tempter, and we've learned to listen to our own ecospiritual inner voices and achieved Atonement with the Father in the process. Now, in preparation for receiving the Ultimate Boon, we must achieve Apotheosis.

As mentioned in previous sessions, Apotheosis in ecospirituality is achieved through integrating Shadow with Persona. When this integration occurs successfully, we are able to recognize *all* parts of ourselves as divine. The reason the Shadow exists in the first place is that we have been conditioned by society to believe that certain feelings are "good" and certain feelings are "bad;" however, all feelings are just feelings. What may be considered "good" or "bad" is the behavior we choose to engage in after experiencing the feeling. So successful integration of Shadow with Persona means being willing to examine and accept all of our feelings without believing we are obliged to act on them. It is a shift from *doing mode* to *being mode.*

In doing mode we're trying to come up with solutions to problems, or trying to stop anxiety or depression, or trying to escape from the repercussions of the problem, or trying to suppress feelings by stuffing them deep into the Shadow. In being mode, we're just allowing ourselves some space to be in the moment, without trying to push the problem away or solve it, and without trying to suppress feelings by hiding them in the Shadow. Trying to stuff feelings, or trying to tell ourselves not to feel what we feel, is doing something. So if we're trying, we're in doing mode.

When we move our attention from the thinking cycle to the sensing cycle, we often find that it is not necessary to do anything right now. When we leave doing, we enter being. From Wise Mind we are able to prepare for Apotheosis by allowing ourselves to just be with our own true nature.

10.3 Apotheosis: Integrating Shadow and Persona

The Shadow is the part of the unconscious mind where all of our suppressed impulses, thoughts and feelings lie. The Persona is the face we choose to show the world. Apotheosis, or becoming "godlike," means recognizing the divinity within ourselves. To acknowledge the divinity within us, we must first accept all parts of ourselves. This includes those parts that have been suppressed in the Shadow. Those suppressed parts are the evidence of our previous injuries received from the voice of the Father. These injuries are probably what caused us to suppress those parts of ourselves in the first place. Once we can acknowledge this, we can integrate Shadow and Persona, and achieve Apotheosis.

This integration is facilitated through being mode. This is largely because the act of suppressing thoughts, feelings, and beliefs in the Shadow is itself a type of doing. If we can learn instead to simply allow ourselves to enter being mode and feel what we feel without having to do anything about it, there is no need to suppress the feelings by stuffing them down into the Shadow. This also means that the energy of such feelings is readily available for channeling into creative and constructive purposes because the feelings haven't been suppressed or repressed.

As you contemplate the things you might have been repressing in your own Shadow, think about how they might be turned into sources of strength instead of sources of injury and pain. Also think about how many of those things have to do with the material world and how many of those things have to do with the spiritual world. For the purposes of ecospirituality, the "spiritual world" means the things that more easily allow you to connect to others, to nature, and to yourself; those awe-inspiring moments of beauty we all live for.

When we achieve rebirth through Apotheosis we have learned to set aside material pleasures in favor of spiritual gifts. We have learned to live a sacred life set apart from the concerns of the mundane world. We have learned how to follow healing energies and to be healed ourselves so that we may help nature to heal others.

10.4 The Golden Road

According to Jung, the Shadow lies within the realm of the unconscious. The problem with trying to tap into the power of the unconscious is that if we could be consciously aware of its workings, it wouldn't be unconscious. So how do we get there from here? Sigmund Freud, Carl Jung's mentor, called dreams the "Golden Road to the unconscious." He believed that the apparently nonsensical content of our dreams was in reality the unconscious mind's attempt to communicate to the conscious mind. Jung expanded on this concept, believing that the symbols we see in dreams could tap into the power of the collective unconscious through the archetypes. A dream about an archetypal image was especially powerful to Jung. Such a dream, to him, was a direct message from the collective unconscious.

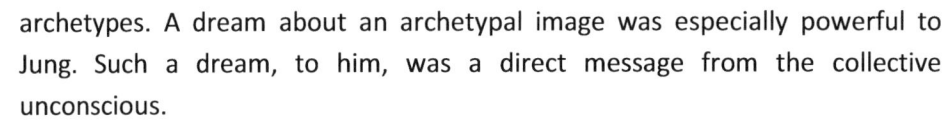

Later psychotherapists began to expand on this idea, especially in the use of projections from the unconscious. You may have seen a Rorschach ink blot test, in which a subject is shown a blot of ink on a piece of paper and is asked to describe what he sees. Such images are attempts by therapists to tap into the subject's unconscious, in much the same way that Freud and Jung used dreams to achieve the same end.

Rorschach Ink Blot

Such techniques are used by therapists to try to gain insight into the unconscious minds of those who have mental health issues, but is it possible for mentally healthy people to do this on our own without having to go through years of psychoanalysis?

Have you ever looked at the clouds and seen faces or other images in them? Most children, and many adults, have played this game from time to time, but have you ever stopped to think about why you saw a certain image and not another? There is no real image there in the clouds, so any image you see is a projection of your own mind onto the pattern in the sky. The next time you see an image in the clouds, ask yourself what that image means to you, and what might be going on in your life that would cause you to see that particular image.

The medieval Celts had an archetype known as the Green Man. This Green Man was the physical embodiment of nature. They often saw faces of the Green Man in the trees in much the same way that we see faces in the clouds. One Celtic legend has it that when an ancestor dies, his or her soul inhabits a tree. According to this legend, each tree has its own properties and personality. If a Celt saw the face of an ancestor in a tree, they noted the type of tree and its qualities. It was believed that the ancestor whose face they saw in the tree was sending a message through the type of tree they chose to manifest in.

Of course, there was no real face in the tree. What was at work here was the observer's own unconscious mind, meeting his or her need to hear from an ancestor from beyond the grave.

When you spend time in nature, notice which things attract your attention. Think about what those things mean to you, and ask yourself why this particular thing should capture your attention at this particular time. When you are able to do this effectively, you've taken the first step on the Golden Road to the unconscious. When you can make the unconscious conscious, you will be able to integrate Shadow and Persona, and achieve apotheosis.

10.5 Connecting through the Green Man

The Green Man is not unique to Celtic folklore. Many cultures throughout the world have some form of Green Man. Because so many cultures recognize this symbol, the Green Man is archetypal. That is, his image is part of the collective unconscious shared by all humans. He is often depicted as a face surrounded by or made of leaves and other greenery. He symbolizes rebirth and the cycle of seasons as the plants return to live in the spring, so the icon of the Green Man is a fitting way to begin your own rebirth to living in True Self.

One way the Celts tapped into the power of the Green Man was to go out into the woods and see shapes in the leaves on the trees, in much the same way that we amuse ourselves by looking for faces and other shapes in the clouds. The Celts would look for the faces of their deceased ancestors in the shapes and patterns the leaves made. Of course, there were no actual ancestors in the leaves, just as there are no actual faces in the clouds when we play the cloud game. What we see is a projection of our own unconscious minds.

The Green Man

This Green Man exercise can be a way to connect to the power of your unconscious mind that lies in your own Shadow. By seeing shapes in the trees, you are allowing your unconscious motivations to come forth so that you may become conscious of them. Becoming conscious of them is the first step in achieving Apotheosis by integrating these unconscious impulses into your consciousness, and therefore into your own ideal True Self.

If you are doing this exercise in the winter months, you will have to use an evergreen tree. If there are no trees in your immediate area, you may use a photograph of a tree, but the exercise works better if you can go outdoors and use a real, living tree.

To begin the Green Man exercise, first perform the Tree of Life meditation, preferably outdoors under a tree. When you have centered yourself by completing the meditation, find the tree you intend to use. It should be a leafy, full tree. Stand or sit near the tree and look at it with soft eyes, relaxing your focus. Observe the tree until a picture forms in it. Picture doing this in the same way you would look for pictures in the clouds in the sky. Don't stop looking at the tree until you can make out a picture hidden in the leaves. When you have the picture firmly in memory, go on to the next page and sketch what you saw. You don't have to be an artist about it. Just sketch enough to give a general impression of what you saw.

WORKSHEET 10.5 THE GREEN MAN

Name _____ Date _____

Sketch a picture below of what you saw when you did the Green Man exercise. It doesn't have to be too detailed, as long as you can tell what the picture represents.

WORKSHEET 10.5 THE GREEN MAN PAGE 2 OF 2

Name _____ Date_____

What did you see in the tree? Use what you drew to answer these questions:

What does the picture you saw in the tree symbolize to you? What is the emotional quality of the picture?

_____
_____
_____
_____
_____

What does the picture you saw tell you about your current emotional state?

_____
_____
_____
_____
_____

How does the picture you saw relate to living in your True Self?

_____
_____
_____
_____

How might the image you saw help you to integrate your Shadow and your Persona?

_____
_____
_____
_____
_____

10.6 Apotheosis through the Green Man

When you have completed the Green Man exercise, you have allowed your unconscious mind to come forth and project itself onto the trees. What did the image you saw tell you about your unconscious motivations? How might this knowledge help you to integrate your Shadow and your Persona? Remember that the Shadow is the unconscious part of the mind where those impulses we've been told not to own dwell. So integrating Shadow and Persona means accepting those "darker" impulses as a means to channel their energy creatively and with purpose. When that balance between chaos and order occurs, Apotheosis is achieved.

Apotheosis simply means remembering you are a divine child of the universe. When you are able to integrate Shadow and Persona, you are able to accept yourself "warts and all." This means accepting that all parts of your psyche are perfect just as they are, even those that have been suppressed in the unconscious world of the Shadow. Acknowledging them gives you the ability to control how you react to them. When you can control your responses to your darker impulses you will have mastered the integration of Shadow and Persona and achieved Apotheosis.

Session 11 The Ultimate Boon

Coyote continued to walk on the snow-covered trail. As he rounded a bend in the forest, he was surprised to see White Buffalo Woman standing in the path ahead.

"Who is this I see before me?" she asked, "The same Coyote who set out to find fire for his People?"

She studied him quietly for a moment, then said in a whisper, "No...not the same Coyote."

Coyote opened his mouth to protest that yes, he was indeed the same Coyote who had learned from her at the Cave of the People of the Ashes, but before he could speak, he looked into his own heart and realized that her words were true. He was not the same Coyote. This journey had changed him.

As this knowledge crossed his mind, he looked up to see a smile spreading on White Buffalo Woman's face.

"Now you are ready to seek the fire," she said. She motioned for Coyote to follow her.

They walked on for most of the morning until they came to a dense forest. The vegetation here was so thick that the narrow path was barely visible. At the edge of the forest, White Buffalo Woman stopped and turned to face Coyote.

"From this point on, you must walk the path alone. Follow the trail through the forest until you come upon the Tribe of the Fire People. I cannot tell you what is to come. I can only tell you that whatever may happen among the Fire People, you must be true to your own nature in order to survive. Trust your own heart and your own mind and you will know what to do."

Her words filled him with a sense of foreboding, but at the same time he felt self-assured. After all, everything that had happened on his journey thus far was leading up to this moment. After taking a deep breath, he stepped on the path and into the forest.

The forest was frozen. Snow lay thick upon the ground. Icicles hung from the trees. The further he walked, the darker the path became. The thick vegetation drowned out almost all of the light of the Sun. But his keen eyes guided him, and by and by he came upon a village in the center of the woods.

Though the forest around him was frigid with cold, here in the center of the village there was warmth. As Coyote entered the village, he could see the reason why. The huts had been arranged in circular fashion around a central fire. The fire before him blazed brighter than the Sun. Around that fire danced all manner of creatures, both two-legged and four-legged. The creatures of the air flew above it. A river ran through the center of the village, and the fishes of the river leapt up out of the water and over the fire, their scales sparkling with the reflected light. All manner of insects were there dancing too. Even the serpents danced around the fire in their own fashion, writhing on the ground near the fire circle.

Coyote approached the fire. As he drew nearer he began to dance just like the others. The music was familiar, as if he'd heard it before. He couldn't seem to help himself as his feet began to move to the beat and the rhythm. For a time he lost himself in the pure joy of the dance, but then he remembered his purpose here and came to his senses.

He decided to steal some of the fire for himself by grasping a twig or branch in his mouth. As he danced through the crowd, inching his way ever closer to the fire, he was almost to the edge of the fire pit when a figure leaped between him and the fire, blocking his path. He looked up to see Coyote Woman standing before him.

At first he didn't recognize her, because there was something different in her eyes. This was the same Coyote Woman who had tricked him on the trail, yet not the same. She smiled at him and began dancing between Coyote and the sacred fire.

As Coyote Woman danced before him, Coyote returned her smile and joined in the dance. But with each move he was ever mindful of his ultimate goal of stealing a flaming twig from the fire. As he danced with Coyote Woman, he feinted to the left and to the right, always trying to circle around her to get to the fire. But no matter how many tricks he employed she was always one step ahead of him. It was as if she could read his mind, for no matter where he turned he found her between him and his goal.

As they danced together around the fire, it occurred to him that the reason she knew his every move was that she too was a Trickster. She knew every prank, every trick, every deception he could use to his advantage because she possessed the same skills and talents as he. Coyote soon came to realize that the only way to defeat an opponent such as this and to obtain his goal would be to do something completely unexpected and out of character for him.

He pondered what this might be. Then, as he danced with Coyote Woman, he noticed that she always met his face, eye-to-eye. If he danced between her and the fire, she didn't notice it as long as his gaze met hers. She was ever watchful of his eyes turning away from hers, because that meant he would easily be able to reach into the fire with his teeth and snatch a flaming branch. Any time he turned his gaze away from hers, she leaped between him and the fire. As they spun around and around each other dancing, she did not try to prevent him from turning his back to the fire as long as he looked her in the eye.

With this revelation, he came up with a plan. As they danced around each other, he placed himself between her and the fire, all the while meeting her gaze eye-to-eye. She relaxed because he did not look away. Seeing this, Coyote then put his plan into play. Without looking where he was going, he darted backwards, plunging his tail into the fire. The tip of his fine bushy tail immediately burst into flame. Yelping with pain, Coyote took flight, running away from the fire circle at top speed.

11.0 The Ultimate Boon - Living in True Self

"All behavior is purposeful if you understand the context."

– Alfred Adler, founder of the School of Individual Psychology

People do all sorts of crazy things. Some people smoke, some people do illicit drugs, some people engage in risky hobbies like skydiving or rock climbing, some engage in criminal activities, and many participate in behaviors that, to an outside observer, might look downright harmful. Have you ever had a friend or family member who insisted on doing things that were potentially dangerous to themselves or to others?

Adler's quote above explains such self-harming behaviors.

To someone without a substance abuse problem, it is difficult to understand how someone could abuse dangerous drugs like crack cocaine or methamphetamine. To someone not in the depths of despair and depression, it might be impossible to understand how suicide might look like a viable option to a person locked in their own personal hell. Suicide might even be considered a selfish act to a person who doesn't understand the harsh effects of depression on the human mind and brain.

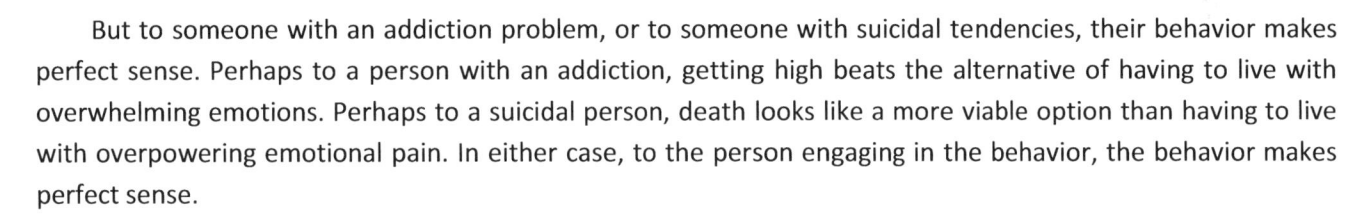

But to someone with an addiction problem, or to someone with suicidal tendencies, their behavior makes perfect sense. Perhaps to a person with an addiction, getting high beats the alternative of having to live with overwhelming emotions. Perhaps to a suicidal person, death looks like a more viable option than having to live with overpowering emotional pain. In either case, to the person engaging in the behavior, the behavior makes perfect sense.

Every human being on the planet has experienced occasional feelings of shame, guilt, blame, or inferiority. Such feelings are a natural part of the human condition. They are the source of many of the problems we experience with our relationships, careers, spiritual endeavors, and day-to-day living.

As human beings we're conditioned to disown certain parts of ourselves. We don't like to admit our feelings of shame or guilt, because doing so might mean that we are less than perfect. But what does "perfect" really mean?

Try this sometime: Ask three of your closest friends or family members what their idea of the "perfect day" is. I'm willing to bet you'll get at least three different answers. So if you do get three different answers to the question, "Describe your perfect day," what does "perfect" really mean?

The obvious answer to this is that the term "perfect" is defined by the individual. This means that your idea of perfect might be completely different from my idea of perfect. Each of us is in charge of what "perfect" means to us.

The good news about this is that if "perfect" is self-defined, and if my own personal idea of what "perfect" means is causing me stress, then I am free to change it at any time. The way to do this is to realize that all of us have feelings of depression, stress or anxiety from time to time. All of us fail to live up to our own expectations for ourselves from time to time. We may choose to beat ourselves up for failing to be "perfect," or we may choose to realize that as human beings, failing to be "perfect" is a natural part of existence.

By learning to love ourselves "warts and all," we learn the art of radical acceptance of the True Self.

The next exercise is for determining who you are and what you would like to become. It is designed to help you identify your True Self, and to accept that this is who you are. You may wish to make several copies of the exercise, doing one each week until you complete the course. Notice how your answers change over time.

The last session in this course and in this workbook is Freedom to Live: Living in True Self. You may re-visit the Radical Acceptance of True Self exercise after completing the last session of this workbook as a means of charting your progress over the duration of the course, so you may wish to hang on to your answers as you do this exercise for the first time.

The freedom to live completely and freely in True Self is the Ultimate Boon. It is the purpose of the quest. When we are truly able to connect with our own True Selves we have achieved the pinnacle of existence in the way of life that is ecotherapy. We will have succeeded in completing the journey that is the Way of the Coyote.

WORKSHEET 11.0 RADICAL ACCEPTANCE OF TRUE SELF   PAGE 1 OF 3

Name _____ Date _____

This exercise will help you to gain practice in accepting yourself for who you are and who you wish to be. Answer the questions below, being as honest as you can. Do this exercise at least once per week for the duration of this course, and see how your answers change as you gain more experience in acceptance.

What do you care about? What gives your life passion and meaning?

_____
_____
_____
_____
_____
_____
_____
_____
_____
_____
_____
_____

What thoughts, feelings and behaviors generate feelings of blame, guilt or shame in you?

_____
_____
_____
_____
_____
_____
_____
_____
_____

WORKSHEET 11.0 RADICAL ACCEPTANCE OF TRUE SELF**PAGE 2 OF 3**

Name _____ Date _____

Of the things about yourself above that generate feelings of blame, guilt or shame, do any of them reveal hidden strengths? How? Example: If you get angry easily, could it be because you are passionate about the things you care about? Could this passion be turned into a strength?

_____
_____
_____
_____
_____
_____

What are some ways that you could accept these feelings of blame, guilt or shame as parts of yourself without having to buy into them? Are there any ways that you could think about these feelings and thoughts so that they are no longer a problem? Be as specific as possible in your answers.

_____
_____
_____
_____
_____
_____

How would these different ways of believing and behaving about your thoughts and feelings create a more compassionate and positive reality in your life?

_____
_____
_____
_____
_____
_____
_____

WORKSHEET 11.0 RADICAL ACCEPTANCE OF TRUE SELF

Name _____ Date _____

What would have to change about the way you view yourself in order for you to be able to live more fully in your True Self?

_____
_____
_____
_____
_____

What strengths do you possess that will allow you to make those changes?

_____
_____
_____
_____
_____

What are some potential things that could go wrong when you plan to make those changes?

_____
_____
_____
_____

What are some potential solutions if those things go wrong?

_____
_____
_____
_____
_____

11.1 True Self and Living in Wise Mind

The more experience we gain in achieving radical acceptance, the more we are able to live in True Self. Such acceptance allows us to deal with ourselves as we really are. There are two ways to achieve this. We may either change the way we see ourselves to bring it more in line with our True Selves, or we may change our concept of True Self to bring it more in line with the way we see ourselves. When we have done so, we will be living in Wise Mind, balanced perfectly between emotion and reason, chaos and order. We will have become the persons we were born to be.

The Ultimate Boon means finally overcoming our greatest personal challenges by casting aside the fear of living according to our own true nature. When we have captured the Ultimate Boon, we will be transformed into a new state, emerging from quest as stronger and more confident persons. This newfound confidence may come in many forms. It may manifest as recognition of our own personal ecospiritual power, greater knowledge or insight, or even reconciliation with a loved one or another ally. Whatever form the Ultimate Boon chooses to take in your life, take a moment to appreciate how far you've come. The journey is now halfway over, and the final phase is about to begin.

11.2 The Ultimate Boon - Vision Quest

What is your own true nature? What is your mission in life? What is your journey to True Self? One way to answer these questions is to undertake a vision quest.

The vision quest is a time-honored rite of passage common to shamanic tribes throughout the world. It is used to determine life's purpose. The vision quest may take on many forms, but for this activity we will be using the form of the vigil.

To perform your own vision quest, first find a place that calls out to you. It may be your own sacred space, or some other place that feels full of energy to you. Make sure it is a place that you will be undisturbed for the duration of the vigil. Dress in comfortable, loose-fitting clothing. You may wish to take a blanket with you to ward off the chill night air if you are planning to stay overnight and make sure that the place you have chosen is a safe place, free of predators of the four-legged, or two-legged, variety. If you are doing this activity as part of an ecospirituality program, your instructor may have already selected a place for this activity.

When you have arrived at your sacred space, first ask permission to use the space, then make an offering to the place and express your gratitude for being able to use the space for your quest. Next, sit or stand comfortably and ground and center yourself. Do this in a place where you will be comfortable but alert for the duration of the vigil.

You may wish to perform a mindful meditation like mindful breathing or the Tree of Life meditation prior to starting your vigil. If you play any instruments like drums or flutes, you may make music a part of your vigil. Some ecospirituality groups use drum circles for this purpose. The rhythm of the music helps to induce trancelike meditative states that are conducive to vision seeking.

It may help to build a campfire or to light a candle to give you a center of focus as you ground and center.

* Once you feel you are ready, ask the Universe to reveal your life purpose to you, and wait for a reply. Sometimes this reply may come as a vision, or a dream, or just as a feeling in your spirit, or as an omen. Stay alert for the duration of the vigil, and greet the conclusion of the rite with open acceptance.

11.3 Preparation for the Vision Quest

To prepare for your vision quest, spend as much of the day prior as possible in quiet contemplation and meditation on your life's purpose and mission. Even if you feel you already have a good understanding about the meaning and purpose of your life, the vision quest may help you to clarify the details, so greet the experience with an open and accepting attitude.

How will your life's purpose be revealed to you? Look for messages from the environment. Do the trees speak to you? Are you visited by any animals? A visit from your totem animal would be especially powerful during a vision quest. Don't forget to look for omens as well. These can be especially powerful in determining your future, since they come from your unconscious mind. And since your dreams, visions, and omens come from you and to you and you alone, nobody else can tell you what they mean but you. There is no "right" or "wrong" message you can receive in a vision quest as long as the message has meaning for you.

11.4 The Vision Quest

The five phases of your Vision Quest are as follows:

1. *Preparation*: Find your sacred space for the Vision Quest and prepare yourself by first asking permission of the spirits or energies there to use the place for your intended purpose. Wait for a reply. When you feel that permission has been given, make an offering in the form of a bit of bread, or some seeds for the local wildlife, or a libation of ale, wine, fruit juice or other potable poured on the ground there to express your gratitude. If you sense that permission has not been given, then put off your Vision Quest until another day.

2. *Separation*: A Vision Quest is a vigil that must be accomplished alone. While your friends, family or pets may accompany you to the site, once the Vision Quest has begun they should leave you alone with the spirit of the location. Make sure that everyone understands this before you begin, so that you are not interrupted. If you are participating in the Vision Quest with an ecospirituality group, your instructor will have all members of the group go off some distance from everyone else so that you may all enjoy isolation for purposes of contemplation.

3. *Isolation*: Once you are alone, sit or stand comfortably and ground and center yourself. You may wish to perform a meditation as you prepare yourself to receive what your chosen site will be sending to you this night. Although this rite is called a "vision" quest, remain open to what all of your senses may be telling you. What sounds, smells, or other physical sensations might you be getting that could be interpreted as a message about your life's purpose? It may help

to build a campfire or to light a candle to give you a center of focus.

4. *Assimilation*: Once you feel you are ready, ask the Universe to reveal your life purpose to you, and wait for a reply. Sometimes this reply may come as a vision, or a dream, or just as a feeling in your spirit. Stay awake all night if possible, and greet the dawn with open acceptance. If you are not able to stay for the night, just remain alert and open for the time you have to complete the quest. Look for messages from the environment. Do the trees speak to you? Are you visited by any animals? Did you receive any omens? A visit from your totem animal would be especially powerful at this time.

5. *Interpretation*: The magical thing about a Vision Quest is that any message you receive is yours, and yours alone. So how you choose to interpret the omens is totally up to you. When your life's mission is revealed, greet the dawn and offer thanks. If your mission is not revealed, try again at another time, after preparing yourself by a period of meditation, fasting, and thanksgiving.

Once you have completed your vision quest, go on to the next page and complete the Reflections on My Vision Quest exercise.

Worksheet 11.4 Reflections on My Vision Quest

Name _____ Date _____

Now that you have completed your Vision Quest, reflect on its meaning and how it has helped you to achieve the Ultimate Boon by answering the questions below.

Was your life's mission and purpose revealed to you on your Vision Quest?   Yes | No

If your answer to the above was "yes," describe the message you received below. If the answer was "no," why do you think your life's mission was not revealed to you?

_____
_____
_____
_____
_____

How might what you experienced on your Vision Quest help you to live more fully according to your own true nature in True Self?

_____
_____
_____
_____
_____

How did your Vision Quest help you to achieve your own Ultimate Boon? In other words, how did it clarify who you are and what you want your life to be about from this day forward?

_____
_____
_____
_____
_____
_____

WORKSHEET 11.4 REFLECTIONS ON MY VISION QUEST   PAGE 2 OF 3

Name _____ Date _____

Who or what came to you during your Vision Quest? An animal totem? An omen? A friend or family member? Did anyone at all show up? If so, what is the meaning of your relationship with this person or entity? If nobody showed up, did anything else of significance occur during your Vision Quest?

_____
_____
_____
_____
_____

Did you see, hear, taste, smell or feel anything that was of personal significance to you? If so, what was it? If not, what did you learn about your own thoughts, feelings and internal states?

_____
_____
_____
_____
_____
_____
_____

If something of significance occurred, when did it happen? Was it towards the beginning of your quest, towards the middle, or towards the end? What message might you interpret from the time that your event happened?

_____
_____
_____
_____
_____
_____

WORKSHEET 11.4 REFLECTIONS ON MY VISION QUEST   PAGE 3 OF 3

Name _____ Date _____

Where specifically did your event occur? Was it in front of you? Behind you? Over your left or right shoulder? Above your head? Below you? What interpretation might you give to the place where your event occurred? If nothing occurred, what interpretation might you give to this?

_____
_____
_____
_____
_____
_____
_____
_____

If you saw an omen, how did it make its presence known? What about it attracted your attention? If you feel that nothing happened during your Vision Quest, is it possible that you may have missed something? Even the smallest events can be omens.

_____
_____
_____
_____
_____
_____
_____
_____

Why did you get the message you received? What is its significance to you?

_____
_____
_____
_____
_____
_____
_____

Phase Three: Return

In the Return Phase, the hero has gained wisdom about the nature of reality and consciousness, and is now faced with the challenge of returning to the world to teach those who are willing to listen. It is the process of coming home with the Holy Grail. It is the act of bringing the Ten Commandments down off the mountaintop. It is the skill of helping others to achieve what the hero has achieved, while avoiding the temptation to turn them into carbon copies of himself. For a spiritual seeker, this means applying lessons learned in the spiritual realm to daily life. It means learning to see the bigger picture and to trust the vision.

Session 12 Refusal of the Return

With his tail ablaze from the sacred fire, Coyote ran for many miles. As he ran, feeling the pain from his burning tail, he thought about all of the things he had experienced on the journey so far. He especially thought of Coyote Woman. She seemed so different at the fire circle than she had when he had met her on the trail.

How could this be?

While he ran, the answer came to him. Like himself, Coyote Woman was a Trickster. What if, when he met her on the trail, she was playing a prank of her own? What if, when she had abandoned him on the trail, she had done so in order to goad him into completing his journey?

As he pondered this he began to smile. The Trickster had been tricked again. He had been given another dose of his own medicine. But Coyote Woman had played her tricks to teach him and to lead him to complete the quest.

With this thought, he stopped running. Exhausted, he flopped down in the snow, breathing heavily. He had come to rest on the side of a mountain with a clear view of the valley below him. The fire from the sacred circle still burned brightly at the tip of his tail, but the pain was now diminishing to a warm glow. It was uncomfortable, but it was not unbearable.

As he rested, Coyote thought about how each creature in his Tribe lived according to his nature. Brother Eagle was a stern hunter and visionary who saw far, so he lived a serious life. Brother Bear was strong and knew the herbs, so he lived a life of ease and healing. Sister Cougar was crafty and wise, and lived the solitary life of the hunter. Sister Salmon was quick and sleek, and lived a busy life jumping from stream to stream.

But Coyote was playful and mischievous, so he spent his days running to and fro about the earth playing tricks on all the other People.

He rested his chin upon his paws as he thought of how he had managed to steal the fire. He had tried all of his usual tricks, but Coyote Woman had seen right through them. Yet when he embraced his own nature as a Trickster, and trusted his own instincts, he was able to find a solution, even though painful. When he closed his eyes and leaped backward into the fire, he had become who he was born to be.

Coyote mulled over his choices. He really should be going soon. He wasn't sure how long the fire on his tail would continue to burn, and he still had a long way to go to bring the fire back to his own tribe.

On the other hand, it felt good just to lie here in the snow. Although the icy ground was cold, the warmth from the fire on his tail was keeping him cozy, helping him to find balance between the fire and the ice.

As Coyote began to regain his breath, he pondered what he saw at Coyote Woman's Village of the Sacred Fire. All of the animals there

were warm and happy despite the chill of winter. They all danced before the flame in their joy. They truly seemed to live a life of ease.

It was so tempting to return to that place. While the return home was long and arduous, Coyote could, if he chose, simply return to Coyote Woman's village and join them forever. There would be no need to face the perils of the road back to his own village. He had found what he was looking for. He had captured the sacred flame. If he didn't return then the People of his own village might freeze to death, but was that really his concern? How would it benefit him personally to bring the fire back to his People, when he could instead just return to Coyote Woman's village, give them their fire back, and beg forgiveness? Perhaps they might even take him into their tribe as a member!

12.0 Refusal of the Return - Nature as Metaphor

We have now come to the third major phase of the Way of the Coyote: The Return. In Phase One, the Departure, we left the familiar to forge a new trail through unknown territory. In Phase Two, the Initiation, we learned to die to the old way of being so that we could live in a new way, with spiritual eyes and spiritual body. Now, in Phase Three, we learn what it means to return from the Otherworld with the knowledge we have gained. But first we must overcome the Refusal of the Return.

When you have tasted the milk and honey of Paradise, why would you want to leave? Once you've journeyed to that place at the center of your being where your True Self dwells, it can be intoxicating. When you've experienced the knowledge of your own perfection, it can be difficult to summon the energy to return to an imperfect world. When you've experienced the bliss of living fully according to your own true nature as the person you were meant to be, it's tempting to think that the journey is over. It can be an enticing thought to wish to stay in the Village of the Sacred Fire, to retreat from the world and to live alone.

We might also be tempted to forget that many others have helped us to this place. What if they had chosen to remain in their own versions of paradise instead of teaching others how to achieve what they have accomplished themselves? Would we have ever found the trail without the guidance of those who had been here before?

It has been said that we don't truly know a subject until we begin to teach it to others. The best way to truly experience living in True Self is to teach others how to do the same. By teaching others we are able to give back to the world while gaining an even deeper understanding of the path.

On the other hand, there is the difficulty of trying to communicate our wisdom to others who have not had the same experience. We will lack a common frame of reference because we have not walked the same path. Once our perceptions have been transformed along the journey to True Self and we learn to see things in new ways and speak a new language of the spirit, it can feel like it's impossible to communicate with those who haven't learned the same language.

Plato's Cave Allegory

In Plato's Cave Allegory, the Seeker learns to see beyond the illusions we live by and into the real nature of things. In the Cave, these illusions take the form of shadows projected on a wall. The shadows are of people and animals. The shadows are not the people or animals; they are merely an illusion and a projection of the real people behind the shadows. In Plato's Cave, the Seeker sees the real people and animals behind the shadows for the first time. But when he tries to explain the concept of real creatures to the others in the cave, who can see only the shadows, they cannot understand what he means. They lack a common frame of reference.

A return to the "real" world of shadows after living for a time in the world of true substance can be a frustrating experience, especially if you hope to share your newfound wisdom with others. Because of this, it is easy to refuse the return, especially if you have attained your own personal paradise along your journey.

But if we never return, we can never share the wisdom we've gained. We can never reach the deeper understanding of the path that comes from teaching it to others. We can become trapped in Xanadu, never to return, and never to help others achieve the same bliss.

How do we resist the temptation to refuse the return? One way to do so is through the use of *Nature as Metaphor*.

12.1 Nature as Metaphor

Fairy tales were used in the past, and are sometimes still used today, as teaching tools (for a great example of a fairy tale being used as a teaching tool in the modern world, see Robert Bly's book, *Iron John*). These stories often contained moral lessons. Another thing most fairy tales contain is archetypal images and elements of nature. Think of your favorite fairy tale. What are the elements of nature in it? Does the fact that it is your favorite fairy tale have anything to do with those elements of nature? Are those elements good like the Goose that Laid the Golden Egg, or bad, like the Big Bad Wolf, or neutral like the beanstalk in Jack and the Beanstalk? What does your fondness for those particular elements of your fairy tale tell you about yourself?

Are there any archetypal elements to your story?

Each of us lives in our own personal fairy tale called "my life." We all have good things that happen to us, and we all have bad things that happen to us. We create our own personal myths by choosing which things to focus on in our own lives. The good news about the myth of our lives is that we are the authors. So if we don't like the way the story is going, we have the power to do a rewrite at any time. We can't always choose the circumstances of our lives, but we can always choose the story we create about those circumstances.

If you go out into the woods and start observing things, you will notice something begin to happen. You will begin to create stories about the events you observe there in the forest.

I remember once when I watched a flock of crows defending their turf against a hawk. I had created personalities for each of the crows, and for the hawk. Before I knew it, I had created back story for each of the characters, and dialogue for the major players. I had watched this show for about ten minutes before I realized that the story I had created in my mind told me a lot more about what was going on inside my own head than what was happening with the birds.

The next time you are able to observe nature for a time, pay attention to what sort of stories come to mind. What could it be that your unconscious mind is trying to tell you? Can you see nature as a metaphor for your own inner journey? To practice the art of observing nature as a metaphor for your own life, go on to the next page and complete the exercise, *A Closer Look*.

WORKSHEET 12.1 A CLOSER LOOK

Name _____ Date _____

This exercise will help you to gain practice in seeing nature as a metaphor. These skills help us to live more fully in True Self by helping us to observe our own inner dialogs and to describe them to ourselves. In this exercise you will observe and describe an experience in nature.

INSTRUCTIONS

You may wish to purchase a Hula Hoop™ or similar toy before trying this exercise.

Weather permitting; go outside on the lawn in a park, your backyard, or other natural area. If you have a toy hoop, place it on the ground in front of you, and sit down on the grass. If you don't have a hoop, mark off an area about 3 feet in diameter with a rope, or by drawing a circle, or by just using your imagination. Now imagine that the entire world is contained within that hoop. See yourself as an artist, about to paint or draw everything you see inside that hoop. At first you may see nothing but blades of grass, but as you pay more attention you may begin to notice how no two blades are different. Each is pointing in a different direction, and each is a slightly different color, texture, and shape. You may notice the soil beneath as well. What color is it? Is it fine or grainy? Do you see any insects in the little world you have created? If so, what are they doing? Are there any stories unfolding in your little patch of grass? Pay attention to what you see before you for at least ten minutes. Shift your attention to what you see, hear, smell, taste, and feel as you sit on the grass. When your time is up, write your response below.

RESPONSE

Write a description of what you saw in the grass. Think of it as a story, from "Once upon a time" to "…and they all lived happily ever after." Imagine you are now documenting the story in the section below. What story did you see unfolding in the grass? Use extra paper if necessary to write your story.

_____
_____
_____
_____
_____
_____
_____
_____
_____
_____
_____
_____

12.2 Reflections on a Closer Look

The story you just created in the *Closer Look* exercise can be seen as a metaphor for your own inner journey.

The idea of living in True Self is that it creates a lasting paradigm shift where we are able to expand our vision and see the bigger picture. Such a change of perspective is a way of changing the way we see the world so that the Refusal of the Return becomes insignificant. The Closer Look exercise can help to achieve this by using our observations and descriptions of nature as a window into our own souls.

The first step in achieving such change is to achieve beginner's mind. Beginner's mind is a way to look at the world anew with a sense of childlike wonder. It is a way of freeing ourselves from the assumptions we have made about the way the world works. If those assumptions are leading us to consequences in our lives that we don't want to experience, the way to change those consequences is to challenge those assumptions that are leading to consequences we don't want.

What assumptions may you have been making that might be creating a barrier to your intention of living fully in your True Self? How might you re-examine those assumptions, using beginner's mind, to see the world in a new way? How might your new vision of the world remove those barriers? How might moving beyond your own Refusal of the Return help you to live more fully in True Self?

Read over the story you created in the *Closer Look* exercise. Now imagine that story as a metaphor for your observations and descriptions of what is going on inside your own mind. See the story you created as a metaphor for your own inner journey as you complete the *Reflections on a Closer Look* activity on the next pages.

Worksheet 12.2 Reflections on A Closer Look

Name_____Date_____

After completing the Closer Look exercise, did you notice any common themes in your observations? Read over the questions below, and write your answers in the spaces provided. Were your observations more about what you saw, or about your own internal state?

_____
_____
_____

If it was more about what you saw, how do these observations relate to your thoughts and feelings?

_____
_____
_____

If it was more about your own internal state, did you discover anything about your assumptions about the workings of your own thoughts and feelings?

_____
_____
_____

Did you engage any of your other senses during the activity? If so, how?

_____
_____
_____

Did you write anything about what you heard?

_____
_____
_____

Did you write anything about what you smelled?

_____
_____
_____

WORKSHEET 12.2 REFLECTIONS ON A CLOSER LOOK   PAGE 2 OF 4

Name_____ Date_____

Did you write anything about what you tasted?
_____
_____
_____

Did you write anything about what you felt (touch, hot, cold, etc.)?
_____
_____
_____

Did you write anything about what you felt emotionally?
_____
_____
_____

Did you write anything about your thoughts?
_____
_____
_____

How do these observations about your own inner experience of the Closer Look exercise relate to what you observed on the ground? In other words, what does your response to the Closer Look exercise tell you about your own inner states?
_____
_____
_____
_____
_____
_____
_____
_____

Worksheet 12.2 Reflections on A Closer Look

Name_____Date_____

Did you find yourself inventing stories about what you saw on the ground?   Yes | No
If so, what can these stories tell you about how you see your own True Self? If not, what did you write?

_____
_____
_____
_____
_____

How did you feel before this exercise? After?

BEFORE

_____
_____
_____

AFTER

_____
_____
_____

Did you use one sense more than others to record your observations (e.g., seeing more than hearing)?

_____
_____
_____

If your observations relied more on one sense than others, how might this experience change if you relied on another sense (e.g., hearing rather than seeing)?

_____
_____
_____
_____

WORKSHEET 12.2 REFLECTIONS ON A CLOSER LOOK

Name_____Date_____

If you focused primarily on observing the natural world during this experience, how might it change if you paid more attention to your own internal state (thoughts and feelings) instead?

_____
_____
_____
_____

If you focused primarily on your own inner state, how might this experience change if you focused more on the natural world?

_____
_____
_____
_____

What did you learn about your True Self and how it relates to the natural world?

_____
_____
_____
_____
_____

Did you learn anything about your assumptions about how the world works? If so, describe the lesson:

_____
_____
_____
_____
_____
_____

12.3 A Closer Look Inside

If we are able to make the paradigm shift from viewing nature as something separate from ourselves, to viewing nature as a part of us, we are better able to re-integrate and to reconnect with the natural world. From this perspective, we are able to gain the knowledge that we are nature, and nature is us. This means that if we find ourselves in Refusal of the Return, we are refusing ourselves by refusing all of nature.

Sometimes those of us who work with ecology and environmentalism like to draw a line between humans and the rest of nature. In doing so we continue to foster the myth that humans and nature are two different things; that humans are not a part of nature.

In the *Reflections on a Closer Look* exercise on the previous pages, it is hopefully made clear that the line we often draw between nature and ourselves is an imaginary line. No such distinction between humans and nature actually exists. In this exercise we are using a small patch of nature to observe and describe our own inner states. The *Closer Look* exercise allows us to use nature as a metaphor for our own inner emotional and spiritual states.

But what if this is a two-way street? What if nature herself could use us as a metaphor? Does nature learn from us and communicate with us in the same way that we learn from her and communicate with her? What if a two-way communication with nature were possible? What if we could use the metaphors we have constructed as a way of connecting to nature?

In the *Closer Look Inside* exercise on the next pages, we will explore communicating with nature through metaphor.

As you complete the *Closer Look Inside* questions, reflect back on the story you created during *the Closer Look* exercise, and to your responses to the questions in the *Reflections on a Closer Look* exercise. Viewing the story you created as a metaphor for your own personal journey to True Self, examine the details of your narrative for clues that might help you to remove your barriers to Crossing the Return Threshold. In other words, look for details in your story that might indicate your own Refusal of the Return. In what ways might you be clinging to the idea of isolating yourself and not teaching what you have learned?

For example, suppose that in your *Closer Look* story you wrote the following: "I saw an inchworm on a blade of grass, struggling to get to the next blade of grass."

Could that sentence be a metaphor for something you are struggling with inside of yourself? If so, how might you remove the barriers that you are struggling with so that you are more freely able to connect with nature, with others, and with your True Self? How might this wisdom help you to cross the return threshold?

Sometimes when I do the *Closer Look* exercises with groups, there are people who don't create a story. These people usually write things like, "I saw a bunch of green grass with several ants, and a few ladybugs." Their responses to the exercise are heavy on observing and describing, but short on narrative content. If your responses to the exercise were of a similar nature, it could be that you have learned to see the world just as it is, without assumptions or perception filters.

Sometimes, however, such observational descriptions of the exercise, without any narrative elements, can be a way of avoiding the inner journey. In such a case, the person may be evading the story elements as a defense mechanism to keep from revealing too much to others or to self. This resistance itself might be a metaphor for the Refusal of the Return.

If you think that you may be doing this, just honestly ask yourself if you are doing so to avoid connecting with your True Self. You're your own best expert on your own inner state, so this is a question that only you can answer. If you are satisfied that the answer to this question is, "no," then go on to the next section, *A Closer Look Inside*.

If the answer to the question, "Did I avoid telling a story because I wanted to avoid describing my own inner journey?" is "yes," then you may wish to go back and try the exercise again.

So what if you truly are not avoiding a narrative in order to avoid connecting with your True Self, but you just wrote a description of your observations with no story elements?

In that case, you may still continue on to the *Closer Look Inside* exercise. If you did not include any story elements, and you are not trying to avoid connecting to your True Self, then simply writing a description of everything you saw in the *Closer Look* exercise means that you can see the world in a non-judgmental fashion, without assumptions. You may use these skills to help you to answer the questions in the *Closer Look Inside* exercise that follows.

WORKSHEET 12.3 A CLOSER LOOK INSIDE

PAGE 1 OF 3

Name _____ Date _____

Are you struggling with your own Refusal of the Return? This refusal manifests itself in resistance to the idea of serving others by sharing the knowledge gained while walking the Way of the Coyote. Think about your own Refusal of the Return while answering the following questions.

What is the exact nature of this barrier? Physical or mental? Why?

_____
_____
_____
_____
_____
_____

Is this barrier a permanent refusal, or a temporary one? Why?

_____
_____
_____
_____
_____
_____

Is this barrier a pervasive one, touching all aspects of your life, or is it a situation-specific one, touching only one or a few areas of your life?

_____
_____
_____
_____
_____
_____

WORKSHEET 12.3 A CLOSER LOOK INSIDE PAGE **2** OF **3**

Name _____ Date _____

Is this barrier a personal one, having something exclusively to do with you, or is it something external to you?

_____
_____
_____
_____
_____

Is this barrier something you can change, or is it something you have to accept?

_____
_____
_____
_____
_____

Is this barrier something you have control over?

_____
_____
_____
_____
_____

Is this barrier something you can re-frame in order to turn it into aid to connection?

_____
_____
_____
_____
_____

Now visualize yourself drawing a circle around this barrier in your own mind.
Allow yourself to move from Doing Mode into Being Mode. Simply observe what's going on inside of this imaginary circle you've drawn around your barrier to Crossing the Return Threshold. Write down any observations about it in the exercise on the next page.

WORKSHEET 12.3 A CLOSER LOOK INSIDE

PAGE 3 OF 3

Name _____ Date _____

In your mind you've drawn an imaginary circle around your number one barrier to connection. This is the one thing that tempts you to the Refusal of the Return, keeping you from Crossing the Return Threshold. Observe it from Being Mode for a few minutes, and write down any observations you get from your thoughts, feelings, memories or senses about this Refusal of the Return Remember that the Refusal of the Return most often manifests in a desire to be separate from nature. It is embodied in the idea that you are not a part of the natural world, and therefore have no obligation to serve others or the natural world.

Prior to doing this, you may wish to ground and center yourself. It may help to engage in a brief mindful meditation before beginning.

Use the space below to note your observations.

_____
_____
_____
_____
_____
_____
_____
_____
_____
_____
_____
_____
_____
_____
_____
_____
_____
_____
_____
_____

12.4 Nature as Metaphor for True Self

The more time we spend in nature, the more we come to realize that we are not separate from nature, and nature is not separate from us. This realization is a Crossing of the Return Threshold in itself. It is a paradigm shift of the mind. When we come to see ourselves as a part of everything that exists, and realize that everything that exists is also a part of us, we can never go back to our old ways of thinking that lead us to believe that we are something separate from, and apart from, nature. We cannot see ourselves as separate and apart from others. Most importantly, we cannot be separate from ourselves. When we come to this wisdom, we have conquered the Refusal of the Return.

This revelation usually comes when we are able to achieve beginner's mind, setting aside our old assumptions about the way the world works, and about our places in it. The western industrialized world has taught us that we are "civilized" beings separate from the wildness of nature, but in beginner's mind we can return to that childlike sense of wonder of the natural world and enjoy the beauty of a sunset or the melody of a mountain stream.

From beginner's mind we are able to ask ourselves what we truly value in this world, and in this life. How much of what I'm worried about today will matter in five years? In ten? How much of what I'm worried about today involves the accumulation of material possessions? How much of it involves my relationship with the natural world, including my friends, my family, and myself? When we are able to determine the answers to these questions for ourselves, we can use our power of intention to move closer to the people we want to be, using nature as our guide.

When we achieve this unity with nature we are able to begin to see nature as a metaphor for our own stories. We are a part of nature, and nature is a part of us. We are on this journey together. When we accept nature into the narrative of our lives, we have moved one step closer to living in True Self, and we will be ready to cross the return threshold.

Session 13 The Magic Flight

As coyote lay there on the side of the mountain, lost in fantasies of returning to Coyote Woman's village, he heard a noise off in the distance like the sound of many animals running. This stirred him from his quiet contemplation and he looked down into the valley to see a whole herd of animals from Coyote Woman's tribe heading in his direction. She was leading them, stopping from time to time to sniff the ground in order to pick up Coyote's scent. While they were still some distance away, they would be upon him before nightfall.

Still weary from his journey, Coyote arose and ran down the other side of the mountain to escape. Seeing a shallow creek before him, he jumped in and walked its length for a while to mask his scent from his pursuers.

The instant his paws touched the icy water he shivered and nearly leapt out again, but after a moment he gathered his will and his wits and forced himself to continue on, taking care not to let his flaming tail dip into the water.

As he ran through the freezing water of the creek, his body gradually became accustomed to the cold and after a time he found it invigorating, giving him energy he didn't knew he had. This newfound energy spurred him on.

13.0 Resurrection

> *"If the hero in his triumph wins the blessing of the goddess or the god and is then explicitly commissioned to return to the world with some elixir for the restoration of society, the final stage of his adventure is supported by all the powers of his supernatural patron. On the other hand, if the trophy has been attained against the opposition of its guardian, or if the hero's wish to return to the world has been resented by the gods or demons, then the last stage of the mythological round becomes a lively, often comical, pursuit. This flight may be complicated by marvels of magical obstruction and evasion."*
>
> --Joseph Campbell

This stage in the Hero's journey is a counterpoint to the Call to Adventure. In that leg of the journey the hero had to cross the first threshold. In this part of the adventure the Magic Flight is undertaken in order to cross the return threshold. The Magic Flight consists of defeating the gatekeeper who guards the way home. The must return home with the Ultimate Boon but this time the anticipation of danger is replaced with visions of sanctuary, the warmth and love of home, and perhaps vindication from those who doubted the hero in the first place.

For the spiritual seeker who walks the Way of the Coyote, the Magic Flight may consist of letting go of forms of spirituality that are no longer meaningful. In ecospirituality, "spirit" simply means "that which inspires." So a spiritual path in ecospirituality is one that inspires. Clinging to forms of spirituality that no longer provide a sense of wonder and awe about our places in the universe can be a type of Refusal of Return. If you find yourself stuck in a spiritual path that is no longer inspiring, you may be in need of the Magic Flight.

The Magic Flight leads to resurrection because it breathes new life into old, dead spiritual paths. It is a re-awakening, or a "revival," if you prefer, that leads to renewed vigor and inspiration. How do we know if we are in need of a Magic Flight? Maybe this story will help to illustrate.

One warm spring day many decades ago I was at a lake with a woman I was dating at the time. We were having a picnic by the lake. She'd brought along her collection of talismans and other New Age paraphernalia and was busily trying to read portents in a deck of Tarot cards. Unfortunately, she had the habit of consulting the deck for every little aspect of her life to the point that it was almost an obsessive-compulsive disorder. It's fine to see portents from time to time, but she couldn't seem to see anything else.

As we sat there enjoying our lunch, she was dealing out her Tarot cards and obsessing over them to the exclusion of all else, missing the joy of the forest surrounding us. Suddenly a cardinal appeared on a tree branch just above our heads. Seeing an opportunity for yet another omen, she looked up at the bird and said, "Hi, do you have a message for me?"

The bird, in response, cocked her head sideways and dumped a prodigious load of excrement right onto her head.

I laughed, looked at her and said, "There's your message."

Spirituality is only good when it isn't taken too seriously. If you find yourself in a space where the tools have become more important than the message, then you may benefit from the Magic Flight.

In the Return Phase of our journey, the hero has gained wisdom about the nature of reality and consciousness, and is now faced with the challenge of returning to the world to teach those who are willing to listen. It is the process of coming home with the Holy Grail. It is the act of bringing the Ten Commandments down off the mountaintop. It is the act of helping others to achieve what the hero has achieved, while avoiding the temptation to turn them into carbon copies of himself. For a spiritual seeker, this means applying lessons learned in the spiritual realm to daily life. It means learning to see the bigger picture and to trust the vision. In ecospirituality, it is gaining the wisdom that we are not separate from nature, and that we are all one. It is the realization that in helping others I help myself.

In most hero stories the Magic Flight is the climax in which the hero (or heroine) must have the final and most dangerous encounter with death. It is Arthur confronting Mordred. It is Moses fighting for the Promised Land. It is Luke Skywalker confronting Darth Vader. The final battle also represents something far greater than the hero's own existence. It is a world-changing event. Its outcome will have far-reaching consequences to the world he left behind and is now re-entering. Once the Magic Flight is undertaken, things can never go back to the way they were before. The hero has learned a new way of seeing and being in the world.

If she fails in her quest, it is not just she who will suffer. All of the members of her tribe who were left behind when she took up the journey will suffer too. But if she succeeds, the Magic Flight will lead her to victory and she will be reborn as the Master of Two Worlds.

13.1 Magic: Confidence in One's True Nature

When I was a child, about seven years old, I dreamed of King Arthur and Merlin. In my childhood sense of awe and mystery, I wished to be a wizard studying under Merlin at Camelot. I remember one Thanksgiving when I was awarded the wishbone from the turkey. My sister and I made a wish, and I got the winning end.

What I wished for was a castle. After I made my wish I ran outside, expecting to find a castle in the back yard. In the childish wonderment of youth, I was actually disappointed when I didn't find one.

We lived in the country back then, on a 400 acre farm owned by my grandfather. As I walked down the dirt road trying to hide my disappointment, I looked into the field next door to my family's house. There was a grove of trees in the middle of the field. The grove had been covered over with kudzu. I'd seen that grove hundreds of times, but this time I saw it with new eyes. Something about the way the kudzu grew on the tallest trees looked like a castle turret. As I looked again, I began to see a fortress wall. The more I looked, the more my imagination transformed the kudzu into a castle. Right there before my eyes, my imagination had allowed my wish to come true!

To me, this is how all magic works. We don't do magic to affect change in our external environment. We do magic to create change within ourselves. The rituals and tools of the shaman work to evoke change within us so that we may see things in a new way. The magic is always there, all around us. We simply have to change ourselves in order to be able to see it. If the way we've been seeing things is causing us to feel stress, or pain, or worry, then magic is the means by which we may heal ourselves so that we may begin to see the world in ways that do not hurt us.

What this ultimately means is that magic is confidence in self. As we become more accustomed to living according to our own true nature, we grow in the confidence that this is the correct way to live. It is a solution-focused approach that draws upon the power of intention.

We can talk about problems all day, but nothing gets solved until we start talking about solutions. To start talking about solutions, we may draw upon the power of intention by asking ourselves two questions:

1. What am I trying to accomplish with my life?

2. Is what I'm doing, thinking, feeling and believing helping me to accomplish this mission?

When we shift our thinking to a solution-focused approach, we create magic in the world for ourselves and for others. This magic, or sense of wonder, is what will allow us to successfully complete the Magic Flight.

13.2 Ancestral Magic

Our ancestors knew hundreds of medicinal uses of local plants and herbs. They knew the seasons, when to plant, when to harvest, how to forecast the weather by the behavior of plants and animals, and a host of other things based on their observations of nature. The lessons our ancestors learned haven't gone away. They're still there, waiting in the forest like an open book. All we have to do is to learn how to read it.

Before the advent of the written word, our ancestors had no books from which to learn; no sacred texts from which to grow their spirituality, and no written history of their peoples. Nature was their sacred text. They studied the forest in the way that we study books today.

Think about applying the power of intention to your studies of nature. Can you see the day-to-day changes in the trees as they grow through the seasons? What could you learn about the medicinal properties of the trees by paying closer attention to them? What can you learn about the qualities of each tree by studying it? Do different trees have different personalities? What can you learn about your own personality by studying the trees?

The more you increase your knowledge of nature by spending time in it and studying it, the more "magic" you gain. From this perspective, "magic" is simply the sense of awe and wonder we get from the beauty to be found in nature. This inspirational sense is the key to the Magic Flight that allows us to seek ecospirituality.

13.3 Animal as Teacher: My Own Animal Legend

If you look at the myths, legends and stories of indigenous peoples, you won't have to look far to find that animals are used quite often as teaching tools. Remember Aesop's Fables? Most of those parables involved animals. Likewise, many of our fairy tales, from Goldilocks and the Three Bears to the Three Little Pigs, involve animals.

You don't have to be a shaman in order to use animals as teaching tools. You already have within you volumes of knowledge on animals and their characteristics. You can draw on these traits to create your own personal stories and legends, just as you draw on the archetypal energy of your own spirit animal.

The *My Own Animal Legend* exercise on the next pages is a method to use the knowledge within you as a way to teach others and yourself. The information and wisdom gained by completing this exercise will help you to gain the magic and the inspiration necessary to achieve your own Magic Flight.

To complete this exercise, first answer the questions provided, then go on to use that information to create your own Animal Legend. Don't worry too much about being elaborate in your creativity. If the story comes from your own heart, it will be a good one.

It's best to complete this exercise outdoors if possible. Use your own sacred space for this purpose, or if you are completing this workbook as part of an ecospirituality program, your instructor may have a place prepared for you. Call upon your own power animal when completing the questions. It may also help to have any personal talismans nearby so you may draw upon their energy when doing the exercise.

Worksheet 13.3 My Own Animal Legend

Name _____ Date_____

We're going to create a story about animals. These animals will be metaphorical for people you know, or people you'd like to know. First answer the questions below, then go on to the next page to create your own story.

If you were an animal, what sort of animal would you be?

_____
_____
_____

Why did you choose this animal?

_____
_____
_____
_____
_____
_____
_____
_____

Think of some people you'd like to include in your Animal Legend. They can either be real or imagined people, living or dead. Think of them as animals, and list them below. You don't have to use all the spaces provided. Just include enough characters for your story to be interesting to you.

Person	Animal Representing this Person
_____	_____
_____	_____
_____	_____
_____	_____
_____	_____

WORKSHEET 13.3 MY OWN ANIMAL LEGEND PAGE 2 OF 6

Name _____ Date _____

For each animal listed above, describe what they are doing in the story:

_____
_____
_____
_____
_____
_____
_____
_____
_____
_____
_____

The animal represented by you is looking for something. What is he/she looking for?

_____
_____
_____
_____
_____

Describe the place in which these animals live:

_____
_____
_____
_____
_____
_____
_____

WORKSHEET 13.3 MY OWN ANIMAL LEGEND

Name _____ Date _____

The animal representing you is going on a journey to find the thing they are looking for. Where is it that you are going?

_____
_____
_____
_____
_____
_____
_____

Something (or someone…possibly one of the animals from the story) is trying to prevent you from reaching your goal. Who or what is it? Why are they trying to keep you from your goal?

_____
_____
_____
_____
_____
_____
_____

There are many trials on your journey, but you finally manage to reach your destination. What happens when you get there?

_____
_____
_____
_____
_____
_____
_____
_____

WORKSHEET 13.3 MY OWN ANIMAL LEGEND PAGE 4 OF 6

Name _____ Date_____

Once you've reached your destination and achieved your goal, you have to return home. What happens on the trip home?

_____
_____
_____
_____
_____
_____
_____
_____

During this journey, you encounter the other animals from above. What are they doing? Are they helping or hindering you on your journey? Why?

_____
_____
_____
_____
_____
_____
_____
_____
_____

Which animal(s) are helping you on your journey? Why?

_____
_____
_____
_____
_____
_____
_____
_____
_____

WORKSHEET 13.3 MY OWN ANIMAL LEGEND

Name _____ Date _____

Which animal(s) are hindering you on your journey? Why?

_____
_____
_____
_____
_____
_____
_____
_____

You've finally arrived home again. What happens when you get there?

_____
_____
_____
_____
_____
_____
_____
_____

What will be the moral of your story?

_____
_____
_____
_____
_____

Now go on to the next page, and write your story out, based on the information provided above. In first blank on the next page, write the name of the animal that represents you in the story.

WORKSHEET 13.3 MY OWN ANIMAL LEGEND

Name _____ Date _____

Once upon a time, there was a _____ who…

_____
_____
_____
_____
_____
_____
_____
_____
_____
_____
_____
_____
_____
_____
_____
_____
_____
_____
_____
_____
_____
_____
_____

(Use more paper if necessary to complete your story)

DON'T GO ON TO THE NEXT SECTION UNTIL YOU'VE FINISHED YOUR STORY!

WORKSHEET 13.3A LESSONS FROM MY OWN ANIMAL LEGEND

Name _____ Date _____

Was this story difficult for you to write, or was it easy? Why?

_____
_____
_____
_____
_____
_____
_____

Let's look at your story again. If you didn't complete it yet, go back and do so before continuing.

Now that you've finished your story, answer the questions below about it in the space provided.

The thing you were looking for in your story is a metaphor for the thing you most need in your life right now. Think about the qualities of the thing you were seeking. What does it symbolize? Why are you looking for it? What is your intention in finding it? Write your answers below:

_____
_____
_____
_____
_____
_____
_____
_____
_____
_____
_____
_____
_____
_____
_____

Worksheet 13.3a Lessons from My Own Animal Legend Page 2 of 6

Name_____ Date_____

The place in which the animals live represents the place where you are right now in your life. Describe your thoughts and feelings on where you live right now. For example, if you said that your animals live in a desert, think about the emotional qualities you associate with a desert, and not its physical qualities. Such answers might include: Lonely, barren, foreboding, etc. If you like deserts, your emotional qualities for this setting might include: Peaceful, quiet, and undisturbed. Write your answers in the space below:

_____
_____
_____
_____
_____
_____
_____
_____
_____
_____

The place you are going on your journey represents where you would like to be in your life. Describe this place in the space below, again focusing on the emotional qualities you associate with this place:

_____
_____
_____
_____
_____
_____
_____
_____
_____
_____

Worksheet 13.3a Lessons from My Own Animal Legend Page 3 of 6

Name _____ Date _____

Think about the animal(s) that tried to prevent you from reaching your goal. This animal represents the barriers to connecting with your True Self. What qualities does this animal possess? How are these qualities keeping you from connecting to who you really are?

_____
_____
_____
_____
_____
_____
_____
_____

Examine what happened to you in your story once you reached your destination. Did you achieve your goal? If you did, describe what happened to the animal representing you when you reached your goal. Use feeling words. If you reached your goal, then this attainment represents what you imagine you will achieve when you connect fully with your True Self:

_____
_____
_____
_____
_____
_____
_____
_____
_____
_____
_____
_____
_____

WORKSHEET 13.3A LESSONS FROM MY OWN ANIMAL LEGEND

Name _____ Date _____

If you didn't achieve your goal in the story, what was the reason? Did the animal who was working against you prevent you from achieving it, or did something else happen? Whatever prevented you from achieving your goal represents your own fears of living in your True Self. Describe these fears below. Use feeling words like sad, empty, frustrated, etc.

_____
_____
_____
_____
_____
_____
_____
_____
_____
_____

Look at what happens in your story when you return home. This represents how you would see your life changing if you were living every day in your True Self. Is it a positive change, or a negative change? If bad things happen in the story when you return home, what would that tell you about your own fears of living in True Self? Describe your thoughts below, using feeling words.

_____
_____
_____
_____
_____
_____
_____
_____
_____
_____

Worksheet 13.3a Lessons from My Own Animal Legend Page 5 of 6

Name _____ Date _____

Did any animals help you on your journey? If so, what are the characteristics of these animals? These helper animals represent the positive qualities you see in yourself. Write these characteristics below.

_____
_____
_____
_____
_____
_____
_____
_____
_____
_____

Did any of the animals hinder you on your journey? These animals represent the barriers to connecting with your True Self. They represent the reasons you see within yourself for not living in True Self. How did these animals hinder you? What could you do to befriend these animals within you so that they no longer hinder you on your journey?

_____
_____
_____
_____
_____
_____
_____
_____
_____
_____

WORKSHEET 13.3A LESSONS FROM MY OWN ANIMAL LEGEND

Name _____ Date _____

What was the moral of your story? This represents the lesson you most need to learn in your life right now in order to "get out of your own way" and live fully in your True Self. Describe your thoughts and feelings on this in the space below.

_____
_____
_____
_____
_____
_____
_____
_____
_____
_____

What did you learn about yourself from this journey? Write any reflections or observations in the space below.

_____
_____
_____
_____
_____
_____
_____
_____
_____
_____
_____
_____
_____
_____
_____

13.4 Nature as Teacher

The *Animal Legend* exercise is an opportunity to allow nature to teach us. It is also an opportunity for us to draw the archetypal energy of various animals into our lives as aids to connection. When I have done this session in workshops in the past, we have occasionally acted out the stories people have written. This has been especially enjoyable when people were able to wear the masks they created in the *Faces and Masks* exercise during the performance.

The techniques applied in the *Animal Legend* exercise may also be used in other aspects of our lives as we learn from nature. Imagine coming upon a stream while walking in the woods. A practitioner of ecospirituality sees the stream and studies its every aspect. How am I like the stream? How am I different? How may its energy be tapped? Why does it reflect the light of the moon? What is its substance? What is the nature of its life force? Is there an Art of Water? How do people feel about the different faces this stream presents? These are just some of the questions one might ask when observing and connecting with a stream. Asking such questions reveals the wonder and awe that is inherent in nature, and leads us to our own ecospiritual power, or "magic."

The basic lesson of the *Animal Legend* exercise when used in the Magic Flight is to keep an open mind about anything you are studying so that you do not allow your preconceptions to cloud what is really there. This is not as easy as it sounds, but it can be accomplished. As with all things, the skill will grow with practice and patience. The key to this is to try to see all sides of a problem before looking for an answer, without judgments or preconceptions.

With nature as your teacher, always strive to find the truth about your universe, and not merely what you wish to see or what your senses tell you. Remember that anything you will ever learn has been filtered through the sieve of your senses. What your body can perceive is but a small fraction of what is really there. The real nature of the Universe is deeper and more mysterious than we can ever know, at least in this present form. But that does not mean that we should stop trying. Your own inner universe is forever limited to the boundaries of your senses, but because of this, you also have the ability to create your own universe. That is the true nature of ecospirituality: The ability to see the world as it really is, free of expectations or assumptions, and to create your own world by changing your beliefs and assumptions. When you have mastered this, you will be ready to teach others what you have learned. You will have mastered the Magic Flight.

Session 14 Rescue from Without

Coyote continued to follow the shallow creek for as long as he could, until it came to a waterfall. Although it was small, the cascade was still too high for him to jump, so he left the creek and continued along the bank, thinking himself to be safe now. He followed the creek to the bottom of the waterfall, taking care not to slip on the ice-covered rocks on the way down. Just as he reached the bottom he was about to enter the forest again when Coyote Woman stepped out from behind a boulder near the creek bed. All of the other members of the Fire Tribe stood behind her, some distance away.

She bared her teeth at him, saying, "You have stolen from me, and now you must pay the price!"

Coyote steeled himself for a battle, but as his hackles rose he remembered that Coyote Woman was a Trickster, just as he was. He could not defeat her by engaging in his usual arsenal of trickery. As he pondered this, he felt his consciousness expanding, burning like the fire in his tail. As the warm awareness spread throughout his body and his mind, he began to see things in a different way. He recognized that Coyote Woman had the same wants and needs that he had. As he thought of this it became clear that all creatures, whether of his tribe or of another, had the same basic goals. He looked at all the members of Coyote Woman's tribe, standing behind her at the top of the hill. All wanted food. All wanted safety. All wanted a warm place to sleep. Most of all, all wanted to love and to be loved.

With this realization, Coyote smiled at Coyote Woman and took a step towards her.

At first she looked confused. She seemed to struggle to keep the angry look on her face, then something within her surrendered and she began instead to laugh. She flopped down into the snow at Coyote's feet and rolled back and forth, giggling uncontrollably.

Unable to help himself, Coyote began to laugh as well. Laying there beside her, they both chuckled until they had to stop to catch their breath, while the Fire Tribe, puzzled, looked on.

When Coyote was able to breathe comfortably again, he asked her, "So you're not really angry with me?"

Coyote Woman smiled at him and replied, "Of course not. Why would I be? The funny thing about fire is that it is like love...as long as you feed it, it continues to grow. The little flame you stole from me is insignificant compared to the source from which it came."

Coyote pondered this in the light of the knowledge that nobody is truly separate from anyone else. By reaching out with his own spirit and touching the aspect of himself that was Coyote Woman, he was able to end the conflict and make peace between them. He was able to use his insight to become what was needed for the situation.

As he smiled at Coyote Woman, the rest of the Fire Tribe looked upon them with love in their hearts.

14.0 Rescue from Without - Nature as Nurture

As the end of the path draws nigh, we may find ourselves exhausted from the journey. The Magic Flight challenges us to use all of our resources to seek inspiration and magic from the natural world instead of from the trinkets and baubles of a modern post-industrialist existence. Once we have learned to stand naked and alone in the wilderness, content and at peace with the natural world, we are probably not in any hurry to return to the mundane 9 to 5 existence.

If this is the case, then the world may have to send for us. For a spiritual seeker, this rescue from without may come from a friend or a family member who needs the wisdom you have gained from your journey. Or it may just come from the need to share the wisdom you've gained as a method of gaining an even deeper understanding of what it means to truly trust your own inner voice.

For the shaman who has walked the Way of the Coyote, this rescue from without comes from the knowledge that he/she is truly not separate from anyone else. So by calling on Supernatural Aid, he/she becomes one with all that is, and is able to shape-shift into whatever is needed for the situation using the magical skills learned during the Magic Flight.

14.1 Nature and Nurturing Relationships

I met my wife online through an Internet Personals site back in 2000. On my Personals page, one of the questions asked on the Profile was, "What is your idea of the perfect date?" For my response, I wrote, "Going camping in the woods...that moonlit beach is getting too crowded!"

Of course, the reason I'd written this is that the majority of responses to the question consisted of, "A romantic walk on a moonlit beach."

The fact that so many people want to take romantic moonlit strolls along the beach with a romantic partner tells me something: That nature has the power to induce romantic feelings.

Real physiological changes occur when we go outdoors. Our heart rates slow down. Our blood pressure drops. We become more focused and aware. Many similar changes occur when we fall in love. Love is a nurturing relationship. When we have similar physiological changes in nature and in love, does it mean that we love nature? Could it mean that nature has the power to nurture?

The moral of the story is that if your intention is to build stronger relationships, to connect with your family, or friends, or with nature, you'll want to do more things that afford you the opportunity to build those connections. Nature is a powerful tool for helping both you and your partner to calm down, slow down, move out of doing mode into being mode, and to simply enjoy each other's company. If you're single, nature can still be a way to receive strong nurturing feelings similar to those of being in love.

Do you have pets? Do you find nurture from animals? Do you nurture and love your pets in return? Animals are a part of nature as well. We nurture them and they nurture us. In the next section we will explore how animals and natural environments can nurture us, and how we can nurture them. The exercises in this session will help us to connect with the nurturing aspects of our True Selves and with the nurturing power of nature.

This healing power of nature will be our Rescue from Without, that helps us to reach the end of our Hero's Journey.

14.2 Non-Verbal Communication

Ecospirituality is all about connection. The Rescue from Without is also about connection. It is about connecting with something larger than ourselves. For the purposes of ecospirituality, that something is the natural world. This means that the Rescue from Without involves learning to connect with nature so that we may tap into its nurturing power and be "rescued" or healed.

People often find it easier to connect with their pets than with other people, because pets are generally non-judgmental and accepting. They have few expectations of their human friends outside of food, shelter, and love. For this reason, when you are practicing your connection skills, it is often easier to practice with animals than with humans.

Nurturing is an aspect of connection. Connecting with nature, animals, others, and with ourselves is a very nurturing act. Some equate connection with love, and love is the most nurturing emotion. The first step in tapping into this two-way stream of nurturing and connecting is through communication.

Do you talk to your pets? Do they seem to understand you at times? Can your pets make their wants and needs known to you? Pets can't speak English. So how do you know what they want?

The answer is that pets communicate to us through the use of their body language. A dog wagging his tail means that the dog is happy. On the other hand, a cat wagging her tail means that someone is probably about to get scratched! We've learned what these signs mean by living with our pets and by paying attention to what their bodies are telling us. The more we pay attention to these non-verbal cues, the more we come to understand our pets.

As much as 70% of communication between human beings is non-verbal in nature. With pets, 100% of how they communicate with us is non-verbal. So if you can learn how to read what your pets are telling you, you have learned the art of nonverbal communication.

The vast majority of therapy and counseling done in the world today is what is called "talk therapy." In this type of therapy, therapists and their patients work on problems and find solutions by talking about them. There is, however, a vast body of experiential awareness that is non-verbal in nature. Because of this, some therapists believe that the ultimate therapy would be one in which you would not have to talk at all. Have you ever been emotionally moved by a beautiful piece of instrumental music, or by a sunset, or by a walk in the woods, or by an affectionate nuzzle from a favorite pet? If so, you've experienced non-verbal therapy.

When exploring the world of animal-assisted ecospirituality, especially when connecting with animals, don't focus so much on using words to describe what you are experiencing. Approach it from being mode rather than from doing mode. Just enjoy the experience. As you do the exercises in this session, explore what it might be like to live in a non-verbal world. Ecospirituality is more about experiences than about talking. It's more of a way of directly being in the world than about verbal communication. Communication with nature is easy once you get past the idea of words.

14.3 Animal as Nurture

Therapists have a saying: "The map is not the territory." One meaning of this phrase is that the greatest psychotherapist in the world can never know all the subtle nuances of her patient's thoughts and feelings. You are your own best expert on what you are feeling or thinking at any given moment. By closely examining your True Self, and learning to trust that knowledge, you journey towards the person you wish to be.

Another meaning of the saying, "The map is not the territory," is that the way we perceive others is not the true way others actually are. Each of us carries within ourselves our own representations of the people we meet. This is also true of the animals in our lives. We see them through our own personal lenses, assigning to them attributes and feelings that come from deep inside us. Think back to the story you created in *My Own Animal Legend.* Which animals were nurturing you on your journey? What qualities did they possess? The qualities you saw are projections of your own feelings and thoughts about these animals. In a way, they are the nurturing qualities you possess within yourself.

If you have pets, you're probably aware that they help you get in touch with your own inner nurturing qualities. Many animals instinctively respond to your own nurturing by nurturing in return. My cats know when I've had a bad day, and they come to me to offer comfort and affection in the same way that I offer my comfort and affection to them. I've learned a lot about myself from the way my animals respond to me, and the way I respond to them.

Even if you don't have pets, you can still take advantage of the nurturing qualities of animals by getting in touch with your own feelings about what nurturing animals represent to you. Symbolically, these thoughts and feelings represent our own primal urges.

Think about the totem animal you selected when you began your journey on the Way of the Coyote. What qualities does this animal possess that are nurturing? What qualities does it possess that aren't nurturing? How can you use these qualities in your journey to your True Self?

14.4 Your Animal True Self

In her book, *Drawing Down the Moon*, Margot Adler tells of an experience she had with catching fish bare-handed. She was having very little success, until a shamanistic friend asked her to think of animals who are natural fishermen. Adler immediately thought of a bear. Her friend then advised her to "become the bear." She then pictured in her mind how bears caught fish. When she adopted the pose and the technique that bears use to catch fish, she began catching them bare-handed at a rapid rate.

From mythology and legend, we all familiar with people who transform themselves into animals. There's the werewolf, and Dracula's ability to transform into a bat. There are legends about witches like Baba Yaga and the Skinwalkers of the Navajo who had the power to shapeshift. Unfortunately, we took those legends literally. What if they weren't about an actual physical transformation, but a transformation of the mind? If you could mentally transform yourself into an animal of your choosing, what would that look like? What would be different about the way you carried yourself? About the way you thought about things? About the way you felt about the world and yourself? What could you do in such a frame of mind that you couldn't do as yourself?

Of course, I'm not talking about barking like a dog at your next business meeting! But what if you could embody the courage of a lion the next time you ask for a raise? What if you could take on the gentleness of a lamb at your next romantic encounter? What if you could be as wise as an owl the next time you needed a solution to a problem?

Think about your totem animal from the *My Animal Totem* exercise. What characteristics of your totem animal could help you to affirm and live in your True Self if you pictured yourself becoming that animal? Could you draw on the power and energy from your totem animal to help you to succeed in transforming yourself into the person you were meant to be? If so, how might the archetypal energy of your spirit animal help you to attain the Rescue from Without?

14.5 An Attitude of Gratitude

Have you ever been thanked for doing something nice for someone? How did you feel afterwards? Did it make you more likely to want to help again in the future? Did it help the person who thanked you by making them more aware and more grateful to you in return for the gesture?

Imagine that you approached life with a sense of entitlement. Suppose you expected life to hand you everything on a silver platter. How long do you imagine it would be, with such an attitude, before you began to take things for granted? How long do you imagine it would be before you started demanding things?

Now imagine you approached life with a sense of gratitude. Suppose you were grateful for the air that you breathe, the food that you eat, the clothes that you wear, and the people in your life. Would it be possible to take things for granted with such an attitude of gratitude? Would it be possible to demand or expect things with such an attitude?

In ecospirituality we teach students to approach life with an attitude of gratitude. Being thankful to others, to nature, or to your own concept of the divine changes the way you think and feel. Even if you have no concept of a higher power or of the divine, being grateful to the Universe for providing for you changes the way you approach things. It changes your thinking.

Nature nurtures us by providing for us. Everything you eat, the air you breathe, the water you drink, the clothes you wear, everything you see, hear, touch, taste or smell is a product of nature. How often do you thank nature for this bounty? If you learned to be more grateful to nature, is it possible that nature might be more willing to help you with your Rescue from Without?

One way to express gratitude is to commit a nurturing act in a spirit of thanksgiving.

Most, if not all, aboriginal peoples around the world provided offerings of one form or another to nature. These offerings could consist of bits of food, or libations (liquid refreshments poured out on the ground), or of colored ribbons, or of any form they chose with which to honor the spirit of nature.

Many Native American tribes offered pinches of sacred tobacco as a sacrifice when gathering healing herbs or plants. The Celtic peoples of Europe often tossed valuable silver vessels or finely crafted tools and weapons into sacred rivers and other bodies of water. This is where we get our tradition of tossing coins into wishing wells. These were called "sacrifices" because it was the custom to only give their best to honor the spirits of nature.

One way to establish a two-way nurturing relationship with nature is to make such offerings. In order to receive nurture from nature, we must be willing to offer our own nurturing in return. This is only natural. Would you stay in a relationship that was not nurturing you? Likewise, we have no reason to expect nurture from nature if we are not willing to give it ourselves.

A first step in establishing this nurturing relationship is to always remember to ask nature for permission before engaging in any outdoor activity, and to thank nature when the activity is over.

How do you know that nature has granted permission? The answer to this question is sort of like trying to explain what it's like to be in love, to a person who has never been in love. The best answer you can give is, "You'll know it when it happens."

One way to know that nature has granted permission is to notice, after asking, what you may feel attracted to. Does something in the environment call for your attention? After asking permission, do you feel at peace, or uneasy? Open your heart and your senses, and be willing to accept the answers you receive.

If you don't feel that nature has given you permission, then find another place, or postpone your activity until another day.

If you do feel that nature has consented, then thank her by offering something. A libation of ale, or wine, or other refreshment may be poured on the ground, or you may leave a bit of bread or cheese or other food item. When I do workshops, we sometimes cover pine cones in peanut butter, and then roll them in birdseed.

Whatever offering you choose, present it in a thankful manner. You may wish to express your thanks out loud, or you may simply remain silent and respectful while placing your offering. Whatever manner you choose to express your thankfulness, the act will change your perceptions about the natural world and your place in it. This act eases the spirit and gives you a sense of peace and gratitude for all that nature has provided.

When you have committed this nurturing act, you have opened the way for a reciprocal exchange of nurturing from nature to you, and back again.

To take the first step in establishing the cycle of nurture, complete the Attitude of Gratitude exercise on the next page.

Worksheet 14.5 An Attitude of Gratitude

Page 1 of 2

Name _____ Date: _____

For this exercise, enter your sacred space. If you have not yet established a sacred space for yourself, find any natural spot outdoors that seems to call to you. This spot will be your sacred space for the purposes of this exercise. Ask the spot's permission before continuing. If you feel that you have been granted permission, express your gratitude by making an offering of some sort. This offering can be food, or a libation, or a colored ribbon, or an act of nurturing like watering or pruning a plant or removing debris from the area. While engaging in this activity, remain open to nature's voice by performing a mindful breathing exercise or some other form of meditation.

After you have made your offering, sit quietly in your sacred spot and observe for a few minutes. Write down your observations by answering the questions below.

Did nature grant you permission for this activity? If so, how did this permission manifest itself?

_____
_____
_____
_____
_____

When you made your offering, how did you feel? Did your perceptions of the location change? How?

_____
_____
_____
_____
_____

When you made your offering, did you notice any changes in your thinking? If so, what changes?

_____
_____
_____
_____
_____

WORKSHEET 14.5 AN ATTITUDE OF GRATITUDE

Name _____ Date: _____

If this is the first time you have ever established a nurturing relationship with nature by making an offering, did this act of gratitude change how you feel about yourself? In what ways?

_____
_____
_____
_____

If this is the not first time you have ever established a nurturing relationship with nature by making an offering, when did you first start the practice? How has the practice helped you to grow in your relationship with nature?

_____
_____
_____
_____

After you made your offering and began observing this sacred space, what did you notice?

_____
_____
_____
_____

How might the things you noticed or observed change how you feel about yourself?

_____
_____
_____

Was anything you noticed nurturing to you? If so, how might it help you to live more fully in your True Self?

_____
_____
_____
_____

14.6 Establishing the Cycle of Nurture

The *Attitude of Gratitude* exercise is a first step in establishing a reciprocal nurturing relationship with nature. The next step is to create a cycle of nurturer. In order to receive nurturing, we must be willing to give nurturing in return. By opening yourself to the idea of being thankful to nature for her bounty, we are able to connect more fully to nature and to ourselves by removing obstacles to connection like ungratefulness, unwillingness, and indifference.

All relationships have difficulties. From time to time we argue with our loved ones, and disagree. The next time you find yourself in such a disagreement, practice the exercise below. It works with romantic relationships, with parents and children, with family members, and with friends. It works with pretty much any relationship where people interact with each other.

The next time another person has a problem with you, try saying this to them:

"I understand that you are suffering. I am here for you. I hear you. I care. Please tell me how I may help."

The next time you have a problem with another person, try saying this to them:

"I am suffering. I see that you are here for me. I hear you. I care. Please help me."

These simple phrases, adapted from the *Four Mantras* by Thic Nhat Hanh, let the other person know that you value the relationship enough not to let the problem interfere. They also let the other person know that they are valued, and that you care for them. They also open the door to helping both partners feel heard and understood.

Practice these phrases with a loved one a few times before going on to the *Cycle of Nurture* exercise on the next page.

Worksheet 14.6 The Cycle of Nurture

Name _____ Date _____

If we expect to receive nurturing from nature, we must first expect to be willing to offer such nurture in return. Nurture is a two-way street. In order to establish the cycle of nurture with your own sacred space, first go to your sacred space and find a comfortable place to sit or stand. Next ground and center yourself by engaging in a brief meditation. Now ask permission for what you are about to do, and wait for a reply. If permission is granted, continue with the exercise below. If permission is not granted, find another place or wait until another day.

When you have received permission from nature, make an offering to express your gratitude, then sit or stand comfortably and recite the following three times to all the life present in your sacred space:

"I understand that you are suffering. I am here for you. I hear you. I care. Please tell me how I may help."

Once you have recited the above three times, open your heart and your mind and wait for an answer. This answer may come in the form of a visit from an animal, or the way the wind moves through the trees, or a sound, or just a feeling within yourself. If you don't receive an answer, end the exercise and try again on another day, following the same formula described above. When you feel you have gotten an answer, write your responses to the questions below.

What answer did you receive?

_____
_____
_____
_____
_____

How do you plan to respond? In what ways may you nurture nature?

_____
_____
_____
_____
_____
_____

WORKSHEET 14.6 THE CYCLE OF NURTURE

Name _____ Date _____

How might the actions described above (your plan to help nature) help you to receive nurturing from nature in return?

_____
_____
_____
_____

How might nature manifest its gratitude to you for your help?

_____
_____
_____
_____

How might you prepare yourself to receive this expression of gratitude?

_____
_____
_____
_____

How might establishing this cycle of nurture with nature help you to become the person you were born to be? To live more fully in your own True Self?

_____
_____
_____
_____
_____
_____

14.7 Reflections on Nature as Nurture

> *"I think over again my small adventures. My fears, those small ones that seemed so big. For all the vital things I had to get and to reach. And yet there is only one great thing. The only thing. To live to see the great day that dawns, and the light that fills the world."*
>
> --Old Inuit Song

Think about all of the things that have stressed you out in your life. How many of them were a product of the mind trap? That is, how many of them had to do with anxiety over things that had happened in the past, or that might happen in the future? How many of them had to do with things that are happening right now at this very second, as you're reading this sentence?

How many of them had to do with words and language? Could you worry about things if you had no words or language with which to fret over them?

As we learned earlier in this session, nature doesn't communicate with words. Plants and animals can't talk. They make their wants and needs known in other ways. To give and receive nurturing from nature, we must be open to learning non-verbal ways of communicating. Actions are more important than words when it comes to nurturing, so in order to establish a nurturing relationship with nature, we must be willing to act instead of merely talking.

While ecospirituality involves leaving doing mode and entering into being mode, nurturing involves leaving talking mode and entering into doing mode. The doing mode of the nurturing cycle is about a different kind of doing than the type of doing that occurs in the mind trap. Nurturing is about doing activities that have positive emotional content rather than negative emotional content. Studies have shown that it is virtually impossible to dwell on our own problems when we are helping others with their problems. The more we nurture others, the more we are nurtured in return.

This is true of nature as well. If we are doing things to help nature, it is difficult to remain focused on the doing of the mind trap. By leaving the world of words behind, we are free to enter into a nurturing relationship with nature and to do things that help both nature and ourselves.

We are a part of nature. The more we embrace our own capacity for nurturing, the more nature will offer nurture in return. The more nurturing give, the more we receive. The more nurturing we receive from nature, the more we participate in the Rescue from Without, and the more we are able to help others in return.

Session 15 The Crossing of the Return Threshold

Coyote began to walk and Coyote Woman walked with him for a time, leaving her Tribe behind to stand guard on the hill. Together they walked until they arrived at the river that marked the boundary to Coyote's home.

When they approached the beaver dam Coyote had crossed at the start of his journey, he looked into Coyote Woman's eyes.

"I must bring the fire back to my People," he said, "If I don't, they will all die."

"I understand," she replied.

He turned to walk away from her, but then an idea struck him.

"Why not come with me?" he asked her.

She smiled hesitantly. For a moment it seemed that she was about to agree to return home with him, but instead she said, "I have my own Tribe to look after. Your path is not my path."

Disappointed, Coyote hung his head.

"But of course," Coyote Woman said, "Just because your path is not my path, that doesn't mean that our paths won't converge on occasion."

Heartened by this, Coyote nuzzled his nose against hers; as if to promise that they would meet again. Thus having said goodbye, he turned towards the river and the beaver dam, recalling the safe path to take to return to his homeland. He looked over his shoulder to watch Coyote Woman disappear into the snow-covered forest, and then with a few well-placed leaps and bounds he made the crossing.

15.0 Nature as Healer

"The society is the enemy when it imposes its structures on the individual. On the dragon there are many scales. Every one of them says 'Thou Shalt.' Kill the dragon 'Thou Shalt.' When one has killed that dragon, one has become The Child."

--Joseph Campbell

"Can miles truly separate you from friends? If you want to be with someone you love, aren't you already there?"

--Richard Bach

The Return Threshold is the doorway that lies between the spiritual world and the "real" world. In order to cross the return threshold, the spiritual seeker must complete three tasks. First, she must retain all the wisdom she gained on the quest so that she may share it with others. Next, she must find a way to integrate that wisdom into a human life without pain or regret. Finally, she must find a way to share that wisdom with the rest of the world in such a way that they receive it with welcome. This last task is especially important, as we humans tend to make martyrs out of messiahs.

This is the final stage of the Hero's Journey. It is the return home from the quest, bringing the knowledge and wisdom learned on the way so that it may be shared with the tribe. The Seeker will have grown as a person and learned many things. The Way of the Coyote teaches the skills of ecospirituality that ultimately lead the seeker to be able to live fully in True Self in both the world of the spiritual and the "real" world.

In our Coyote story, his return may bring fresh hope to those he left behind when he took up the quest, a direct solution to their problems and perhaps a new perspective for everyone to consider. One the Way of the Coyote that leads to ecospirituality, the Seeker returns with the knowledge that he/she and nature are not separate things. It is the wisdom to know that we are all connected. We are all one. Because of this we cannot ever truly be separate from one another. What we do to nature we do to ourselves. The more we harm nature, the more we harm ourselves. But the good news is that the more we care for nature, the more we care for ourselves as well, by establishing a cycle of nurture. These cycles lead to healing...for self, for others, and for the entire natural world.

When we have gained the power to establish these healing cycles of nurture consistently, we will have crossed the return threshold.

15.1 Animal as Healer

One of the purposes of Crossing the Return Threshold is to share the healing that we have learned while traveling the Way of the Coyote. In ecospirituality this means tapping into the healing powers of nature so that it may be shared with others.

Humans are mammals. Mammals nurture and care for their young. During this period of nurturing in infancy, we form bonds that affect how we approach others for the rest of our lives. There is a whole area of psychology, called *Attachment Theory*, that studies how these relationships are formed, and how they cause us to act in the ways we do. If you've had negative attachments in your childhood, it may be difficult for you to connect with other people in positive ways. Pets afford people who've experienced negative attachments the opportunity to form positive attachments in non-threatening ways.

Animals have been used in schools, in therapeutic settings, and in nursing homes to help individuals form positive attachments. The reason this works is that people have a natural instinct to nurture and to be nurtured. Through this nurturing, we are healed. Through this healing, we return home by Crossing the Return Threshold.

15.2 Animal Assisted Healing

There is a branch of psychotherapy known as Animal-Assisted Therapy. In this broad category of ecopsychology, animals help to facilitate therapeutic interventions. When animals nurture us in this manner, healing takes place in a realm beyond the words of traditional "talk therapy."

Since animals cannot rely on words for communication, they are much more sensitive to other means of communication. They can read our body language, our pheromones, our facial expressions, and the tone of our voices. This ability makes them excellent assistants in more experiential forms of therapy.

Studies compiled by Palley, et al in 2010 have shown that spending time with pets has the following effects on humans:

- The breathing rate slows down
- The heart rate slows down
- The blood pressure decreases
- Stress hormones are reduced
- Endorphins (the body's natural painkillers) are increased
- The immune system is strengthened
- People become calmer and more relaxed
- Perhaps not surprisingly, the animals also become more relaxed!

All of the characteristics listed above are obviously healing characteristics, so animals are great natural physicians!

To experience some of the healing power that animals can offer, try the Animal-Assisted Healing exercise on the next page. If you do not have a pet of your own, you may borrow one from a friend or visit a petting zoo. If you are completing this workbook as part of an ecospirituality program, your instructor may have already selected an animal assistant for you. This exercise may be performed with any friendly four-legged friend. If you have allergies, take that into consideration when selecting your animal "therapist."

WORKSHEET 15.2 ANIMAL ASSISTED HEALING

Name _____ Date_____

For this exercise you will need an animal assistant. You may use your own pet for the exercise. If you do not have a pet, you may wish to borrow one from a friend or neighbor, or visit a petting zoo if there is one near you. Don't attempt this exercise with a wild animal. If you have allergies, select an animal you're not allergic to.

To engage in the Animal Assisted Healing exercise, complete the following steps, then go on to answer the questions on the next page.

1. Find a space, preferably outdoors, where you and your animal assistant may be undisturbed for the duration of the exercise.

2. Begin by taking your pulse. Write down your heart rate on the worksheet on the next page, or just make a mental note of it for now.

3. Ask your animal assistant for its permission and help in completing this exercise, and wait for a reply. Read the animal assistant's body language for signs that permission has been granted. If it has not, or if the animal seems uneasy in any way, postpone the activity until another time.

4. Once permission has been granted, thank your animal assistant by giving him or her a treat of some sort.

5. Bond with your animal assistant by grooming or petting it.

6. When you feel a bond has been established, think of a situation in which you need healing help. If you do not have such a situation, just enjoy the experience of being with your animal assistant.

7. Play with your animal assistant in some way. If your animal assistant is a dog, you may toss a ball or a stick. If a cat, you may offer it a bit of string. If some other animal, find a way to engage in a playful activity with it.

8. When you have finished playing with the animal assistant, thank it once again and express your gratitude by offering it another treat.

9. Take your pulse again.

10. Dismiss your animal assistant in a kind and gentle way.

When you have completed all 10 steps above, go to the worksheet on the next page and answer the questions.

WORKSHEET 15.2 ANIMAL ASSISTED HEALING PAGE 2 OF 3

Name _____ Date_____

RESTING HEART RATE AT THE BEGINNING OF THE EXERCISE: _____ beats per minute

How did your animal assistant grant you permission to do the exercise?

_____
_____
_____
_____
_____

How did choose to bond with your animal assistant? How did he/she respond?

_____
_____
_____
_____
_____

How did your animal assistant grant you permission to do the exercise?

_____
_____
_____
_____

Before playing with your animal assistant, did you think of a situation in which you needed help? Did playing with your animal assistant change the way you thought about the situation? How?

_____
_____
_____

WORKSHEET 15.2 ANIMAL ASSISTED HEALING　　　　　　　　PAGE 3 OF 3

Name _____ Date _____

Did you notice any change in your thoughts, feelings, or overall mood after the exercise? If so, what?

_____
_____
_____
_____
_____
_____
_____
_____
_____

How might animal assisted healing help you to live more fully in your True Self?

_____
_____
_____
_____
_____
_____
_____
_____
_____

RESTING HEART RATE AT THE END OF THE EXERCISE: _____ beats per minute

Did your resting heart rate increase or decrease during the exercise (circle one)?

INCREASE | DECREASE

15.3 Reflections on Animal Assisted Healing

If you are like most people who engage in the *Animal Assisted Healing* exercise, you probably experienced a decrease in your heart rate from the beginning of the exercise until the end of the exercise. Of course, if your play with your animal assistant involved running or jumping, the opposite may have been true, but overall most people become calmer and more relaxed after engaging in animal assisted healing.

There's a reason that humans have had relationships with our four-legged brothers and sisters for millennia. They nurture us, and we nurture them. By their nurturing, we are healed. This healing is what Crossing the Return Threshold is all about. First we heal ourselves, then we heal others. Sometimes we can heal others…and ourselves…by caring for and healing the natural world around us.

15.4 Material Possessions and Healing

The only things we really need are food, clothing, shelter, healing, and love. Everything else is a luxury item. The society we live in conditions us to believe that material possessions are the key to happiness. We tend to reinforce this when we buy each other gifts in an attempt to purchase love and affection. But what we're really teaching each other when we do this is that the gifts are more important than the giver.

This belief that owning things is the key to happiness is not very conducive to developing healing relationships with other people, or with nature. In fact, many of the things that cause us stress come from our desire to purchase more and more in our never-ending pursuit of happiness.

Think about some things that have kept you from connecting to your own True Self in the past. How many of those things might have to do with material possessions? List them in the exercise on the next page.

WORKSHEET 15.4 ANXIETY FROM MATERIAL POSSESSIONS   PAGE 1 OF 2

Name _____ Date _____

Think about some things that stress you out. How many of those things have to do with material possessions? That is, on your list of things that cause you stressful or depressing thoughts, how many of them have to do with the purchase, rental, or ownership of material goods? For purposes of this exercise, "material goods" may also include intangible goods such as stocks, bonds, insurance policies, medical bills, rental and lease fees, etc.
Once you have identified these items write them below:

1. _____
2. _____
3. _____
4. _____
5. _____
6. _____
7. _____
8. _____
9. _____
10. _____
11. _____
12. _____
13. _____
14. _____
15. _____
16. _____
17. _____
18. _____
19. _____
20. _____
21. _____
22. _____
23. _____
24. _____
25. _____

WORKSHEET 15.4 ANXIETY FROM MATERIAL POSSESSIONS   PAGE 2 OF 2

Name _____ Date _____

Now think about some things that have led you to deny your own true nature in the past. In other words, things that have kept you from connecting to your True Self. How many of those things have to do with material possessions or the worries they cause? List them below:

1. _____
2. _____
3. _____
4. _____
5. _____
6. _____
7. _____
8. _____
9. _____
10. _____
11. _____
12. _____
13. _____
14. _____
15. _____
16. _____
17. _____
18. _____
19. _____
20. _____
21. _____
22. _____
23. _____
24. _____
25. _____

What did you learn about yourself from doing these lists? What did you learn about your relationship to material goods?

15.5 Connecting and Healing

There is a relationship between feeling spiritually connected and healing. In a 2007 meta-analysis on this relationship, Dyer found that the odds of survival for people who scored highly on spiritual measures were 29% higher than those who scored lower in spiritual involvement.

Dyer also examined a number of studies that indicated that meditation is associated with positive changes in immune function, reductions in cardiopulmonary and gastrointestinal tract symptoms in cancer patients, beneficial changes in blood pressure and heart rate, and decreased mortality risk, all of which may be related to long-term health.

This meta-study also found that the type of spirituality wasn't as important as the fact that participants had some sort of spiritual practice. For purposes of this study, agnostic and atheist Buddhists were included, with similar results. Using our definition of "spiritual" as "connected to something larger than self," even people who have no concept of a higher power or of the divine can reap the healing benefits of connecting through ecospirituality.

Looking back on your lists on the exercises *Anxiety from Material Possessions*, did you learn anything about the relationships between material possessions and spirituality? Do material possessions act more often as aids to spiritual connection, or as deterrents to spiritual connection?

If spirituality leads to healing, and material possessions often act to hinder us from achieving high levels of spiritual connection, what does that say about the relationship between material possessions and healing? Perhaps there is a reason that so many advanced practitioners of spiritual paths around the world practice asceticism. That's not to say that the only true path to happiness lies in running off to live alone in a cave in the woods somewhere. It's just saying that material goods rarely lead to true happiness. True happiness comes from within, and from our connections to nature, to others, and to self.

15.6 Chaos and Order

Nature is all about balance. In order for new life to begin, old life must pass away. The seeds that fall in autumn contain the beginnings of new life in the spring. The circle of life and death is neither good nor bad. It just is. Each half of the cycle depends on the other for its existence.

Consider the seasons. The winter solstice marks the longest night of the year. From that day forward, days get longer and longer until the summer solstice, which is the shortest night of the year. At midsummer the days begin to grow shorter and the nights grow longer until the winter solstice returns again, marking off a lighter part of the year and a darker part of the year.

All life on earth exists in a perpetual balance of chaos and order. Chaos represents the forces of death, darkness and decay, and order represents the forces of life, light, and growth.

Humans and animals live balanced between these forces of chaos and order. The ideal life is one that strives for a balance between these forces. To live a life ruled by chaos is to live without direction and purpose. Such a life is one of death, darkness, and decay. On the other hand, to live a life ruled by order is to become obsessive about everything, always chasing after an orderly perfection that does not exist in the natural world. Finding balance between the forces of chaos and order allows one to live a life of purpose without engaging in compulsive, controlling behavior.

In ecospirituality we seek to restore balance by acknowledging this impulse. Instead of swallowing our anger, we would recognize it as a darker impulse. But instead of returning anger for anger, we strive to express that anger in positive ways; perhaps by confronting the source of the anger and saying to the person, "I really felt angry when you did _____. I don't want to be angry with you. What can we do to resolve this situation?"

As much as we might sometimes like to think otherwise, we are not separate from nature. A huge body of research confirms that our environment and the seasons affect our moods and behavior. If you think about it for a moment, you will probably find this to be true for yourself as well. Do you find yourself becoming more contemplative and introspective during the winter months? Do you become happier and more outgoing in the summer months? Does a walk in the woods improve your mood? If so, you are not alone.

The tools of ecospirituality allow us a tangible symbolic representation of these inner states of being. Just as the seasons move back and forth between cycles of light and darkness, so our own moods and feelings cycle between lighter and darker times. Celebrating the changes of the seasons and the cycle of life allows us to acknowledge both our lighter and our darker impulses in a contemplative and meditative way. By acknowledging them, we restore balance to our lives and to our own spiritual journeys. When we achieve this balance consistently we have crossed the return threshold.

15.7 True Self and Healing

We are nearing the end of our journey together. The next session, Master of Two Worlds, has been the ultimate destination, and we are almost there. Upon finishing the final session and the epilogue that follows you should have a much better understanding of who you are, and how to live as the person you were meant to be. You will understand the essence of ecospirituality and you will be free to live in True Self.

So how does one live in True Self?

When a person has learned to connect to the healing power of nature through the skills of ecospirituality that person has the ability to live in True Self.

We all have a vision of how we see ourselves, called the Perceived Self. We all also have a vision of how we would like to be. This vision is called the True Self. When the Perceived Self and the True Self are evenly matched, a person feels calm and at peace with herself and with the world. But the farther apart the Perceived Self and the True Self are the more chaotic and stressful her journey will be.

When the Perceived Self and the True Self are far apart, there are two possible solutions to bring them back into balance. The first is to bring the Perceived Self more closely in alignment with the True Self. The second is to bring the True Self more closely into alignment with the Perceived Self. In reality, most people achieve individuation, and therefore the ability to live in True Self, by moving the Perceived Self and the True Self more closely towards each other so that they meet in the middle.

The Perceived Self is ruled by chaos, and the True Self is ruled by order. The way to move the Perceived Self more closely towards the True Self is to see that a truly balanced person needs a little chaos in their lives, because that's where the creativity comes from. The way to move the True Self more closely to the Perceived Self is to see that a person needs a little order in their lives as well, because that's where stability and confidence come from.

The way to determine which direction to go when aligning your Perceived Self and your True Self is to think about the seasons of the year, and the cycles of life and death they bring. These cycles are a dance between the forces of chaos and the forces of order. Both light and dark are necessary in order to find balance, as are life and death, growth and decay, Shadow and Persona. Do you have more chaos in your life, or more order? Do you have a balance between the two? Are you comfortable with finding that balance if you do not have it?

A person who is perfectly balanced between the Perceived Self and the True Self is a person who is spiritually connected. Such a spiritually connected person does not need material possessions to feel better about themselves. Their self-esteem and self-confidence are generated from within. Their sense of value comes from what they are, and not from what they own.

When we attain this level of balance and mastery, the power of nature has healed us. We will have walked the Way of the Coyote to find the meaning of ecospirituality.

Chapter 16 Master of Two Worlds

Coyote journeyed for a few more days until he arrived at the boundary of his Tribe's village. He had grown so accustomed to the pain that the blaze on his tail caused that he barely noticed it anymore. So he was surprised for a moment when Sister Cougar greeted him in amazement at the luminous orange flower blossoming from his tail.

"What is this strange thing?" she exclaimed, leaping backwards.

"This is called 'fire,'" said Coyote, "and it will keep us warm through the winter until the spring returns."

Hearing the commotion at Coyote's arrival, Chief Buffalo had stepped out of his lodge to see what was going on. He approached Coyote just in time to hear him answer Sister Cougar's question.

"What is 'winter'? What is 'spring'?" Chief Buffalo asked.

Coyote began to teach Chief Buffalo all of the things that White Buffalo Woman had taught him. As he continued to speak, all the rest of the members of his Tribe gathered 'round, listening.

As he spoke, Coyote gathered sticks and twigs and placed them in a pile in the center of the village. Chief Buffalo and the rest of the Tribe followed him as he continued to teach them, helping him assemble wood for the fire.

Coyote remembered the giant pile of firewood he had seen at the center of Coyote Woman's village. Using this memory as a model, he directed his People until they had made a similar pile. Prior to lighting it, Coyote turned and addressed his People.

"Henceforth this will be known as the Fire Circle. The fire here will remain lit at all times so that all of the People may come and light their own torches. They may take their own fire home to keep warm and to be a light in the darkness. This fire shall belong to all, and all may partake of it."

With that, Coyote stuck his tail in the woodpile and watched the fire leap forth. As the People watched, a shout of joy and amazement rose up from them, and Coyote was well-pleased.

16.0 Master of Two Worlds - Seeker as Teacher

"Even a happy life cannot be without a measure of darkness, and the word happy would lose its meaning if it were not balanced by sadness. It is far better take things as they come along with patience and equanimity."

--Carl Jung

Once your basic needs of food, clothing, shelter, healing and love have been satisfied, how much do you truly need? We often confuse our wants with our needs. The Master of Two Worlds has learned to reconcile duality. Such a Master has found a balance between the spiritual world and the material world. This seeker has also found a balance between his Shadow and his Persona; his "light half" and his "dark half." Such a person has moved beyond seeing the world in black-and-white terms, and can see the gray areas.

Many modern nature-centered spiritual traditions follow the calendar known as the Wheel of the Year. In Western cultures, time is seen as linear; but in nature-centered spiritual paths, time is seen as cyclical. In such paths the cycle of the year is divided up into eight Sabbats, or High Days. These eight High Days consist of the solstices and equinoxes and the midpoints between each solstice and equinox. The summer and winter solstice, combined with the spring and fall equinoxes, are called the "Quarter Days" The midpoints between each are referred to as the "Cross-Quarter Days."

It is easy to miss the spiritual significance of the Wheel of the Year. We get our food from supermarkets and fast food restaurants, and most of us don't depend on agriculture and animal husbandry for our wellbeing. In an agrarian society, though, not knowing the proper times to plant and harvest could literally have been a matter of life and death. So it is only natural that our Pagan ancestors gave the Wheel of the Year a central place in their spiritual and religious practices.

For today's Neopagan followers of nature-centered spirituality, each High Day on the Wheel marks a different phase of spiritual development as well as a holiday. Taken altogether, the holidays of the Wheel of the Year are symbolic of the cycle of birth-death-rebirth found throughout nature, and within an individual's spiritual and personal grown. The circular nature of the Wheel reminds us that all of this has happened before, and all of this will happen again. The teaching of reincarnation is a theme in many of the surviving epics of the Celts, the Hindus, the Buddhists, some Germanic tribes, and many other nature-centered spiritual paths, and the Wheel also serves as a living representation of this concept, as the cycle of death, life and rebirth plays out through the course of a year.

On another level, the Wheel can be taken as a metaphor for life's journey. The Wheel tracks the Sun as it waxes and wanes throughout the year. With sunrise on the Winter Solstice, the days begin to grow in length, reaching their peak at the Summer Solstice. From there, the days begin to get shorter and shorter until the next Winter Solstice. So the period from Winter Solstice to Vernal Equinox represents youth, the period from the Vernal Equinox to the Summer Solstice represents young adulthood, the period from the Summer Solstice to the Autumnal Equinox represents middle age, and the period from the Autumnal Equinox to the Winter Solstice represents old age.

Further symbolic meaning in the Wheel of the Year can be seen in the balance between light and dark. The brighter months of summer give way to the darker months of winter, and then the cycle begins anew. This can be seen as a metaphorical representation of one's own life journey. We all have periods of darkness and periods of light. When in a period of darkness, it helps to remember that the light will come again. Also, when in a period of light, it helps to remember that darkness will come again.

So like the Wheel of the Year, human beings have a dark half and a light half.

The Wheel teaches us that we are not separate from nature. As the seasons of nature rise and fall, so do the seasons of our lives. The seasons of the year affect our moods and behavior. Do you find yourself becoming more contemplative and introspective during the winter months? Do you become happier and more outgoing in the summer months? Does a walk in the woods improve your mood? If so, you are not alone.

The Wheel of the Year allows us a tangible symbolic representation of these inner states of our being. Just as the seasons move back and forth between cycles of light and darkness, so our own moods and feelings cycle between lighter and darker times. Celebrating the Wheel of the Year allows us to acknowledge both our lighter and our darker impulses in a sacramental way. By acknowledging them, we restore balance to our lives and to our spiritual journey.

The Wheel of the Year is symbolic of the lighter and darker seasons of the cycle of the year. It can also be used as a metaphor for finding the balance between the lighter and darker aspects of ourselves. It can help us to integrate the Shadow and the Persona.

The Way of the Coyote is the way that acknowledges that we all have these darker impulses. We all have a Shadow side. The Way of the Coyote is the means by which we seek the divine in our own lives, and the Wheel of the Year is the living physical embodiment of that divine inspiration, written upon the sky. So the celebration of the Wheel of the Year is the celebration of our path of seeking divine inspiration by answering the Call of the Coyote. As we walk in the Coyote Way, we learn to balance our lives by integrating the dark and light within us through the Wheel of the Year. As we balance the Shadow and the Persona, we become more fully individuated. We become the Masters of Two Worlds.

16.1 *Per Ardua ad Astra*

I was born the year after the United States entered the space race. My childhood was spent watching rocket launches and lunar landings. Television and movies of the time were filled with spacemen exploring strange new worlds and seeking out new life and new civilization. More than anything else, I wanted to join them and to be an astronaut when I grew up.

Then I had my first eye exam.

It turns out that I had astigmatism. Astronauts have to have perfect vision, so at the ripe old age of nine years old, when men were walking on the moon for the first time, I was told that I had no chance of being an astronaut.

I was depressed about it for several years, until I decided that there was no use beating myself up over a minor twist of fate. So instead I asked myself what it was about being an astronaut that was attractive to me, and what other careers might offer the same or similar experiences.

The answer I came up with was that it was the adventure of seeing places and things that nobody had ever seen before that made being an astronaut so desirable. So would it be possible to do that here on Earth?

The next step was to think about what sorts of careers might give me the chance to be an explorer. I examined several possibilities before deciding to major in Experimental Psychology. The idea of discovering things about the mind that no one had ever experienced before excited me even more than the idea of walking on the moon!

The final skill of ecospirituality is living in True Self. My experience with having to change career directions very early in life taught me to look behind the mask to find the meaning. I thought that being an astronaut was the only way to live in my own True Self, until that option was no longer available to me. But after a little soul searching I found a career that was even more exciting.

In this session we will discuss what it truly means to live in True Self, and how to find all of the characteristics and traits that make us who we are. We'll also talk about how to dig a little deeper to find the meaning behind the masks we wear with others and with ourselves.

16.2 Mindful Awareness of the True Self

Ponder this phrase for a moment: "I truly love myself."

What sort of feelings did that sentence generate? What sort of thoughts? Sometimes we get caught up in the idea that loving ourselves is somehow selfish or egotistical. But let's think about that for a moment. If you don't love yourself, is it really fair of you to expect anybody else to love you? Not only that, but if you don't love yourself, and you're in a relationship with someone who loves you, eventually you might find yourself thinking along these lines, either consciously or unconsciously:

"I don't really love myself, yet this person says they love me. If I don't love myself, yet this person says they love me, then there must be something wrong with him/her! How could a 'normal' person love someone like me, when I can't even love me?"

Of course, the above paragraph is exaggerated just a bit, but there is some truth to it from time to time. If you don't really love yourself, then you can't really show others how to love you in the way you'd like to be loved.

16.3 Personal Truths

Think about the image of your True Self that you have been creating since you began this course. Take off all the masks you present to the rest of the world, and ask yourself, "Who am I, really?" Be as honest as possible when answering this question.

The purpose of the exercise in the next section is to discover your personal truths. Personal truths are the unwritten rules we have chosen to live our lives by. Some examples of personal truths would be:

"I am a creative person"

"I care about those around me"

"My relationships end in disaster"

Think about your own personal truths for a moment before going on to the next page. This should be an open and honest "warts and all" assessment that includes all of your thoughts about yourself and your own identity. List both your positive qualities and negative qualities.

It may help to center yourself first by taking a few deep breaths, and to ground yourself by stating a few personal affirmations. If necessary, try a little basic mindful meditation before looking deeply inside of yourself to discover your personal truths. When you feel you are ready, go on to the next page and complete the exercise there.

WORKSHEET 16.3 MY PERSONAL TRUTHS

Name_____ Date_____

What are some of the personal truths by which you live your life? List as many as you feel necessary in the space below. Use extra paper if needed:

1. _____
2. _____
3. _____
4. _____
5. _____

In what positive ways have your personal truths helped you to live the life you want to live? List them below:

1. _____
2. _____
3. _____
4. _____
5. _____

In what ways have your own personal truths hindered you from living up to your own potential? From living the life you would like to lead?

1. _____
2. _____
3. _____
4. _____
5. _____

In what ways could you change your personal truths to help you to live up to your own full potential? List those changes below:

1. _____
2. _____
3. _____
4. _____
5. _____

16.4 Turning Negatives into Positives

What did you learn about yourself in the previous exercise? Were you surprised by anything you learned?

Now go back to your list of personal truths, and put a check mark beside the ones that are helpful. Circle the ones that are less helpful. Take the less helpful ones, the ones you have circled, and try to change them into more positive personal truths in the space below. For example, one of the personal truths you listed might say, "All my relationships end in disaster."

A more positive way of stating this might be: "In the past, I've had relationships that have disappointed me, but I choose to learn from my mistakes and move on so that I may grow as a person."

A few pointers to look for while rephrasing these statements:

Try to avoid rephrasing in ways that are global, external, and permanent. A global statement is one that is true in all situations at all times.

An example of global thinking would be, "I am an unlovable person." A better way to phrase it might be, "I am a lovable person who sometimes does unlovable things."

An external statement would be one in which your personal truth is derived from circumstances which are beyond your control; i.e., things external to you. An example would be, "People treat me with disrespect."

While this may be true on occasion, you really have no control over how other people treat you. The behavior of others is an external event beyond your control. What you can control is how you react to the way you are treated. One way to rephrase the above statement would be, "I can't change the way others treat me, but I can change the way I react to them."

A permanent statement is one that assumes that this is the way things have always been, and this is the way they will always be. An example would be, "I can't help it, that's just the way I am." One possible way to rephrase that statement would be, "I've usually reacted a certain way in the past, but I am in control of my life, and from this moment forward, I choose to react in a different manner this time and every time in the future so that I may get different results."

Think about your circled responses from the previous page, then go on to the next exercise, *Positive Affirmations of My Personal Truths.*

Rephrase all of your circled responses on the next page so that they are positive affirmations rather than negative ones. Remember to keep away from global, external, and permanent thinking.

WORKSHEET 16.4 POSITIVE AFFIRMATIONS OF MY PERSONAL TRUTHS

Name _____ Date _____

Rephrase any circled responses from the previous exercise, My Personal Truths, so that they are more helpful to you in achieving the life you would like to live:

1. _____
2. _____
3. _____
4. _____
5. _____
6. _____
7. _____
8. _____
9. _____
10. _____

Was this exercise difficult for you? Why or why not?

_____
_____
_____

Did you notice any recurring themes? Were these themes positive or negative?

_____
_____
_____

How could you adapt more positive personal truths to help you live the life you would like to live?

_____
_____
_____
_____
_____

16.5 Radical Acceptance of Your True Self

You can never love another until you truly love yourself. The first step in learning to love yourself is to truly accept who you are. The first step in learning to accept who you are is to accept yourself with all your perceived flaws and imperfections, but also with all your good qualities. Give yourself permission to make mistakes once in a while. When you are able to do so, and to teach others to do so as well, you will have become the Master of Two Worlds.

It's been said, "When you lose, don't lose the lesson." The idea here is that each mistake can be an opportunity for learning and growth. The *Positive Affirmations of My Personal Truths* exercise is a way to turn perceived negative qualities about yourself into positive personal truths.

Now go back to all the personal truths you placed a check mark by on the *My Personal Truths* page. Add those to the ones you rephrased from the *Positive Affirmations of My Personal Truths* page. The list you've created is a basic sketch of your True Self. One way to look at your True Self is to accept that your True Self is the person inside of you that feels loved by others, and feels loved by you. When problems arise in our lives, it is usually because we have lost sight of our True Selves, so it is important to know who we really are and what we really want.

The way this often plays out in relationships, is that we sometimes become so involved with the other person that we give up our True Selves in the process. Think back on any negative relationships you may have had in the past. Did you give up a part of your True Self in an effort to sustain that relationship? If so, how did that turn out?

Healthy relationships do not require that we sacrifice who we really are for the sake of another. We can compromise with our partners or other loved ones, but that compromise should never come at the cost of a part of ourselves, especially if we are living in True Self. One way to prevent this from happening is to ask yourself, "Am I doing this because this is what I want to do, or am I doing it because I'm afraid I'll lose this person if I don't?"

It's one thing to do things for another person because you want to do it; it is quite another thing to do things for another person because you feel obligated to do it. One way to tell the difference between doing it because you want to and doing it because you have to is to ask yourself, "Would I feel guilty if I didn't do this?"

If the answer to this question is, "yes," then it is likely that the other person has asked you to step outside of your True Self and do something out of character for you. In other words, you have been asked to deny your own true nature.

16.6 Nature and the Mindful Body

In early childhood, we are not aware of ourselves as separate beings. We see ourselves as a part of our parents. The moods and feelings of our primary caretakers become our moods and feelings, and vice-versa. It's like language. If you grew up in a Spanish-speaking household, you'd speak Spanish. If you grew up in an English-speaking household, you'd speak English. Likewise, we learn our emotional language from the people who shape our childhood.

As we mature, we gradually develop a sense of identity; a sense that we are individuals. We become separate from the people who raised us. There are positive aspects to this idea of separation. If we develop our own sense of identity, we learn to be responsible for our own physical and emotional wellbeing. We learn that we are responsible for our own happiness, and that others are responsible for their own emotions as well. However, sometimes we can take this idea of separation too far. When this happens, we come to think that the environment around us has no impact on us, and that we have no impact on the environment.

In reality, we are not separate from the environment in which we live. When we go out into nature, physiological changes occur. Our heart rates slow down, our blood pressure decreases. Our minds become more open and accepting. In short, nature gives us a sense of calmness and wellbeing. Even if you live in an urban environment, you can reap the benefits of these physiological changes by incorporating houseplants into your living space, or by listening to recordings of natural sounds like waterfalls, rainstorms, or crickets chirping.

Our actions change our environment. What we do to the Web of Life, we do to ourselves. If we pollute the water table, we eventually find ourselves drinking polluted water. If we poison the food chain, we eventually find ourselves eating tainted food. These toxins then become a part of us. This idea can be extended to emotional pollution as well. If we act in emotionally toxic ways, we will eventually find that others respond to us in the same way. Could it be that our tendency to emotionally pollute the environment is somehow linked to our tendency to physically pollute the environment?

Nature teaches us that we are not separate from the natural world, and that the natural world is not separate from ourselves. We need nature to survive. We need nature to thrive. And nature needs us. Part of living in True Self is the simple acceptance of these facts.

As you bring your consciousness into closer alignment with your own image of your True Self, meditate on the role nature has to play in teaching you more about your body and the way it interacts with the natural world. You may try meditating both indoors and outdoors. If you do this, note any differences in the way your body experiences itself indoors and outdoors. In doing so, you will learn more about how your True Self manifests itself. You will also learn more about your own place in the world.

16.7 Wise Mind and Communication

"Allow others to live as they choose, and allow yourself to live as you choose."

–Richard Bach

Without communication, there could be no relationships. The main, if not the only, cause that relationships develop difficulties is poor or misunderstood communication. Thinking back to the concept of Wise Mind as a harmony of Emotional Mind and Rational Mind, let's apply Wise Mind to communication. What would a balance of emotional and rational communication look like? Could it be that the Wise Mind of communication is the ability to make our emotional needs known in a calm and rational manner, without blaming, shaming or trying to blame, shame, or guilt-trip our partners into submission?

A part of this Wise Mind of Communication is to take responsibility for our own emotional wellbeing, and to expect the same of others. To be the Master of Two Worlds is to be able to share the wisdom you have gained on the quest with others. The first step in learning to be a mentor is learning to communicate from Wise Mind.

When you communicate from Wise Mind, you come to realize that you are responsible for your own emotional wellbeing, and that is all you are responsible for. Likewise, when you communicate from Wise Mind, you are aware that your partners are responsible for their own emotional wellbeing, and that is all they are responsible for. No matter how much you try, you cannot force someone to see things your way unless they are willing for it to happen, and vice-versa. Wise Mind realizes that you're each entitled to your own viewpoint of the situation. Wise Mind realizes that what you are not entitled to is the right to invalidate your partner's thoughts, feelings or opinions. Wise Mind knows how to agree to disagree.

A part of living in True Self is learning to free yourself from emotional dependence and codependence on your family and/or romantic relationships. Living in True Self involves taking responsibility for your own emotional wellbeing, and allowing others to be responsible for their own emotional wellbeing. Ecospirituality means using your own power of intention to achieve this.

16.8 True Self and the Power of Intention

The ultimate goal of ecospirituality is to free yourself from the assumptions and barriers to connection that keep you from living fully in your True Self. In ecospirituality, spirituality just means "connection." Specifically, it means finding those moments of connection that are awe-inspiring. In order to connect with those moments we must first eliminate our barriers to connection. How many of those barriers to connection have to do with your own assumptions about the way things work in your life?

What paradigm shifts would have to take place in order for you to be able to live according to your own true nature? How many assumptions have you made about life that may not be helpful to your living fully in True Self? Is there a way you could change your own personal story that would lead you to be more accepting of yourself? If you did so, would it help you to become the person you were meant to be? Would it help you to become the Master of Two Worlds?

Imagine this scene:

You're walking alone in the forest one day. Suddenly your Fairy Godmother appears before you.

"Greetings," she says. "You have found my secret hiding place, and now you will be granted a single wish."

You protest, "But I thought Fairy Godmothers granted three wishes?"

"Ahhh," your Fairy Godmother says, "But I am a special Fairy. I have but one power…the power to give you the life you have always wanted. I cannot grant you material possessions, or change other people, or make any changes in the environment around you. All I can do is to change you into the person you want to be."

Your Fairy Godmother waits for your reply. What would you tell her? Go on to the next page and answer the questions on the *What I Would Tell My Fairy Godmother* exercise.

WORKSHEET 16.8 WHAT I WOULD TELL MY FAIRY GODMOTHER PAGE 1 OF 1

Name _____ Date _____

You're walking in the woods when you meet your own special Fairy Godmother. She offers to grant you a single wish, but this Fairy Godmother cannot change other people. She cannot change the world. This Fairy Godmother can only change things about the way you think and feel. The Fairy Godmother asks you what you would like to change about yourself.
What would you tell your Fairy Godmother? Answer the questions below in the space provided:

What would you ask the Fairy Godmother to change about the way you think?

_____
_____
_____
_____

What would you ask the Fairy Godmother to change about the way you feel?

_____
_____
_____
_____

What would you ask the Fairy Godmother to change about the assumptions you have made concerning your life?

_____
_____
_____
_____

What would you ask the Fairy Godmother to change about the assumptions you have made about your ability to live fully in your True Self?

_____
_____
_____
_____

16.9 Becoming the Fairy Godmother

What did you learn about yourself from the Fairy Godmother? Of course, the above is a fanciful scenario, but the good news is that the Fairy Godmother is real! The Fairy Godmother is your own True Self. Look again at your answers to the questions on the *What I Would Tell My Fairy Godmother* exercise. Are there any answers there that are beyond your own ability to change? Why? Why not?

16.10 Killing the Goose

"Love people, not things; use things, not people."

— Spencer W. Kimball

There's a fairy tale called The Goose Who Laid the Golden Egg. For you who are unfamiliar with the story, it's about a farmer who had a magical goose. This magical goose laid one golden egg per day. The farmer sold these eggs and made quite a comfortable living for himself and his family. But one day the farmer began thinking that instead of just having the one egg every day, wouldn't it be nice to have a whole bunch of golden eggs all at once?

The farmer began to have many sleepless nights thinking of all the things he could buy if he could get all the eggs at once.

Finally one day his greed got the better of him, and he decided to kill the goose, cut it open, and take all the eggs at once for himself. So this is what he did.

But when he killed the goose and cut it open, there were no eggs inside. The goose produced a fresh new golden egg every day, but it took a day for the goose to produce it. Now that the farmer had killed the goose, not only did he not have a big pile of golden eggs, but the one golden egg per day that he had gotten in the past was gone as well. So for the rest of his life he had to work and scratch in the dirt just to get by.

We do not live in a sustainable society. Most of the resources that we take for granted are finite in quantity. Many cannot be replenished. Once they're gone, they're gone. Little by little, we are killing off the goose that laid the golden egg. Even the most dyed-in-the-wool materialist must know this deep in the back of his or her mind. What sort of impact does this have on our individual psyches? On our collective conscious? A quick glance at the popularity of movies with apocalyptic themes will tell you that this meme is deeply imbedded within us.

What sort of impact does this knowledge have on the way we live our day-to-day lives?

The quote from Spencer W. Kimball reminds us to think about what's truly important in life. How much of your own personal happiness comes from things? How much of it comes from your relationship with people? With nature? With yourself? Yes, a certain amount of material possessions are necessary to survive in life, but as the Beatles reminded us, "Money can't buy me love."

16.11 What's Possible

What if you could create the whole world all over again? Think about the Fairy Godmother exercise. Suppose you had another Fairy Godmother who would restore the world to its primal state, with all the people and all the animals, and all the forests, but without all the factories, traffic, and industries that pollute the Earth, our Mother. Suppose you could start over with all the knowledge and technology we have right now. But imagine the technology would be applied in appropriate, sustainable ways that focused on people and nature instead of rabid materialism. What sort of world would you create?

There are a lot of top-down environmental efforts through legislation to improve our ecological situation. There is a place for such actions, but I don't think that a top-down approach will yield results quickly enough to avert environmental catastrophe. I believe that what is needed is a bottom-up approach.

The game we're playing right now with the environment is a no-win game. We need to change the rules of the game if humankind, and the planet, are going to survive and thrive. The way we change the rules of the game is to change the culture itself by changing our values. Material possessions are a necessity, but they are not a solution to all of life's problems. If we change our values to respect the things that are truly important in our lives, then I believe that a sustainable culture will automatically emerge from the bottom-up.

Can you imagine a whole culture of people living mindfully and caring about themselves by caring about the environment? If that culture swept over the planet, what would that do for the mental and physical wellbeing of every person on this earth? Imagine a whole world full of people in touch with their own True Selves, living out the lives they were born to have! I personally cannot imagine a greater adventure.

This workbook contains the basic tools you need to bring about such a paradigm shift for you and your family. Take the lessons you've learned here. Apply them to your own life, and help your family and friends to apply them to their lives as well. If the whole world learned to live in an ecospiritual manner, in balance with and a part of nature, then the global environmental crisis would take care of itself. We would all be Masters of Two Worlds.

16.12 Walking the Path

We're now coming to the end of our journey together. Whether you are completing this workbook as part of a class, or on your own, congratulations for all you hard work! You've learned a great deal about yourself, your relationship with others, and your relationship with nature. You've developed and created some tools that will help you along your journey. Now go out and do something nice for yourself...you deserve it!

If you completed this workbook on your own, and are interested in taking a live series with a trained facilitator, visit www.mindfulecotherapy.org for a list of trained facilitators in your area and registration information.

Now go forth and enjoy living as the person you were meant to be!

Epilogue - Freedom to Live

As Coyote watched the people light their torches one by one from the Fire Circle, a figure approached from the darkness. As she drew closer and closer to the flame, she was gradually more illuminated. When she was near enough, Coyote recognized her as White Buffalo Woman.

He greeted her with a smile as members of his Tribe danced around the fire.

As they sat side-by-side, watching his Tribe dance, a thought occurred to him.

"Grandmother Buffalo Woman," he began, "at the beginning of my journey you told me that each person must find his own fire, yet all of the People are lighting their torches from the fire I brought them. How can this be?"

White Buffalo Woman smiled at him and said, "Yes, it is true that they lighting their torches from the fire you brought to them, but each person will use it in their own way. Eventually each will learn to make his or her own fire. Some, like you, are meant to be the Seekers who will find fire of their own. Others, like those lighting their torches, are meant to be Followers...at least until their own time comes to seek. Their time to seek may come in this life, or in the next. Who can know? That is for them to decide. Everyone's own journey is ultimately up to them. What I do know is that you have opened the path for others to follow. The lesson of the journey is that we are all born of the same fire. And since we are all One, and we all come from the same Source, in a way they have all found their own fire through you."

"I know the path you have trod has been a long and difficult one," she continued, "but it was your path, and not theirs, to walk. Besides, if I had not told you to seek your own fire, you would have never set out on the journey in the first place, and you would not have become the strong and powerful Trickster that I now see before me. You brought back something far more powerful than the fire. You brought back the wisdom of who you truly are."

Coyote though long and hard about this before replying. He thought about all he had learned on the journey. He recognized that although he was still a Trickster at heart, he could never go back to the way things were before. The quest had changed him, giving him the confidence to live according to his own true nature as a Trickster and a teacher. All of this happened because White Buffalo Woman had deceived him into finding his own fire.

After a time, he grinned at her and said, "So you played a trick on me?"

White Buffalo Woman laughed and said, "Yes, I did. What do you think?"

Coyote, the Master Trickster, laughed with her as he said, "It was a very good trick. A very good trick indeed."

"The hero is the champion of things becoming, not of things become, because he is. 'Before Abraham was, I AM.' He does not mistake apparent changelessness in time for the permanence of Being, nor is he fearful of the next moment (or of the 'other thing'), as destroying the permanent with its change. 'Nothing retains its own form; but Nature, the greater renewer, ever makes up forms from forms. Be sure there's nothing perishes in the whole universe; it does but vary and renew its form.' Thus the next moment is permitted to come to pass."

--Joseph Campbell

"Show me a sane man and I will cure him for you."

--Carl Jung

"The true master does not seek to run away from Death. He accepts that he must die, and understands that there are far, far worse things in the living world than dying."

- - Albus Dumbledore, *Harry Potter and the Deathly Hallows*

What is the freedom to live? Can we ever truly be free to live until we come to grips with the fact that we are going to die? Once you've conquered your fear of death, what else can stand in your way? If the soul is the only thing in the Universe that is truly indestructible, then death is just another way of being. Even if you are atheist or agnostic, and have no belief in an afterlife, this is still true from the point of view of your own consciousness. If this life is all you will ever know, and there is no afterlife, then it is impossible to ever be conscious of your own death; therefore there is no way you could ever know that you have died. How can you be conscious of your own death, if death is the end to consciousness? So from the perspective of your own consciousness, you are immortal for all practical purposes. If there is no afterlife, then you die, your Universe ceases to exist, and you are no longer the Center.

With this knowledge of death comes the Freedom to Live. Soul musician Ray Charles said, *"Live every day like it's going to be your last, because one of these days you'll be right."*

Freedom to Live means that you have mastered death. If you have gone to the land of the dead and returned, what more is there to fear?

If you are not already outdoors while you're reading this, you may wish to step outside. If your sacred space is convenient nearby, step into it before you finish this book. Once you are in your sacred space, look around you. Take in all the wonderful things that nature has provided for you while you think about the fact that the only things necessary for survival are food, clothing, shelter, healing and love. Just for a moment, make a quick mental inventory of all of your possessions. How many of them would it be impossible, truly impossible, for you to live without? How many are unwanted or unnecessary items? How much of your life is spent working to make money to buy unwanted, unnecessary, and sometimes expensive items that, once purchased, sit in the corner and gather dust?

As you think about these questions, also think about the things that truly give your life meaning. How many of those things have to do with material possessions? How many of those things have to do with yourself? With those you care about? With the natural world?

In my hometown, there's an old cemetery in a forest. The graves go back to pre-Civil War times. Whenever I'm in town, I like to visit that cemetery just to enjoy the silence and the beauty of the surrounding forest. Once as I was walking through this cemetery and reading the ancient tombstones, it struck me that the messages were all about how much this or that person was loved and how much they would be missed. I didn't see any tombstones that said, "Here lies Joe Smith. He had a two-story, five-bedroom house and a Mercedes-Benz." Most of the tombstones I read talked about how much the departed was loved and how much he or she will be missed.

Imagine that you are lying on your deathbed, looking back on your life. What would you like to have written on your own tombstone? What sort of legacy would you like to leave behind for your loved ones? If you knew that you were near to drawing your last breath, what would you regret leaving left undone?

The answers you have to these questions will tell you who you truly are. When you know who you are, you know how to be in the world. That's where the true Freedom to Live lies. That's what is important in life. That is the kind of legacy I'd like to leave.

References

Achterberg, Jeanne (2002). *Imagery in Healing: Shamanism and Modern Magic*. Shambhala, Boston, MA.

Adler, Margot (2006). *Drawing Down the Moon: Witches, Druids, Goddess-Worshippers, and Other Pagans in America*. Penguin Books, New York, NY.

Bach, Richard (1970). *Jonathan Livingston Seagull*, Scribner, New York, NY.

Berry, T. (1988). *The Dream of the Earth*. San Francisco, CA: Sierra Club Books.

Bly, Robert (1990). *Iron John: A Book about Men*, Addison-Wesley, New York, NY.

Campbell, Joseph (1990). *The Hero's Journey: Joseph Campbell on His Life and Work (The Collected Works of Joseph Campbell)*, New World Library, Novato, CA.

Campbell, Joseph (2008). *The Hero with a Thousand Faces: Collected Works of Joseph Campbell, Third Edition*, New World Library, Novaro, CA.

Campbell, Joseph (1990). *Transformations of Myth through Time*, Harper & Row, New York, NY.

Clottes, Jean, and Lewis-Williams, David (1998). *The Shamans of Prehistory: Trance and Magic in the Painted Caves*. Translated by Sophie Hawkes. Harry N. Abrams, New York, NY.

Dyer, Jade (2007). How Does Spirituality Affect Physical Health? A Conceptual Review, *Holistic Nursing Practice 2007; 21(6):324–328*

Eliade, M. (1964). *Shamanism: Archaic Techniques of Ecstasy (W.R. Trask, trans.)*. Princeton, NJ: Princeton University Press (Original publication 1951).

Encyclopedia of Religion, Second Edition (2004). MacMillan Reference, New York, NY.

Feinstein, D., & Krippner, S. (1988). *Personal Mythology: Using Ritual, Dreams, and Imagination to Discover Your Inner Story*. Jeremy P. Tarcher, Inc., Los Angeles, CA.

Gribbin, J. (1986). *In Search of the Big Bang: Quantum Physics and Cosmology*. New York, NY: Bantam Books.

Harner, Michael (1980). *The Way of the Shaman*. Harper & Row, New York, NY.

Harvey, G. (Ed.). (2003). *Shamanism: A Reader*. New York: Routledge.

Hillman, J., & Ventura, M. (1992). *We've Had a Hundred Years of Psychotherapy and the World's Getting Worse*. San Francisco: Harper San Francisco.

Krippner, S. (2002). Conflicting Perspectives on Shamans and Shamanism: Points and Counterpoints. *American Psychologist, 57(11), 962–977.*

Lewis, I. M. (1971). *Ecstatic Religion: A Study of Shamanism and Spirit Possession*, Routledge, New York, NY.

Matrix, The (1999). Warner Brothers Films.

Metzner, R. (1998). *The Unfolding Self: Varieties of Transformative Experience*. Novato, CA: Origin Press.

Metzner, R. (1999). *Green Psychology: Transforming Our Relationship to the Earth.* Rochester, VT: Park Street Press.

Naess, A. (1989). *Ecology, Community and Lifestyle: Outline of an Ecosophy* (*D. Rothenberg, trans.*). New York: Cambridge University Press. (Original publication 1976).

Niehardt, John G. (1932). *Black Elk Speaks: Being the Life Story of a Holy Man of the Oglala Sioux,* New York: State University of New York Press.

Noll, Richard (1985). Mental Imagery Cultivation as a Cultural Phenomenon: The Role of Visions in Shamanism. *Current Anthropology 26 (1985): 443–451.*

Palley, Lori S.; O'Rourke, P. Pearl; & Niemi, Steven M. (2010). Mainstreaming Animal-Assisted Therapy. *ILAR Journal, Volume 51, Number 3 2010.*

Prigogine, I., & Stengers, I. (1984). *Order out of Chaos: Man's New Dialogue with Nature.* New York: Bantam Books.

Rowling, J.K. (2009). *Harry Potter and the Deathly Hallows*, New York: Arthur A. Levine Books.

Schroll, M. A. (2011). Neo-shamanism, psi, and their relationship with transpersonal psychology. *Paranthropology: Journal of Anthropological Approaches to the Paranormal, 2(4), 26–36.*

Singer, J. (1990). *Seeing through the Visible World: Jung, Gnosis, and Chaos.* San Francisco: Harper & Row, Publishers.

Taylor, Bron (2010). *Dark Green Religion: Nature Spirituality and the Planetary Future*, University of California Press, Berkeley, CA.

Van den Berg, A. E., & Ter Heijne, M. (2005). Fear versus fascination: Emotional responses to natural threats. *Journal of Environmental Psychology, 25 (3), 261- 272.*

Vitebsky, P. (2001). *The Shaman: Voyages of the Soul, Trance, Ecstasy and Healing from Siberia to the Amazon.* London: Duncan Baird Publishers.

Watts, A. W. (1972). *On the Taboo against Knowing Who you Are.* New York: Vintage Books.

ABOUT THE ECOSPIRITUALITY PROGRAM

The Ecospirituality Program is available for use at any organization that teaches principles of ecology and/or mental and spiritual health. If you are interested in presenting the program at your organization, training is available for facilitators at www.mindfulecotherapy.org.

If your organization would like to implement the Ecospirituality Program, Charlton Hall, MMFT, LMFT/S, RPT-S, CHt also offers facilitated live instruction and consultation on the program, as well as volume discounts on copies of the *Ecospirituality Workbook*.

Learn more at the Mindful Ecotherapy Center's website at www.mindfulecotherapy.org.

ABOUT THE AUTHOR

Charlton (Chuck) Hall, MMFT, LMFT/S, RPT-S, CHt is a Licensed Marriage and Family Therapist. Chuck's area of research and interest is using Mindfulness and Ecopsychology to facilitate acceptance and change strategies within a family systemic framework, and he has presented research at several conferences and seminars on this and other topics. He facilitates workshops on Mindfulness and Ecospirituality throughout the Southeast. Chuck's approach to therapy involves helping individuals and families to facilitate change through Mindfulness and Ecopsychology techniques in a non-judgmental, patient-centered, positive environment.

Books by Charlton Hall, MMFT, LMFT/S, RPT-S, CHt

The Mindfulness-Based Ecotherapy Workbook

This workbook introduces the 12 skills of Mindfulness-Based Ecotherapy (MBE) and introduces one of these skills at each of the 12 sessions in the program. Although this book is designed to accompany the 12-week Mindfulness-Based Ecotherapy workshop series, it may also be completed on your own at home. The experiential nature of the work allows anyone with access to outdoor spaces the opportunity to complete the series. Mindfulness-Based Ecotherapy allows you to embrace the healing power of nature in an experiential way.

5.0 out of 5 stars

By M. Neuman on March 31, 2016

"As a therapist and outdoor enthusiast I have always dreamed of combining the two. Finally a resource I can use to develop a nature/forest therapy curriculum. I love the book, the author's writing style, and the resources on his website."

Available at Amazon, Barnes and Noble, and most major media outlets. For more information, please visit the Mindful Ecotherapy Center's website at www.mindfulecotherapy.org

Printed in Great Britain
by Amazon